RETHINKING ANTISEMITISM IN NINETEENTH-CENTURY FRANCE

Rethinking Antisemitism in Nineteenth-Century France provides a history of the stories the French told about the Jews in their midst during the early nineteenth century. Using a novel cultural analysis that brings together pamphlets, newspaper articles, novels, and works of art, Julie Kalman focuses on the period that historians have explored the least, encompassing the years 1815–1848. Kalman reveals that there were significant discussions surrounding France's Jewish population taking place during this period and argues that these discussions are central to our understanding of the history of the Jew's place in France. These stories also allow us to reflect on core questions of French history during this period, a time when the French were questioning the fundamental nature of their own identity.

Julie Kalman lectures in Jewish history at the University of New South Wales in Sydney, Australia.

"In this thoroughly researched and persuasively argued study, Julie Kalman skillfully traces the evolution of the Jew in the French imagination. Her important book succeeds admirably in elucidating the role of antisemitism in the cultural formation of modern France."

– Jay R. Berkovitz, University of Massachusetts Amherst

"Julie Kalman's study fills an important gap in the histories of both nineteenth-century France and French Jews. In addition to focusing on the Restoration and July Monarchy (relatively understudied in both fields), Kalman demonstrates why debates about Jews must be seen as far more than a footnote in the era's overall history. In beautifully written prose, she charts the development of anti-Jewish representations in the early nineteenth century and reveals how discourse about Jews reflected the anxieties of a population struggling to make sense of the legacy of the French Revolution."

– Alyssa Goldstein Sepinwall, California State University–San Marcos

"This brilliantly sensitive and thoughtful book shows the 'quiet tolerance' of 1814–48 as the refusal by many to envisage their Jewish compatriots as French citizens."

– Pamela Pilbeam, Royal Holloway, University of London

Rethinking Antisemitism in Nineteenth-Century France

JULIE KALMAN

CAMBRIDGE
UNIVERSITY PRESS

CAMBRIDGE UNIVERSITY PRESS
Cambridge, New York, Melbourne, Madrid, Cape Town, Singapore,
São Paulo, Delhi, Dubai, Tokyo

Cambridge University Press
32 Avenue of the Americas, New York, NY 10013-2473, USA

www.cambridge.org
Information on this title: www.cambridge.org/9780521897327

First published 2010

Printed in the United States of America

A catalog record for this publication is available from the British Library.

Library of Congress Cataloging in Publication data
Kalman, Julie, 1969–
Rethinking antisemitism in nineteenth-century France / Julie Kalman.
p.   cm.
Includes bibliographical references and index.
ISBN 978-0-521-89732-7 (hardback)
1. Antisemitism – France – History – 19th century.   2. Jews – France – Social conditions –
19th century.   3. France – History – 19th century.   4. France – Intellectual life – 19th
century.   5. National characteristics, French.   6. France – Ethnic relations.   I. Title.
DS146.F8K356   2010
305.892′404409034 – dc22   2009031863

ISBN 978-0-521-89732-7 Hardback

To my Joy and to my Delight

Contents

List of Illustrations

Acknowledgements

This piece of writing has travelled far with me since it began life as a doctoral thesis. Many people have given all sorts of invaluable help along the way, and I would like to acknowledge them here. I must start with Peter McPhee, the most wonderful of supervisors, who brought inspiring commitment and infectious enthusiasm to the doctoral project that he oversaw. I wish also to acknowledge other friends and colleagues at The University of Melbourne, where I completed my Ph.D.: Ian Coller was a wonderful sounding board, Chips Sowerwine read an early draft of the manuscript, and I will forever be indebted to Helen Davies for her eye for a good postcard. At the University of New South Wales, where I now teach, I would like to thank my colleagues Martyn Lyons, Sally Cove, and Ruth Balint. Others, such as Pam Pilbeam, David Garrioch, John Merriman, Carol Harrison, Kerry Murphy, and Phyllis Albert Cohen, have been generous with their input, and I am grateful to them for this.

I would like to thank the Australian Academy of the Humanities, which has provided support with a grant to meet publishing costs. At the Rothschild Archive, Barbra Ruperto has made the process of gaining necessary permissions a straightforward and pleasant one. Sections of this manuscript developed through articles, and I gratefully acknowledge the permission of the relevant presses for me to include this material here: parts of Chapters 2 and 3 appeared in an earlier form as "The Unyielding Wall: Jews and Catholics in Restoration and July Monarchy France," in *French Historical Studies* (Volume 26, no. 4, pp. 661–86). This is reprinted by permission of the publisher, Duke University Press. Parts of Chapter 4 appeared as "Sensuality, Depravity and Ritual Murder: The Damascus Blood Libel and Jews in France," in *Jewish Social*

Studies (Volume 13, no. 3, pp. 35–58). This is reprinted by permission of the publisher, Indiana University Press. Sections of the Introduction and Conclusion contributed to "A Life of Evolutions: Félicité de Lamennais and Jews in Early-Nineteenth Century France," published in the *Proceedings of the Western Society for French History* (Volume 35, 2007). An earlier version of Chapter 5 was published as "Rothschildian Greed: This New Variety of Despotism," in *French History and Civilisation: Papers from the George Rude Seminar* (http://www.h-france.net, 2006).

I am sitting in my study looking out on the sort of glorious afternoon that is a feature of life in Sydney. The local kookaburra is proclaiming his authority from the jacaranda in the back garden. The writing of a book is a work of sacrifice and dedication. And if I provided the dedication, all the sacrifice came from my family. My husband has supported me, and this project, in ways that are both too vast to adequately describe, and too numerous to properly list. He knows what he is responsible for, and that will have to do. My children have no idea of their role, and so I wish to devote a rather long last word to them. Explaining to a four- and a six-year-old that you can't come to the park because you have to finish your so-called book (which is actually just a pile of paper) is as effective an exercise in the achieving of perspective as I have ever encountered. For this most important gift; for the times when they have been forced to play second fiddle and managed to assume the role with resignation and dignity; and for the simple fact that they *are*, this book is dedicated to them.

Introduction: Charting a Noisy Silence

*I*T IS WELL DOCUMENTED THAT IN TIMES OF CRISIS, THE FRENCH have made use of Jews to think through change and upheaval. The French Revolution was one such moment. We know that during that time, as well as the Napoleonic period, there was disproportionate discussion of Jews, as they were used to explore and enunciate new concepts such as citizenship and nationhood.[1] A similar process occurred a century later, with the Dreyfus Affair. Yet little or nothing has been written about the intervening period, and especially the early years of the nineteenth century. Did people simply stop using Jews, once they had been emancipated, as one way to decipher their world? Was this truly the "tranquil century" of French Jewry, as one historian has put it?[2] My exploration of this question begins with the premiere in 1823 of a short comic play entitled *Le Juif, comédie anecdotique*.[3]

Le Juif is set a decade before the French Revolution. The Jew of the title, known as Samuel, is the character around whom the action turns, and the night he spends in an inn, together with his fellow travellers, forms the setting for the play. The play opens as all of the characters arrive at the inn on the road to Orléans, where they are obliged to take refuge following an accident involving the coach in which they were travelling.

---

[1] See, in particular, Ronald Schechter, *Obstinate Hebrews: Representations of Jews in France, 1715–1815* (Berkeley, 2003).

[2] This was the title given by Jean-Jacques Becker to his chapter on the nineteenth century, in Jean-Jacques Becker and Annette Wieviorka, ed., *Les Juifs de France, De la Révolution française à nos jours* (Paris, 1998).

[3] Auguste Rousseau, Marc-Antoine-Madeleine Désaugiers, and Jean-Baptiste Mesnard, "Le Juif: Comédie anecdotique en deux actes, mêlée de vaudevilles," in *Fin du répertoire du théâtre français* (Paris, 1824).

Samuel stands out almost immediately from the other characters through their reactions to him. They distrust him: he is secretive. His foreignness is announced by his pidgin French and his awkward Germanic accent. (Another character notes that he speaks a "French-German gibberish.")[4] No physical description is given of him, but his appearance inspires disgust in the other characters, and they react to him with caution and suspicion. He appears greedy and scheming: when thieves descend on the inn and rob the passengers, the travellers' worst suspicions appear to be confirmed. Samuel alerts the thieves to a sum of money being carried by a fellow traveller, a young, naïve girl named Lucette, and he negotiates a portion of this money for himself. But by the end of the play, Samuel has become a hero. His secrecy, it would seem, was none other than prudence, and his treachery quick thinking. In directing the robbers to Lucette's money, he safeguarded his own sum, much greater, which he reveals himself to have been carrying for none other than Lucette, an embroiderer whose father is away fighting in the American War of Independence. Indeed, Samuel is in fact the Paris banker who, on behalf of her distant father, anonymously sent Lucette the sum she herself was carrying. And Samuel's sphere of influence is shown to reach far and wide, for not only does he magically produce a fortune, intact, for Lucette and her fiancé Charles, but he also, by dint of one letter, has Charles released from his military obligations. Thus, while Samuel is initially painted negatively, by the end of the play, his actions show him to be quite a different character altogether. Samuel turns out to be loyal and trustworthy, he shows an astounding lack of greed and disinterested fondness for Lucette; he uses the expectations of him as a Jew (he in fact calls himself "un pauvre chuif [juif] allemand"[5]) to do good to a non-Jew.

The playwrights were clearly making use of Samuel to manipulate their audience. (That the prolific and celebrated playwright and songwriter Marc-Antoine Désaugiers was counted among the authors would very probably have ensured the play's success.) They were drawing on concepts that would, at the least, have been meaningful to their audience, using a stereotype that, if not instantly recognizable, was reinforced by the

---

[4]   Ibid., 166. Samuel's words are transcribed thus: "Vous pien heureuse" ; "Vous li être pas plessée?" Ibid., 77. "Che me être trompé" Ibid., 79.

[5]   "A poor German Jew." Ibid., 204.

reactions of other members of the cast. But were the authors seeking to make some commentary on the pitfalls of stereotyping, or were they merely finding a new use for the common practice of making the selfish and speculating character a Jew?[6] Either way, *Le Juif* provides a fascinating insight into the codes and images understood by the theatre-going public of Restoration France to mean Jew, and there is no overcoming their ambiguity. For, although many of Samuel's acts turn out to have been calculated to have a positive outcome, his character is not neatly resolved. We are not told what happens to the thousand francs of Lucette's money that Samuel bargained from the thieves. Nor is it explained what power he has that makes him able to convince Charles's commanding officer to write the letter that frees him. Why did the authors choose to leave these ends untied? Was it so as to avoid an overly neat ending? Or did these issues simply not figure high on the list of questions central to the plot? Either way, the effect of these outstanding matters is to leave the audience (or the reader) with a feeling of ambivalence and complexity surrounding the character of this Jew, and from here it is not a difficult step to find that, as it is being subverted, the stereotype is also being reinforced. The audience could easily have chosen to understand from this play that behind every powerful banker, however good his character might appear, lurked the foreign and secretive Jew. Moreover, as a tool for the manipulation of the audience, Samuel has clearly exhausted his usefulness by the end of the play. As they climb back into the coach to resume their journey, the characters sing a song entitled "Vite en route" ("Quick let's go"). Each character sings a verse about his ideal place. Lucette's fiancé Charles sings of a utopia where all men would live together as brothers.[7] In contrast, Samuel, his French encumbered by his accent and the many grammatical errors he makes, sings pure nonsense:

> If I knew a country
> Where the windows are rounded
> The arms and hands the same shape
> The faces enormous
> The calves conforming

---

[6] Luce Klein, *Portrait de la juive dans la littérature française* (Paris, 1970), 110.

[7] Charles: If I knew a country/ Where all the inhabitants, united/ Artisans, bourgeois and military/ Without opposing parties/ Lived as brothers/ Ah! How I would go/ And how I would say/ Quick let's go. Rousseau, 264.

Ah! How I would go
And how I would say
Quick, let's go
Gentlemen, let it be said in confidence
The father to whom I owe my presence on this Earth
Floats at the moment
Between fear and hope, from one to the other
Ah! Prove to him, as he suspects
Whatever the row, whatever the debate
That Wednesday for my religion
Is not the Sabbath day.[8]

In the final image we are given of him, then, he reverts to the stereotype, becoming once again a figure for ridicule. Is it possible that stereotypical Jewish Samuels were so deeply entrenched in early-nineteenth-century French society that playwrights could call on such figures readily in order to subvert them?

The historiography suggests the opposite. The narrative follows a well-established path that states, overwhelmingly, that in terms of the persistence of stereotypical notions of Jews, there is little of significance to tell during this period, as though figures such as Alphonse Toussenel, for whom the Jews were the hated kings of the era, were aberrations in an otherwise "tranquil" nineteenth century.[9] Historians of French Jewry have traditionally tended to focus on prominent events where anti-Jewish

---

[8]   This is written in French as: Si che gonnaissais un pays/ où les fenêtres soient arrondis/ Les bras, les mains de mêmes formes/ Les faces énormes/ Les mollets conformes/ Ah! gomme j'irais/ et gomme che dirais: Vite en route. Messieurs, soit dit en confidence, Le père à qui che dois le chour/ Entre la crainte et l'espérance/ Flotte en ce moment tour à tour/ Ah! proufez-lui, comme il suspecte/ Quelque orache, quelque débat/ Que le mercredi pour ma secte/ N'être pas le chour du sabbat. Ibid., 265–6.

[9]   On tranquillity in particular, see Léon Poliakov, *The History of Anti-Semitism*, vol. 3, *From Voltaire to Wagner*, trans. Miriam Kochan (London, 1975), 364. François Delpech, "De 1815 à 1894," in Bernard Blumenkranz, ed., *Histoire des juifs en France*, 305–46 (Toulouse, 1972); Jean-Jacques Becker and Annette Wieviorka, ed., *Les Juifs de France, De la Révolution française à nos jours* (Paris, 1998), 42, 46. For this approach in more general terms, see Jacob Katz, *From Prejudice to Destruction: Anti-Semitism, 1700–1933* (Cambridge, MA, 1980); and idem, *Out of the Ghetto: The Social Background of Jewish Emancipation, 1770–1870* (Cambridge, MA, 1973); Pierre Birnbaum, *Jewish Destinies; Citizenship, State, and Community in Modern France* (New York, 2000); Michel Winock, "Emancipation et exclusion: La France et la question juive," *Histoire. Spécial: l'antisémitisme*, October 2002, 46; Ilana Zinguer and Sam Bloom, ed., *L'Antisémitisme Éclairé: Inclusion and Exclusion: Perspectives on Jews from the Enlightenment to the Dreyfus Affair* (Leiden, 2003).

sentiment has been illustrated most spectacularly, such as Napoleon's Infamous Decree of 1808, and the Dreyfus Affair.[10] The first half of the nineteenth century – particularly the period of the Restoration, from 1815 to 1830 – contains no such dramatic event and as such has received little attention. With some exceptions, historians from all disciplines have followed this lead.[11] In histories of religion, for example, the place of Jews in nineteenth-century France, if treated at all, is seen as having nothing to contribute to the principal narrative. Jews tend to be placed alongside Protestants under a separate heading that deals with their level of assimilation, or government rulings that concerned them.[12] Thus, the ways Jews have lived out modernity in France, their interactions with French non-Jews, and how the latter saw the former, have also, for the most part, been told as a series of separate stories. In this way, the history of France is kept separate from that of the Jews in France, and both, in turn, are distinct from the discipline that encompasses the history of antisemitism. Where this latter is concerned, the story of antisemitism in nineteenth-century France has, at best, been told uprooted from its context, or treated as a peripheral part of either histories of French Jewry or of France.[13] Overall, the history of nineteenth-century France is simply not told as a story where some French citizens took account of their Jewish fellow citizens.[14]

[10] See, for example, Patrick Girard, *Les Juifs de France de 1789 à 1860: de l'émancipation à l'égalité* (Paris, 1976); Simon Schwarzfuchs, *Du Juif à l'israélite: histoire d'une mutation (1770–1870)* (Paris, 1989); François Delpech, "De 1815 à 1894"; or more recently Jean-Jacques Becker and Annette Wieviorka, ed., *Les Juifs de France, De la Révolution française à nos jours* (Paris, 1998).

[11] Some historians of Jews in France, such as Jay Berkovitz, Michael Graetz, and Paula Hyman, have incorporated incidences of Jewish–non-Jewish interactions where these feature in their histories of Jews in France. See Jay Berkovitz, *The Shaping of Jewish Identity in Nineteenth-Century France* (Detroit, 1989); Michael Graetz, *The Jews in Nineteenth-Century France: From the French Revolution to the Alliance israélite universelle*, trans. Jane Marie Todd (Stanford, 1996); Paula Hyman, *The Jews of Modern France* (Berkeley, 1998); and idem, *The Emancipation of the Jews of Alsace: Acculturation and Tradition in the Nineteenth Century* (New Haven, 1991).

[12] See, for example, Adrien Dansette, *Religious History of Modern France*, vol. 1: *From the Revolution to the Third Republic*, trans. John Dingle (New York, 1961); and Gérard Cholvy and Yves-Marie Hilaire, *Histoire religieuse de la France contemporaine* (Toulouse, 1985).

[13] See, for example, as well as Léon Poliakov, Jacob Katz, *From Prejudice to Destruction.*

[14] See, for example, H. A. C. Collingham, *The July Monarchy: A Political History of France 1830–1848* (London, 1988); André Jardin and André-Jean Tudesq, *Restoration and Reaction, 1815–1848*, trans. Elborg Forster (Cambridge, 1983); Sheryl Kroen, *Politics and Theater: The Crisis of Legitimacy in Restoration France, 1815–1830* (Berkeley, 2000);

David Nirenberg has argued that since the Holocaust, the idea that Jewish history is written by Jews, for Jews, to be ignored by others, has become "untenable."[15] But it would seem that, where early-nineteenth-century France is concerned, perhaps because the historiography has not been driven by a sense of urgency, Jewish history has remained marginal.

This process of teasing out the story into separate strands has not allowed us to understand it fully. The way a majority culture makes sense of the minorities in its midst is the story of the majority, and thus the history of French attitudes towards French Jews must be considered as French history. People in early-nineteenth-century France did construct the Jew as a way to think through the vertiginous changes taking place around them. And if we examine how such people used Jews to make sense of their world, we are offered a window on their vision of their world: in this case, competing ideas of what France could and should be. For as *Le Juif* suggests, the French continued to think with the Jew right throughout the quiet nineteenth century. My intention, here, is to bring this thinking to light. I take up where the narrative generally stops, with the aftermath of the Napoleonic regime. I focus specifically on the period that has been the most easily dismissed: the Restoration and July Monarchy, encompassing the years 1815–48. I explore how the idea of the Jew in the nineteenth century allows us to reflect on core questions of French history during this period.

Nonetheless, while I take issue with the direction the historiography has tended to take, I must acknowledge the scholarship on which I have drawn. And indeed, the historians whose work I discuss here do have a point: relative to other moments in their history in France, this was indeed a tranquil time for the Jews of France; a golden age. In 1818, one of the last remaining pieces of state-sanctioned discrimination, in the form of Napoleon's Infamous Decree, expired. Jews could now enjoy

---

Bernard Moss, *The Origins of the French Labor Movement, 1830–1914; The Socialism of Skilled Workers* (Berkeley, 1976); Pamela Pilbeam, *Republicanism in Nineteenth-Century France, 1814–1871* (London, 1995); idem, *The 1830 Revolution in France* (New York, 1991); Roger Price, *A Social History of Nineteenth-Century France* (London, 1987); William Sewell, *Work and Revolution in France; the Language of Labor from the Old Regime to 1848* (Cambridge, 1980); and André-Jean Tudesq, *Les Grands notables en France (1840–1849). Etude historique d'une psychologie sociale* (Paris, 1964).

[15] David Nirenberg, *Communities of Violence: Persecution of Minorities in the Middle Ages* (Princeton, 1996), 3.

rights and opportunities that had never before been presented to them. They were citizens of a state that afforded them complete protection, and in such an atmosphere, occasional acts of violence – verbal or physical – could be viewed much as they have been depicted: random and idiosyncratic. Perhaps in this sense, there simply is no story. Perhaps the historiography is a reflection of the reality of life for the lucky Jews of early-nineteenth-century France: if stories of Jews and Protestants are reserved for confessional histories and treated on the same terms, could this simply be a reflection of the state's treatment of these two confessions? Nonetheless, acts against Jews – be they random or not – cannot be left to fall through the cracks of historical analysis. So in what sense can they be understood? Can we see a play such as *Le Juif* as antisemitism, sufficient to complicate, or even negate, the story of tranquility?

This question begs another: what should qualify as antisemitism? Much of the scholarship on antisemitism has focused on achieving a definition of this hatred, and perhaps also with it some understanding. The size of the body of work on the subject is a reflection of the sense of urgency that comes across at times in this writing. Could one "live after Auschwitz"?[16] This was the agonized question that Theodor Adorno posed in the immediate postwar period, in his intimate psychoanalysis of the antisemite. In fact, works on antisemitism range from close, careful dissection of the hatred to broad surveys of antisemitic figures and moments through history.[17]

But is the term antisemitism the most appropriate for this context? I do not believe so. Quite apart from the risk of anachronism that the use of this term presents, it also invites us to deny the complexity – and ambiguity – in much of the stereotyping that dates from this period. To simply lay out the sentiment and its adherents is to present a story that, in Nirenberg's words, "resists interpretation."[18] There are works contained within these pages that, strictly speaking, cannot be labeled as antisemitic, because their authors did not necessarily write hatefully or see the Jews as

---

[16] Theodor Adorno, *Can One Live after Auschwitz? A Philosophical Reader*, ed. Rolf Tiedemann, trans. Rodney Livingstone and others (Stanford, 2003).

[17] For examples of the former, see ibid.; idem *et al.*, *The Authoritarian Personality* (New York, 1969); and Jean-Paul Sartre, *Réflexions sur la question juive* (Paris, 1954). For the latter, see, for example, Poliakov, *History of Anti-Semitism*, or Robert Wistrich, *Antisemitism: The Longest Hatred* (New York, 1991).

[18] Nirenberg, 68.

evil. In their eyes, the presence of Jews in modern society was a problem that could, under certain circumstances, be solved. Although their consideration of this question may appear to be negative and condescending from the vantage point of our sensibilities, they did not write in a spirit of hatred. The title character of *Le Juif* is, in turn, repugnant, powerful, and ridiculous, but there is a fundamental ambiguity surrounding him, as – particularly from our distance – the authors' intentions in his regard are unclear. So how should Samuel be understood? I would like to suggest that we can view him in terms of what Zygmunt Bauman has called ambivalence. That is, that non-Jews find that the Jews in their midst, or for that matter Judaism, cannot be described or comprehended according to what Bauman calls their "orderly world," and thus the Jew comes to signify what challenges this order.[19] This could be taken a step further: if Jews can be understood as challenging the system, they also serve to explain it. In early-nineteenth-century France, this means that as French men and women deliberated on and debated the meanings of citizenship and nation in their new world, the Jew, who so often constituted the site of anti-citizenship, or anti-nationhood, helped the French to make sense of this new world. In this book, I approach discourses of alterity as being composed in this spirit of ambivalence. In this usage, the term does not denote ambivalence as it is commonly understood; rather, it indicates a sort of discomfort (which can at times be expressed in the most hateful of terms) at the prospect of the Jew who, in so many ways, challenges and defies categorization and who, because of this, takes on a much greater significance. How did the defiant messiness of the Jew help to explain an apparently streamlined ideological system, be it Christianity, Enlightenment thought, or indeed, the post-Revolutionary world?[20]

[19] Zygmunt Bauman, "Allosemitism: Premodern, Modern, Postmodern," in Brian Cheyette and Laura Marcus, ed., *Modernity, Culture, and 'the Jew'* (Stanford, 1998), 144. Bauman argues for the use of the term "allosemitism" to replace the binary pair of anti- and philo-semitism. Kenneth Stow argues that there is a fundamental ambivalence – in the sense closer to the true definition of the term – towards Judaism at the very root of Christianity, stemming from Paul's notion that the Jews should at once be "pushed away," yet also "brought close and loved." Kenneth Stow, *Jewish Dogs: An Image and its Interpreters. Continuity in the Catholic-Jewish Encounter* (Stanford, 2006), 34.

[20] Adam Sutcliffe, *Judaism and Enlightenment* (New York, 2003), 9. A similar approach has been taken to a much earlier period by David Nirenberg in his *Communities of Violence*, in which he argues that atrocities committed against Jews in fourteenth-century France are best understood in the context of social conflict and competing discourses around notions such as "kingship, bodies, Jews, and the nature of evil in a Christian society" (Nirenberg, 68).

How was the Jew used to explain its failure, or indeed, at times, its success?

Refusing a framework of analysis that separates antisemitism, not only from its context, but also from its supposed opposite, also allows for greater contextualisation of the story. We can understand expressions of ambivalence towards Jews as attempts to deny or define that which threatens to break through the borders of a tidy world. In turn, the way in which this alterity is defined, offers insights into what was to constitute inclusion and what was seen to pose the greatest threat to this system. Thus, if rather than separating a figure's ambivalence towards Jews from their belief system and the ideas of the time that influenced their thinking, we focus precisely on that link, we can examine the ways in which such writers sought to negotiate their own identity in the changing world of early-nineteenth-century France, and what this then suggests to us about this period. For, in the context of nineteenth-century France, when we take works that explore the idea of the Jew as problematising the idea of the nation, and using the Jew to think this through, then it becomes clear that they constitute a vital aspect of the construction of the many different worlds that made up this place and time. Thus, I would like to shift the focus away from questions of the precise nature of antisemitism, or of how intense hatred must be before it qualifies as antisemitism. Rather, I would like to shine a light on those who chose to use Judaism to define alterity and examine their words in the context of their world. How did this latter influence the choices they made? How did they make sense of it? In other words, I examine how the Jew was constructed, as Sartre put it, to explain experience.[21]

The question to consider here, then, is not one of relative intensity. Rather, the issue is *in what terms* alterity was framed, and what this, in turn, reveals about the experience of French men and women in nineteenth-century France. This is a fertile period for research, for in fact it was anything but quiet. In 1815, the assembled powers of Europe, wishing perhaps that France might leave them in peace, restored a member of the Bourbon Monarchy to the throne. King Louis XVIII, a younger brother of the beheaded Louis XVI, saw in the period of fifteen years that was known as the Restoration. Recent scholarship has challenged the prevailing notion that the Restoration was a period of stability. Rather,

[21] Sartre, 18.

this scholarship suggests that between 1815 and 1830, negotiations over what the past represented and what the present and future of France should be were intense and ongoing.[22] The Catholic hierarchy sought to persuade the population that the previous twenty-five years of ferment had been nothing more than a parenthesis, which could now be closed, and that French society had been "restored" to the unquestioned hierarchy in which the Church took its rightful place at the top. But however much conservative Catholics may have longed for a return to the world of ancien régime society, too much had occurred during the interregnum for all of French society to simply take up where it had left off before 1789. The Revolution had shown that the three pillars of ancien régime society that were Church, monarchy, and nobility could no longer lay claim to unchallenged legitimacy. The reign of the conservative, devoutly Catholic, and royalist Charles X brought this tension to its climax and resulted in what were to be known as "three glorious days" in July 1830. This, the 1830 Revolution, brought the restorative experiment to an end and put in its place an era of pragmatism. At its head was the so-called bourgeois king Louis-Philippe. Louis-Philippe was of the house of Orléans, a cousin of the Bourbons, and seen by conservative Catholics as the regicide king, whose father Philippe-Egalité had voted for the beheading of his relative Louis XVI. Men such as Charles X, called Ultras, were now to become Legitimists, planning and longing for the return of a legitimate, Bourbon king. But those who maintained their close identification with Catholicism were not the only ones alienated by the new regime. Indeed, if during the Restoration Catholics and Republicans had competed, during the July Monarchy, they were in agreement over their disgust with the succession of pragmatic and materialist governments that now held power.

In nineteenth-century France, therefore, successive regimes faced nothing less than the imposing task of negotiating the meaning and significance of the Revolution in the context of their own times and beliefs. And different groups for whom the Revolution had been a reference point variously for wonder or disaster were forced to do the same. Republicans, for whom citizenship was a privilege and Jews its

---

[22] See, for example, Kroen, *Politics and Theater*, and Bettina Frederking, "'Il ne faut pas être le roi de deux peuples': Strategies of National Reconciliation in Restoration France," *French History* 22, no. 4 (2008): 446–68.

happy recipients, spent the nineteenth century seeking to situate the Jew in relation to their understanding of citizenship and the ideal citizen. Catholics, whose Church had been irrevocably weakened, were forced to renegotiate their place in a world forever changed – one in which, for example, Jews were nominally their equals. All had legacies on which to draw. In Catholic teaching, Jews had for centuries been representative of all that lay beyond the bounds of the safety of the Church. Christian teachings vilifying Judaism reached back into the origins of Christianity itself, to the era when the first followers of Jesus' teachings sought to differentiate themselves from Jews by demonizing them. In 1789 in France, the world changed for the Catholic Church as it had never done before. The Catholic hierarchy could no longer claim its place at the top of the tree of privilege. And among the ancien régime hierarchies that fell was one that maintained a clear delineation between the Catholic and the Jew and that had served to make the latter easily identifiable. Now, with interaction, intermarriage, and conversion, those lines were no longer so clear-cut. Catholics did not form a homogenous group any more than did Jews. Nevertheless, more than one Catholic intellectual found it necessary to continue to ascribe a specific role to the Jew so that, in the changing world, the Jew continued to represent alterity in Church teaching.

But the Church was not the only body that had specific notions of what place the Jew should occupy. It was arguably the Deists, with their writings that brought religion into question, who sparked the development of a secularised way to understand the Jew.[23] But just as economic, social, and cultural development occurred concurrently in the eighteenth century, this secularisation of Jewish alterity, which we could also see as the development of a Jewish question, also had economic roots. In the seventeenth and eighteenth centuries, the spirit and practice of mercantilism spread throughout Europe, sweeping up in its momentum Jews, who for centuries had practised trade. In a stagnant French economy, men such as Colbert and Turgot realised – a century

---

[23] Deism grew out of the so-called rational approach to the study of the natural world that characterised the Enlightenment. The movement, which was highly influential during the late seventeenth and the eighteenth centuries, included among its adherents Rousseau and Voltaire. Deists believed that the Bible contained important truths, but they rejected the concept that it was divinely inspired.

apart – that the strength of countries such as Holland and England had partly to do with the presence of Jewish traders, and therefore in France the Jewish question at this time was to a great extent based on economics: could the Jews be financially useful to France, and, if so, should they be given greater freedoms, and what form ought these to take?

With the Enlightenment came a further – new – perspective on Jews. Enlightenment notions of religious tolerance opened the way for a new evaluation of the status of the Jewish communities resident in France, particularly when those in what Jay Berkovitz has called the "enlightened bureaucracy"[24] could no longer ignore the contradiction between Enlightenment principles and the existence of a population excluded from the privileges enjoyed by subjects of the king on the basis of its religion. This, added to the awareness of the Jews' economic utility, meant that the 1781 work of the Prussian councillor and scholar Christian Wilhelm Dohm, which opened up discussions on Jewish emancipation in Europe, found a receptive audience in France.[25] The attention given to his work and the debate it raised prompted the Société des arts et sciences of Metz to set an essay competition in 1785, the central question of which was whether "there were means of making the Jews happy and more useful in France,"[26] to which the Abbé Grégoire wrote his celebrated response.[27] Grégoire, and others like him, envisaged the gradual emergence of a new type of Jew once civic rights were bestowed. This Jew would be an individual like all other citizens, enjoying the benefits of citizenship and taking on his share of civic responsibilities. Thus, in the years leading up to the Revolutionary debates, this question was no longer one of what the Jew could do for the state, but rather, what the

---

[24] Berkovitz, *Shaping*, 29.

[25] Christian Wilhelm Dohm, *Über die bürgerliche Verbesserung der Juden* (Berlin, 1781–3). This was translated into French and appeared in 1782 as *De la réforme politique des Juifs*. Dohm's work was revisited in 1787 by Honoré Gabriel Mirabeau, whose *Sur Moses Mendelssohn, sur la réforme politique des Juifs* (London, 1787) gave the former's work further exposure in France.

[26] The path from Dohm's work to that of Mirabeau, and then to the essay competition and Grégoire's winning essay, is a well-traced one. See, for example, Berkovitz, 29–31, Hyman, *Modern France*, 19–20. Schechter has also covered this period in *Obstinate Hebrews*, 87–101.

[27] Henri Grégoire (abbé), *Essai sur la régénération physique, morale et politique des Juifs* (Metz, 1789).

state might do for – and with – the Jew. Yet this question was anything but straightforward, for what precisely constituted the state?

The revolutionary concept of France as a nation of free citizens followed Montesquieu's notion of a social equilibrium in which no single force could be allowed to gain ascendancy. Along the lines of the Lockean idea of the social contract, this understanding of the nation emphasised the role of each citizen as an individual sharing a common interest – the nation – and thus forming the national will.[28] For this conceptualisation of nationality to be successful – that is, to ensure the performance of the national will – it was necessary for all citizens to share a primary loyalty to the nation. Thus, the performance by each citizen of his duties to the nation was of paramount importance. These duties included the citizen's responsibility to accept the same standing as his fellow citizens and not to expect or request special status. No citizen could maintain allegiance to any other nation or corporation. Institutions could be disbanded, as were the craftsmen's guilds, or integrated into the nation, as in the case of the Church. Double nationality was a different and far more serious matter. When the Constituent Assembly came to debate whether the proposition that "all men are born free and equal in rights" applied to the Jewish population in France, they did so in the context of this understanding of citizenship. That is, they posed the question of what precisely it meant to be a French citizen, and whether, therefore, the Jew could fit this mould.[29] Debates regarding the suitability of Jews for emancipation centred on the question of their perceived double allegiance, that is: "Did Jews constitute a nation distinct from the French (and thus could not be part of the new sovereign body)? Or were Jewish communities essentially autonomous corporations, like any other in the Old Regime?"[30] It is impossible to generalise regarding the status of supporters and opponents of Jewish emancipation.[31] For example, nobles such as the Count de Clermont-Tonnerre supported Grégoire's push for the Jews to be granted civic equality. However, the overwhelming majority of their

[28] See Gary Kates, "Jews into Frenchmen: Nationality and Representation in Revolutionary France," in *The French Revolution and the Birth of Modernity*, ed. Ferenc Fehér (Berkeley, 1990), 113.

[29] See Schechter, 162–3, and Kates, 109.

[30] Kates, 112–13. Pierre Birnbaum defines the question of whether to emancipate Jews as being "where to draw the line between the public and private spheres." Birnbaum, 19.

[31] See, for example, Schechter's careful discussion of this point. Schechter, 156–8.

confreres of the First and Second Estates did not agree with these two men. At the National Assembly, the spokesmen of the Catholic Church, such as the conservative Abbé Maury and the bishop of Nancy, A.-L.-H. de la Fare, presented arguments against granting citizenship to the Jews. They were supported by nobles such as Prince Claude de Broglie and members of the Third Estate, such as the Alsatian deputy Jean-François Rewbell. His objections echoed the *cahiers de doléances* from the east.

Although the Assembly found it difficult to accept that Jews, with their other national allegiance, could be true loyal citizens of the nation, its successor, the National Convention, had no such qualms about other foreigners. In 1792, the National Convention granted French citizenship to eighteen foreigners, among them Tom Paine and George Washington, "who, through their writings and through their courage," had "served the cause of liberty and prepared the emancipation of peoples."[32] Tom Paine was elected to the Convention. It was not expected that any of these eighteen men would renounce their other nationality.[33] Rather, they were an indication of the cosmopolitanism inherent to Revolutionary ideals and its understanding of patriotism. Although this sentiment would later turn in on itself and give way to the potential within it for xenophobic nationalism, in 1792, the Convention understood its goals as having international significance and the capacity to include all those who shared its ideals.[34] Schechter has equated this "symbolic gesture of inclusion" with the bestowal of citizenship on Jews, as "grand gestures of inclusiveness" that masked moments of exclusion, such as, for example, the reluctance to liberate slaves.[35] Yet can we ignore the influence of the unique place of the Jew in Catholicism, in a nation that had for many centuries been overwhelmingly Catholic, and the influence of pure ideology: the truly "contagious" nature of notions such as equality and

---

[32] *Moniteur universel*, no. 241, 23 August 1792, vol. 13, 540–1. Quoted in Peter McPhee, *The French Revolution, 1789–1799* (Oxford, 2002), 103.

[33] Michael Rapport notes that the deputies Claude Basire and Jacques Thuriot expressed concern that naturalised foreigners might be tempted to favour the national interest of their land of origin over that of their adopted *patrie*. Michael Rapport, *Nationality and Citizenship in Revolutionary France* (Oxford, 2000), 137.

[34] See Michael Rapport, "Robespierre and the Universal Rights of Man, 1789–1794," *French History* 10, no. 3 (1996): 303–33.

[35] Schechter, 160–1.

liberty?[36] The ease with which the Assembly welcomed foreigners into the nation, as opposed to the difficulty with which they did the same for Jews, could be an indication that deputies to the Assembly could not divest themselves of an influence that may well have been Catholic teaching, or perhaps simply Enlightenment thought: that Jew in fact meant much more than simple alternative allegiance or nationhood. After all, Protestants and even Jesuits were viewed with suspicion and at times hostility because it was perceived that their primary allegiance might not be to the nation. But only the Jews carried the millstone of the deicide, and it would seem that the sustained efforts of the Church, beginning in the Middle Ages, to teach Christians to see their Jewish neighbours as foreign and separate, had borne success, for well into the nineteenth century, Jews living within France continued to be referred to as either German or Portuguese. Indeed, it was perhaps the perception of Jews living as a separate nation *within* the nation that was so significant in the debates on their emancipation. As the noble deputy to the National Assembly Clermont-Tonnerre so famously put it in debates about Jewish emancipation in December 1789:

One must refuse everything to the Jews as a nation, and give everything to the Jews as individuals. [...] It would be repugnant to have a society of non-citizens in a state, and a nation within a nation.[37]

Did Judaism itself present an obstacle to the performance of civic duties? Was there a place for emancipated Jews in French society? Was it possible to "fuse" Jews into society, thus effacing any perception of them as a separate nation?[38] "Anti-emancipators," according to Gary Kates, believed that the Jews were both a corporation and a separate nation, while their opponents argued that Jews were a corporation like any other and could thus be disbanded.[39] This was the spirit of "possibilism" that Robert Darnton has described as characterizing the Revolution,[40] and

---

[36] For a discussion of the "Contagion of Liberty" in the context of the American Revolution, see Bernard Bailyn, *The Ideological Origins of the American Revolution* (Cambridge, MA, 1992), 230–319.

[37] *Opinion du Comte Stanislas de Clermont-Tonnère, député de Paris*, 23 December 1789.

[38] Phyllis Albert, *The Modernization of French Jewry: Consistory and Community in the Nineteenth Century* (Hanover, NH, 1977), 40.

[39] Kates, 113.

[40] Robert Darnton, *The Kiss of Lamourette: Reflections in Cultural History* (New York, 1990), 17. On competing ideas of the nation, see also Caroline Ford, *Creating the Nation*

ultimately it was this spirit: optimism and faith in the integrating power of the nation that prevailed. The Jews of France were granted citizenship. Nonetheless, this citizenship did not come without delays. Although the Jews of the southwest became citizens in January 1790, their co-religionists in the east were obliged to wait more than eighteen months longer to be granted this privilege. Even some pro-emancipators did not believe that all Jews would become worthy of citizenship if left to their own devices. Some members of the National Assembly, as well as citizens in their *cahiers*, argued that the Jews of France – and Alsace in particular – were not capable of forming an attachment to France, because the deleterious effects of their religion prevented them from doing so.

It is important to underscore the fact that there was more than one image of French Jewry. The Sephardic population of the southwest was almost always depicted as having successfully taken on citizenship. In stark contrast to this were the Jews of Alsace, the model of failure, who provided the prototype for negative depictions. The thick Germanic accent with which the authors of *Le Juif* saddled Samuel was not a random choice. The Jews of Alsace and neighboring Lorraine, numbering some 25,000, formed the largest group of the approximately 40,000 Jews who lived in France. Physically, they were present throughout the region; they lived in small communities, scattered throughout the villages and small towns that fill the Alsatian landscape. But socially, they lived at a distance: Jews could not own land, nor could they manage a business, and membership of guilds was denied them. The majority of Alsatian Jews were middlemen: travelling peddlers and moneylenders. They formed a vital part of the local economy, and yet they were met with ambivalence, or even outright hostility. Paula Hyman has described the contact between Jews and non-Jews (both Catholic and Protestant) in Alsace as "utilitarian and instrumental," most often as seller-customer and, on the rare occasion that a Jew had some economic success, as competitor.[41] The idea that Alsatian Jews lived among their non-Jewish fellow Alsatians, but not of them, is well illustrated in linguistic terms. In the eighteenth century, Alsatians spoke their own Germanic dialect. Alsatian Jews had their own variant of this, known as Judeo-Alsatian, a dialect close to Yiddish.

---

    in Provincial France: Religion and Political Identity in Brittany (Princeton, NJ, 1993), esp. 10.

[41] Paula Hyman, *The Emancipation of the Jews of Alsace* (New Haven, CT, 1991), 13.

Nonetheless, it was not language, but rather the practice of loaning money at interest that was the particular preoccupation of critics of the Alsatian Jew. Small cash loans were vital for a peasantry that had little or no access to credit in any other form, and Jews were not the only ones to offer this service. Christian notaries, too, made loans to the peasantry. But usury, the damning term by which the practice came to be known – was an evil that was seen to be the specific domain of the Alsatian Jew. In 1777, François-Antoine-Joseph Hell famously attacked the Jews of Alsace for their alleged usury, originating forged receipts that were to release Alsatian peasants from loans outstanding to Jews. A decade later, it was still widely believed that as much as one-third of all mortgages in Alsace were in the hands of Jews,[42] the expression of a generalised fear that Jews were disproportionately, and unreasonably, dominant in Alsatian economic life. In 1789, as the new National Assembly began to discuss whether Jews should be included in the nation, some new citizens from the region of Alsace did not hesitate to make their feelings clear. In April 1790, the Strasbourg municipality sent an *Adresse* to the National Assembly, in which Jewish usurers were described as "growing fat from the food of others." In their *cahier*, the clergy of Colmar-Sélestat made the same complaint.[43] Following the emancipation of the Jews of Alsace, citizens in the Bas-Rhin complained to that department's General Council, fearing a "partial seizure by the Jews" of communal land in the countryside when it was divided up.[44] Most, in fact, found it difficult to feel confident that the Jews of Alsace could become worthy citizens. Nor did this particular view disappear with the granting of citizenship. Schechter has argued that eighteenth-century political thinkers saw citizenship in terms of a series of moral attributes (as opposed to rights); the ideal citizen would "display selflessness over egotism, courage over cowardice, productive utility over sterile idleness, transparency over opacity." For the Jew, generally defined by the negative quality of each duality, this type of conceptualisation suggested that it might be almost impossible for him to be anything

---

[42] Baruch Hagani, *L'Emancipation des juifs* (Paris, 1928), 167, quoted in Hyman, *Alsace*, 13. On the historical background to the association of Jews with usury in Alsace, see Marx, "La Régénération économique des Juifs d'Alsace." In his article "Les Juifs et l'usure en Alsace," Marx has shown that this perception was in fact false.

[43] Marx, 107.

[44] A.D. Bas-Rhin, 1L 491, quoted in ibid., 110

other than the ideal "anti-citizen."[45] That the Jews of Alsace were the last of the four Jewish populations of France to be granted citizenship, nearly two years after this gift had been bestowed upon their Sephardic coreligionists in the southwest, was no coincidence. The National Assembly required many hours of debate before its members could envisage Alsatian Jews as citizens. And this body's decision to grant citizenship to the Jewish population of Alsace was to be criticized constantly over the ensuing years. Alsatian Jews, it was thought, did not live up to the expectations inherent in their emancipation, and the question of what was to be done with them was to be examined and discussed many times over throughout the nineteenth century.

One such discussion was introduced by the Alsatian lawyer Louis Poujol, one of many Alsatian commentators who wrote to decry Jewish usury. Fifteen years after emancipation, Poujol remained convinced that the Jews of Alsace were still unprepared to take on the duties of citizenship along with its benefits, maintaining instead their medieval obstinacy and continuing to profit from the Alsatian population through money lending.[46] In response to heartfelt complaints on this matter emanating from Alsace, Napoleon – who could perhaps more than anything else be called a political opportunist in his relationship with the Jews – was, having first engaged French Jews in lengthy discussions regarding the place of French law in Judaism, ultimately to promulgate a decree that specifically targeted and discriminated against the largest group of Jews in France: those in Alsace.

Poujol argued for the punitive temporary withdrawal of citizenship from the Jews of that region and for strict controlling measures. Although Napoleon did not follow Poujol's recommendations to the letter and allowed the Jews of Alsace to remain citizens, he did enshrine in law the notion that punishment and control were necessary to make the Jews of Alsace useful members of the nation. In 1808, following the convocation of the Assembly of Jewish Notables and the Sanhedrin, he set out the ten-year decree that would come to be known as nothing less than "infamous": in an attempt to curb the usury that was thought to be overwhelmingly practiced by Jews in Alsace, any loan granted at a rate

---

[45] Schechter, 101.
[46] Louis Poujol, *Quelques observations concernant les Juifs en général et plus particulièrement ceux d'Alsace* (Paris, 1806).

of interest beyond ten per cent was cancelled, and all outstanding debts owed to Jews by soldiers, minors, and women were declared invalid. The laws also prohibited any movement of Alsatian Jews to other departments and forbade Jewish immigrants from settling in Alsace. Finally, the decree prevented Jews from supplying replacements for those conscripted for military service.[47] Napoleon's actions underscored the ambiguity at the heart of emancipation. As far as Jews were concerned, their emancipation could simply be understood as an end to limitations and discrimination – the beginning of an era of choices. But even for those non-Jews who supported Jewish emancipation, the bestowal of citizenship was no free gift. It came with responsibilities and, specifically, with the expectation that Jews, once emancipated, would become citizens, with all that that implied. When in 1806 Napoleon saw Jews who had seemingly chosen to make no changes at all in their lives, he reacted as though they had not fulfilled their end of the bargain. If Jews did not want to take on the duties of citizenship of their own free will, they would have to be forced to do so.

Thus, emancipation was not merely the final climactic upheaval for the Jews of France in a chain of events that had begun with the Enlightenment and Moses Mendelssohn and the wondrous beginning of a glorious existence in France. Rather, emancipation in one sense was the beginning of years of assessment and redefinition of France's Jews by their non-Jewish fellow citizens. The foreign, secretive, scheming, and repulsive Samuel is one such attempt at definition. What *Le Juif* suggests is that more than one sector of French society was grappling to make sense of the presence of newly emancipated Jews in French society. What can Samuel, the Jew of the title, tell us about France in 1823? What was it about the world of those who felt discomfort with the Jews in their midst that enticed them to say the things they did? *Who* wrote about Jews in France? *To what end* did they do so, that is, what place did they allot the Jew in their understanding of the world? And *what* can this tell us about nineteenth-century France? How was the ongoing competition for the public space that characterized these years manifested in expressions of ambivalence towards Jews? Did the Catholicism that had informed

---

[47] During this period, conscripts with sufficient means could buy someone to replace them.

peoples' lives for centuries simply wither away following the upheavals of the last decade of the eighteenth century? Or alongside new notions such as nationhood and capitalism, did Catholic ideology continue to influence the way many French men and women saw fit to understand the ongoing controversies that marked the nineteenth century?

In this book, I trace these questions in a loose chronology, beginning with the Restoration and concluding with the later years of the July Monarchy. A wide variety of sources provide the material for my discussion: from the pamphlets of learned figures, self-interested parties, utopians, and charlatans; to newspaper articles, novels, and works of art. Nonetheless, although I have sought out and explored writings from this period that feature Jews, it must be emphasised that this work makes no claim to be an exhaustive study. Rather, I have chosen certain specific events or figures as illustrative of the way in which the Jew was imagined. For example, the many social manifestations of hatred towards Jews in Alsace such as the Hep Hep riots of 1819 or the anti-Jewish riots in Alsace of 1848 do not fall within its scope.[48] Nor have I considered questions of receptivity in any consistent way. The number of copies a work or a newspaper sold might give us an indication of the penetration of the ideas contained within it. It tells us nothing about the ways in which it was received. We know that Le Juif was performed, but what did the audience make of Samuel? Conversely, the very creation of a work is also evidence of the existence of an idea, and this is what concerns me here, as well as the ways in which that idea changed or maintained its form. To this end, where possible I have sought to show how ideas or approaches were shared across ideological systems or bureaucracies. Finally, I am not seeking to amplify the drama of anti-Jewish hatred in France: in examining hateful ambivalence closely, I am not implying that this was a sentiment shared by all French people. Jews were understood in myriad ways during this period, ranging from the positive to the hateful, with the truly ambivalent in between. While I have sought to explore this full gamut, the reader might find a preponderance of negative depictions. This is partly a reflection of the state of affairs. It stems mostly from the fact that I seek here to trouble two assumptions: that the emancipation somehow resolved hatred of Jews for the first part, at least, of the nineteenth century,

[48]   On anti-Jewish riots in Alsace, see Hyman, *Jews of Alsace*, 24–6.

and that tales of this hatred constitute a discrete discipline in the French historiographical canon. Nonetheless, I have sought, throughout this work, to balance my findings in small ways, if only to remind the reader that I am not describing a monolithic sentiment. For this reason, also, France's Jews are given some voice here, but strictly speaking, this is not their story.[49] This is a history of France; of how some French sought to come to terms with life in the early nineteenth century by using Jews to think, to dream, and to make sense of change.

Thus, it is my intention here to trace the evolution of the Jew in the French imaginary in the early years of the nineteenth century. But I will not draw a long bow and link this to the later expressions of the same sentiment with which we are all so familiar. A longer historical perspective is a good way to test a theory, and it offers readers a way to make links between their own world and the world that is being described to them. But in this context, this poses a problem. The reader, armed with only too thorough a knowledge of the appalling end to which understandings of Jews as other were to be taken, is – just like the author – faced with a challenge in a work that traces the history of the framing of alterity in the nineteenth century. For example, what are we – author and reader alike – to make of the words of one Alphonse Toussenel, who in 1844, discussing Jewish-owned railways, told the reader that their travellers were "stuffed into cattle trucks?"[50] If we bring the Holocaust with us to this tale, we risk obscuring the true significance of this ambivalence. Discourses in which the Jew represented alterity that date from this time did not set out on an inevitable journey to a horrible climax. They were an expression of anxieties that relate specifically to 1823, to the 1830 Revolution, to the materialism of the July Monarchy, and so on. My wish for the reader of this work, then, is that they immerse themselves in the world of Samuel and his creators, of Alphonse Toussenel, David Drach, Félicité de Lamennais, and the other characters who feature here, to emerge with a greater understanding of what drove these figures, of the way they interpreted their world, and the reasons why they assigned the Jew a specific place in it. In France of the early nineteenth century, ordinary men and women were forced to confront enormous changes,

[49] For a fuller exploration of Jewish responses, see Leff.
[50] Alphonse Toussenel, *Les Juifs, rois de l'époque; histoire de la féodalité financière* (Paris, 1847), 200.

and many chose to make sense of this through the Jew. I propose to accompany them on this journey. Throughout, untrustworthy, secretive, and repellent *juifs* like Samuel offer a fascinating perspective into the ways in which theatre-goers of 1823 – among many others – chose to make sense of an era of challenge and change.

1

ℒ

Competing Solutions to a Jewish Question

*I*N 1817, DUKE SILVESTRE DE SACY SET ASIDE THE STUDIES OF
the Orient for which he was to become so celebrated to put to
paper his thoughts on Jews in France.[1] He had received a request from a
counsellor to the king of Saxony to write a critique of a pamphlet that was
achieving extensive sales and exciting much attention. In this pamphlet,
the military careerist Charles-Joseph Bail had followed the lead of the
emperor Napoleon, in whose army he had served, to evaluate Jewish
emancipation, to conclude that its pace was insufficient and suggest ways
to remedy this problem.[2] Sacy took another view. A devout Catholic and
dedicated monarchist, commander of the Legion of Honour, rector of
the royal university, and peer of France, Sacy was resolutely absolutist:
there was no place for emancipated Jews in Restoration society.

Indeed, Sacy's confidence in the strength of religious doctrine was
such that he based his argument on the assumption that Judaism was
as absolutist as the Catholicism to which he adhered. Thus, while he
agreed with the stance generally taken by writers on this topic – that long
centuries of debasement were the cause of any apparent vices among
Jews (and he even went so far as to state that similar conditions would
have had the same effect on any nation) – it did not follow that the
granting of civil rights to Jews would bring about their amelioration.
Sacy believed that any attempt to encourage the fusion of the Jewish

---

[1] Silvestre de Sacy, *Lettre à M. ***, Conseiller de S.M. le Roi de Saxe, relativement à l'ouvrage
intitulé: Des Juifs au XIXe siècle, Par M. le B^on. S. de S.* (Paris, 1817).

[2] Charles-Joseph Bail, *Des Juifs au dix-neuvième siècle, ou Considérations sur leur état civil
et politique en Europe, suivies de la Notice biographique des Juifs anciens et modernes qui
se sont illustrés dans les sciences et les arts, par M. Bail,* 2d ed. (Paris, 1816).

and French nations would be to submit Jews to the indignity of being forced to "violate their belief and transgress the obligations their religion imposes on them."[3] Sacy argued that partisans of fusion between Jews and Christians based their assumptions on the assimilated Jew – the one who, "seduced by the attraction of posts and dignities and encouraged by liberal ideas, themselves make all the concessions that one should not dare ask of them."[4] Yet assimilated Jews represented only a tiny minority, and in the eyes of Sacy, speaking for the religiously observant Jewish masses, their quest for political freedom constituted "reckless audacity and a veritable apostasy."[5]

For Sacy, the matter was straightforward: what counted was the observant Jew, the man who could not doubt "that he is of God's chosen people and has been separated by Him from all other peoples,"[6] and who, because he was a Jew, would one day regain the autonomy and political independence that had been promised him. This Jew would naturally share Sacy's belief that the Jews must remain a separate and foreign nation. For Sacy, the very laws – not only of religious tolerance, but also of Judaism and Christianity themselves – precluded the fusion of the Jewish nation with other nations, and those writers who advocated the granting of full civil rights to Jews misjudged these laws. Jews and Christians could only be brought together if both sides renounced the major tenets of their respective religions, that is, if Jews ceased to be Jews and Christians ceased to be Christians. Because Sacy could not condone such an idea, he concluded that the Jew had only two real options: either to embrace Christianity or to remain Jewish in the sense that Sacy understood it – forever foreign and separate.

Alyssa Sepinwall, in her study of the Abbé Grégoire, describes as "conditionalist" her protagonist and others, such as Christian Wilhelm Dohm, who saw Jewish emancipation as possible, but only on the condition that Jews, "in the long run," would shed their particularity. Grégoire, of course, had been one of those to take up the challenge set in 1787 by the Société royale des sciences et des arts de Metz to consider whether there were "ways of making the Jews more useful and happier in France." (*Est-il*

---

[3] Sacy, 10.
[4] Ibid., 8.
[5] Ibid., 12.
[6] Ibid., 9.

des moyens de rendre les Juifs plus utiles et plus heureux en France?) Initially no essays were deemed worthy of recognition, but Grégoire chose to revise and resubmit his essay and was ultimately declared one of the winners. In his work, Grégoire argued that what he called Jewish degeneracy could be understood as the result of their long history of suffering. This degeneracy was particularly evident in their treatment of the peasantry: for Grégoire, this was a moral as well as a financial mistreatment. Sepinwall argues that one aim of Grégoire's essay was a defence of Catholicism. Certainly, as he was decrying the treatment that his fellow Christians had reserved for Jews, he also sought to highlight Christian benevolence towards Jews throughout history. And he took a familiar approach to Judaism itself: Jews had brought their inferior status upon themselves because of their obstinate adherence to a Talmud that was "ridiculous" and evil. He provided detailed information to show that the Jewish population was multiplying at a dangerous rate – if unchecked, he warned, Jews would "inundate and infest" the country.[7] Ultimately Grégoire, like Sacy, wished for the conversion of Jews to Catholicism. But while the revolutionary Abbé could allow for the initial admission of Jews into society as Jews, Sacy's conditionalism called for a literal shedding of Judaism as the condition for inclusion.

Sacy's arguments reflected common attitudes among his fellow Catholic monarchists in the Restoration. Catholics, whose Church had been irrevocably weakened, were forced to renegotiate their place in a world forever changed: one in which, for example, Jews were seen as fellow citizens. By the time that Napoleon had been definitively defeated at Waterloo in 1815 and the Bourbon Louis XVIII was restored to the throne for the second time, the Jews of France had been emancipated for twenty-four years. The granting of citizenship to France's Jews had been an upheaval not only for the Jewish population, but also for French non-Jews, for it had broken down a hierarchy by which, through its very existence, they had ordered their world. The pariah status of the Jewish population, whatever one's moral position, had been one reliable and

---

[7] Grégoire, *Essai sur la régénération physique, morale et politique des Juifs*, 189n8, 83, 85, quoted in Alyssa Sepinwall, *The Abbé Grégoire and the French Revolution: The Making of Modern Universalism* (Berkeley, 2005), 68–71. By the Restoration, Grégoire was writing in ever more frustrated terms at what he saw as continued Jewish exclusivity and, in particular, the ongoing refusal of Jews to convert.

thus reassuring the way ancien régime society was ordered. Jews had been generally identifiable, and their place in society had been clear. As the world changed around Sacy, he maintained this image of the Jew as a foreign, separate entity. He was expressing his rejection of the Revolutionary legacy through his disapproval of the assimilated Jew. In other words, the Jew could bring certainty. Darrin McMahon has described the counter-Enlightenment and later the Right, from the end of the eighteenth century onwards, as being characterised by its "visionary desire" to remould a world it was unable to accept.[8] And indeed, for Catholics and Ultras, the Restoration was the moment for the Church to return to a romanticised and mythological France, harmoniously ruled by a trinity of (Bourbon) king, Church, and nobility.[9]

But this was not the world of the ancien régime. Napoleon was gone, and the crowned heads of Europe had returned a Bourbon king to the throne, yet the Restoration was hardly a straightforward return to the world of the ancien régime. Too much had occurred during the interregnum between a deposed king and a returned one for all of French society to simply take up where it had left off before 1789. The three pillars of Church, monarchy, and nobility, which had shaped and ordered life under the ancien régime, had been shaken to their very foundations by the Revolution. They could no longer lay claim to legitimate and unquestioned authority, and thus they were lost to the French as points of reference, or, at best, they were merely points of yearning.

What was it that now constituted legitimate authority in France? Restoration governments could only respond with ambiguity, for at the heart of the era was a Charter that left the door open to varying interpretations of what Restoration France should – or could – be. Those in the Church, for example, saw the return of the Bourbon Louis XVIII as their own. Under his rule, Catholicism was named the State religion (as opposed to "the religion of the great majority of Frenchmen," as it had been named in Napoleon's Concordat of 1801). The noble and explicitly counter-revolutionary episcopacy that led the Church was aided by ultraroyalist nobles who had turned in exile "from scepticism

---

[8] Darrin McMahon, *Enemies of the Enlightenment: The French Counter-Enlightenment as the Making of Modernity* (New York, 2001), 156.
[9] Pilbeam, *Republicanism*, 66.

to Catholicism,"[10] and these groups were inclined to see a direct connection between monarchy and religion. After all, a France that was ruled by a Most Christian King was a France that was Catholic. And the reinstatement of Catholicism as the religion of the state was the opportunity for the Church to remake its close relationship with royalty, once again anointing the Bourbon kings as leaders of the Christian world. During the Restoration, the National Missionaries of France would send out clergymen to regional centres, where they would seek to bring the population back to the Church. Men and women would be engaged in penitence and expiation, at once both religious and political. Liberty trees that had been planted during the Revolution would be pulled down and either burned or their wood used to repair the local Church. A giant mission cross would be erected in their place, or where a guillotine had stood. The aim of the missionaries was to cleanse the people of the previous twenty-five years, so as to re-establish the reign in France of a Most Christian King. Catholicism would once more be the national faith. Thus, although their stated goal may have been to revive Christianity in the hearts and minds of the French, their intention to do this by recreating a Christian kingdom, headed by a monarch whose legitimacy could not be questioned, was overtly political. More than 1,500 such events were staged throughout France during the Restoration, to the extent that Sheryl Kroen has called the missions "the mass spectacles of the Restoration period."[11] In the parliaments of Louis XVIII and Charles X, Ultras worked to cleanse the years of Revolution from public memory. In doing so, they were to make Restoration France a place which, for Jews, was not unlike Sacy's ideal world in which reigned what Jay Berkovitz has called an "ideology of social isolation."[12]

One such Ultra was Viscount Louis de Bonald, "more royalist than the king, more Catholic than the Pope."[13] Bonald was dedicated to the idea of the central importance of the State. His desire to see France become an absolutely powerful State was evidenced by his actions as a minister under Charles X during the Restoration. What was Bonald's ideal? It was

---

[10] Dansette, 181.
[11] Kroen, 82.
[12] Berkovitz, *Shaping*, 113.
[13] Marvin Cox, "The Liberal Legitimists and the Party of Order under the Second French Republic," *French Historical Studies* 5 (1968): 450.

a France where the Church dominated and government was absolute, if not dictatorial. For Bonald, the presence of Jews in French society was one of the evils of the Revolution's legacy, and a return to a Catholic nation would also be a return to a world in which boundaries between Catholics and others would be clearly delineated. Indeed, Bonald, as absolute in his conditionalism as Sacy, stated quite plainly that Jews could never be citizens in the type of Christian nation that he worked to reinstate.[14] (He could, however, envisage a place for them, on the condition that they convert.) However, Bonald saw no reason to stop at segregation. As a Jansenist, Bonald believed that the most worthy of human experiences involved suffering and sacrifice, and the greatest possible self-sacrifice was that made in the service of the nation. Private life and individual human beings must be subordinate to the state and its needs, and thus it was justifiable, if not necessary, to remove categories of people undesirable to the state.[15] Jews had already proven themselves to be "undesirable," and for Bonald the only question to be resolved was the method of their removal from society. In his article "Sur les Juifs," published in 1806, Bonald outlined a scheme to this end. He suggested that Jews be restricted in their right to marry and produce children, with a view to their virtual disappearance. It is not surprising to find that, like Sacy, Bonald saw only one way to redemption for the Jews: to become Christians.

Another prominent Catholic writer of the time concurred with Bonald's view that Jews had no place in a Catholic France. The priest Félicité de Lamennais was born in St Malo in 1782 in, of all places, the rue des Juifs.[16] Mostly self-taught, he came late to ordination, although he had entered the priesthood by 1817 when the first volume of his *Essai sur l'indifférence en matière de religion* appeared. It was a rapid success, selling forty thousand copies in a few years. (Three more volumes were to follow.) A competitor noted that it would "wake the dead."[17] In these four

---

[14] Louis de Bonald, "Sur les Juifs," reproduced in *Mélanges littéraires, politiques et philosophiques*, 3d ed (Paris, 1852), 369.

[15] David Klinck, *The French Counterrevolutionary Theorist, Louis de Bonald (1754–1840)* (New York, 1996), 230.

[16] On Lamennais and the Jews, see Arnold Ages, "Lamennais and the Jews," *Jewish Quarterly Review* 63 (1972): 158–70. On Lamennais, see Cholvy and Hilaire, 81–91; and René Rémond, *Lamennais et la démocratie* (Paris, 1948).

[17] Gérard Cholvy and Yves-Marie Hilaire, *Histoire religieuse de la France contemporaine* (Toulouse: Privat, 1985), 1: 81.

volumes, Lamennais drew on Bonald's writings and sought to continue what the latter had begun, working for the re-acceptance of Catholic truth in French intellectual life. Lamennais's admiration for Bonald led him to describe the latter as the greatest philosopher the world had seen since the Cartesian Nicolas Malebranche, and in 1818, the two came together as contributors to the newspaper the *Conservateur*. One of Bonald's arguments with which Lamennais agreed – and, indeed, that most Catholics thinkers shared – was the denunciation of the idea of tolerance, a dangerous idea in that it invited relativism and thus challenged the supremacy of Christianity.[18] This was reflected in Lamennais's view on the place of Jews in France, which was consistent with that of Bonald.

For Lamennais, the story of the Jews was divided into two epochs before and after Jesus, with a central, pivotal section focusing on Jesus' life and death. In his view of biblical Judaism (pre-Jesus), Lamennais was similar to Bonald. Both shared with their pre-Enlightenment forebears the understanding of Judaism as a dichotomy of ancient biblical virtue – and modern evil. Thus, Lamennais saw a divine imprint on early Israelite society, describing the Jews before Jesus Christ as a "model people"; "miraculous in its entire existence."[19] The Hebrews and their ritual, chosen by God, served as an example to idolaters. Yet if the ancient Hebrews were worthy of admiration, it was because they were destined to be the precursor to Christianity. Lamennais drew on another aspect of Church ideology, almost as old as Christianity itself. He took care to stress that if God's presence was discernible in biblical Judaism, it was because, at the same time as he had revealed Judaism to his chosen people through the ritual involved, he had also entrusted them with a vital role, to prepare humanity to recognise its Saviour. Judaism was bound together with Christianity, existing only to foretell and ultimately be superseded by it.[20] And although the Synagogue as an institution was exclusive and recognised only the Jewish people, Christianity was God's way of giving all men a chance of salvation, and thus it had been – and still was – the only true religion.

[18] Frederick Artz, *France under the Bourbon Restoration, 1814–1830* (New York, 1963), 155; Sutcliffe, 213.
[19] Lamennais, *Essai sur l'indifférence en matière de religion*, vol. 3, in *Oeuvres complètes*, (Geneva, 1980), 2: 38, 39.
[20] On the ideology of supercession in Catholicism, see Kenneth Stow, *Jewish Dogs*. The frequency with which the Catholic thinkers explored here called on this notion would appear to support Stow's thesis regarding its centrality in Church ideology.

It is unsurprising, therefore, that in Lamennais's eyes, the pivotal moment in the history of the Jewish people was their rejection of Jesus as Saviour and their subsequent guilt for his death. It was from Jesus' time, we are told, that the Jews ceased to be a people. Yet although the deicide had been committed eighteen centuries before Lamennais was writing, the Jews that Lamennais saw around him still "rebelled" against the doctrine and the laws of Jesus, and this persistent refusal meant that they suffered continued punishment.[21] They were strangers in the heart of the French nation, isolated, and followed by disdain and outrage. They waited obstinately for a messiah who had already come. Centuries of living with the enormity of their crime had left them degraded. But since the time of Augustine, Christians had allotted Jews the role of witness to the supremacy of Christianity, and for Lamennais, predictably, the Jews of his time were an example of God's promise of final deliverance. For God had not abandoned the Jews for eternity: "he will stretch out his hand to gather up the debris of his people," and "the day of repentance and misericord will come for them."[22] Predictably, to be "gathered up," it was necessary to convert to Catholicism. For those who chose to remain Jewish, there was no redemption:

They will always be foreigners, distinguishable by the mark on their foreheads, which horrifies all who see them. The mark is written by an iron hand and is more terrible than the mark of Cain: it is DEICIDE![23]

Lamennais and Bonald did disagree on certain important points. Unlike the Catholic hierarchy, Lamennais did not believe that the road leading back to the past was the best way for the Church. Rather, he sought to persuade his fellow Catholics that the Church had to adapt to a changed world if it was to thrive once more. This belief distinguished him among Catholics. Ultimately, in fact, Lamennais came to express a liberalism that would have been anathema to someone like Bonald. Nevertheless, the two men would have remained in complete agreement on the place of Jews in French society (or indeed, that there was no such place). For his part, Lamennais argued that religion was a type of society, and in every fully formed society, there had always been – and could only be – one

---

[21] Lamennais, *Essai*, vol. 3, in *Oeuvres complètes*, 2: 41.
[22] Ibid., vol. 4, 2: 232.
[23] Ibid., 2: 44.

dominant religion. Two religions could not exist side by side any more than could two societies. It followed from this that it was not enough, if one wished to be a member of a society, simply to obey its political and civil laws: the Jews, "in society only with themselves," were a "striking" example of this.[24] In Clermont-Tonnerre's oft-quoted speech, made on 23 December, 1789 in debates in the National Assembly regarding the possible eligibility of Jews – and other non-Catholics – for citizenship, he argued that Jews, as individuals, deserved everything. But for Lamennais, neither the Jew nor Judaism had a place in France.[25] In his writing, he expressed what might be described as a Catholic nationalism. Insofar as he was concerned, Catholicism was not merely the state religion. The State could not exist without Catholicism; it constituted the state; and in such a state, there was no room for the Jew or Judaism.

Louis XVIII's charter did not echo the wishes of men such as Bonald and Lamennais, for although it established Catholicism as the State religion, it also guaranteed freedom of worship for all religions. Indeed, if this period has been generally seen as a quiet time in terms of anti-Jewish writings or acts, it is perhaps because the position of the government on Jews was, at worst, neutral, and at best, favourable. Yet if Louis XVIII's policies could be called favourably disposed towards the Jews, once he was replaced by his brother, the Ultra Charles X, in 1824, the face of government changed, and it appeared that the desires of the Church were indeed to be realised. In celebrating his ascension to the throne on 29 May 1825 with an elaborate coronation evocative of the ancien régime, Charles X announced his determination to resurrect this world. In fact, the Church coronation had been progressively falling out of practice during the eighteenth century, and Louis XVIII held no religious ceremony to sanctify his rule during his reign. Thus, the efforts of Charles X were all the more striking: his coronation specifically emphasised the divine origin of his appointment.[26]

The Church now had an ally in power, and it became ever more pervasive. In 1825, Charles X passed the highly unpopular Sacrilege Law,

---

[24] Lamennais, *Essai*, vol. 3, in *Oeuvres complètes*, 2: 48.
[25] Lisa Leff discusses Clermont-Tonnerre's vision of citizenship in *Sacred Bonds of Solidarity: The Rise of Jewish Internationalism in Nineteenth-Century France* (Stanford, 2006), 24.
[26] Kroen, 118.

under which theft from Churches and profanation of the Host were made criminal offences, the latter being defined as a crime "against God and King." In this equating of the sacred Host with the person of the king, the government of Charles X and the Church appeared to be moving ever closer to one another.[27] And governmental expressions of sympathy with the Church were not limited to legislation. Under Charles X, domains such as education once again came under the aegis of the Church, as they had done during the ancien régime. In 1817, Louis XVIII had allowed the Jesuits to return to France and create an alternative secondary schooling system; under Charles X, the entire education system was thoroughly catholicised. "Overnight," as Adrien Dansette has described it, changes occurred in schools. "Awakening was by the church bell. There was daily Mass, catechism twice a week, and the recitation of the *Veni sancta spiritu* at the beginning of classes and of the *Sub tuum praesidium* at the end. The *Angelus* was said and grace before and after meals in the refectory."[28] By the end of the Restoration, one-third of secondary students were educated in ecclesiastical colleges, and an equal proportion of university teaching positions were held by the clergy. In 1824, Mgr Frayssinous was appointed minister of public instruction (he was already minister of ecclesiastical affairs), and he set out to restore Catholic values to the education system, dissolving the School of Medicine, suppressing the École normale, and removing those professors who were seen as inappropriate. Jews did not escape this purge. From the date of Charles X's ascension to the throne, no Jews were admitted to the Société asiatique.[29] Between 1813, when Myrtil Maas and S.-A. Lévy entered the Ecole normale supérieure, and 1816, when they graduated, a regime had been overturned – twice – and in the Restoration, they were unable to find teaching positions because of their religion. (Maas may well have been grateful in retrospect for this discriminatory act, because he moved into insurance and became a giant in this field.) Olinde Rodrigues, who sought to study at the school sometime later, was refused even admission, on the same basis.[30]

[27] Mary Hartman, "The Sacrilege Law of 1825 in France: A Study in Anticlericalism and Mythmaking," *Journal of Modern History* 44, no. 1 (1972): 21–37.
[28] Dansette, 190.
[29] Berkovitz, "Jewish Scholarship and Identity in Nineteenth-Century France," *Modern Judaism* 18, no. 1 (1998), 15.
[30] Christine Piette, *Les Juifs de Paris (1808–1840): la marche vers l'assimilation* (Québec, 1983), 75. In fact, this type of discrimination continued beyond the regime. In 1834,

But Jews who sought inclusion and acceptance could also find this in the Restoration. For the Revolution had left a spiritual void: many people, most of them young, sought a code of spiritual morality that they felt would enable society to function and to help them build the new world. For Louis de Bonald, Restoration society was atomised: French men and women were alienated from one another, and what he called the "elementary bonds of society" had been dissolved.[31] It was industrialisation that could be found at the root of this evil. Yet although Bonald saw the strong, central Catholic state as the answer to this ill, for many, Catholicism was no longer a meaningful way to fill the gap. What might take its place?

One figure, Count Henri de Saint-Simon proposed his own system of spiritual morality. The majority of Catholics may have sought either to restore or remake the Church, but liberals such as Saint-Simon proposed alternatives to Catholicism. Saint-Simon envisaged a society that would be brought together through work. Merit would be based not on birth or inheritance, but rather on competence and wisdom. Thus would egoism be replaced. On his death in 1825, a movement was founded in his name by a group of students and recent graduates of the École Polytechnique for whom he had been a revered mentor. This group of young men, who called themselves the Saint-Simonians, accorded a special place in their movement for Jews. And Jews participated enthusiastically in the creation of the movement: they were welcomed into it not merely as equals, but as central to its functioning. Here was a space in which they could define society as they would have it be. Indeed, Jews were an intrinsic part of the Saint Simonian movement: they were proof that the Saint-Simonian religion was truly universal and tolerant in a way that Catholicism had never been, that it was appropriate to the new world, and that it had, therefore, effectively superseded Catholicism.[32] The movement's leader, Prosper Enfantin, was also using Jews to define his world, and in his case,

Léon Halevy, known as a brilliant scholar, was overlooked for a chair at the Ecole polytechnique. Jules Clarétie, who remembered this event on the occasion of Halevy's death in 1883, made the claim that Halevy, who had in fact acted in the position for three years, was "put to one side" because of his Judaism. Jules Clarétie, *La Vie à Paris, 1881* (Paris, 1883), 326.

[31] David Cohen, "The Vicomte de Bonald's Critique of Industrialism," *Journal of Modern History* 41 (December 1969), 479.

[32] Leff, 75.

they helped him to think through inclusion. For Enfantin, Jews were included as an indication of what was right about his utopia, rather than being excluded as a sign of what was wrong with it.

Nonetheless, there were some French Jews for whom Saint-Simonian liberalism was not an option. Indeed, some Jews chose to follow the advice of men like Sacy and Bonald and embrace Catholicism. Exactly how many Jews did convert in the generations after emancipation has been a subject of debate.[33] Most recently, Thomas Kselman has found records of 315 baptisms of Jews between 1833 and 1875 in the register of abjurations held in the archives of the archdiocese of France. In a purely statistical sense, this number is of little significance, given that by 1861, the Jewish population of Paris had reached 25,000.[34] Overall, it is probably safe to say that in terms of numbers, Jewish conversions to Christianity in early-nineteenth-century France did not have the same significance as Germany, where historians have generally characterised apostasy in terms of a wave.[35] Nonetheless, some French Jews, confronted with what was in one respect a return to ancien régime (and thus pre-emancipation) France, must have experienced growing frustration and social isolation, only aggravated by the fact of their legal equality. I would like to consider how those Jews who converted to Christianity – apostates to the often bewildered and angry community they left behind them – were received by the Church. What can this tell us about Catholic perceptions of Judaism at this time?

Conversions of Jews to Catholicism were publicised through the leading Catholic periodical of the era, the conservative *Ami de la religion et du roi*. Sometimes only the briefest facts were given. Thus in 1825, readers were told that two Jewish ladies, "from an orthodox family in their nation," received baptism at the church of Notre Dame and that

---

[33] See, for example, Jonathan Helfand, "Passports and Piety: Apostasy in Nineteenth-Century France," *Jewish History* 3, no. 2 (1988): 59–83; and the debate featured in *Jewish History* 5, no. 2 (1991). Paula Hyman has also contributed to this debate, finding conversion among French Jews to be of "little statistical importance" (Paula Hyman, *The Jews of Modern France*, n. 5, p. 229).

[34] Thomas Kselman, "Turbulent Souls in Modern France: Jewish Conversion and the Terquem Affair," *Historical Reflections/Réflexions historiques* 32 no. 1 (2006), 88. The way in which these conversions were perceived is discussed in Chapter 2.

[35] For discussion on this, see Deborah Hertz, "Seductive Conversion in Berlin, 1770–1809," in *Jewish Apostasy in the Modern World*, ed. Todd Endelman (New York, 1987), 48–82.

they were the fourteenth and fifteenth persons that the presiding priest had had the happiness of receiving into the Church in the previous two years.[36] Other incidents were given full coverage. The conversion in 1823 of a Jew who was well known in the Jewish community, described as "an important and glorious conquest," merited two articles.[37] The Abbé Jean Labouderie, vicar of Notre Dame Cathedral in Paris, presided over several conversions between 1815 and 1819, and published six of the sermons he delivered on these occasions.[38] Labouderie placed the Jews in an historic context that had been clearly defined by centuries of Catholic belief in the Jews' crime and punishment. Thus, in his sermons, the Jews were assigned the role of perpetrators of the greatest of all crimes, for which they were eternally punished. Labouderie called down fire and brimstone on blasphemous Jews and condemned Jewish blindness and obstinacy, the Jewish hatred of Christ and Christians, and the evil Talmud. The themes of the sermons did not vary greatly: Labouderie generally began by condemning the deicide Jews to eternal damnation, and then he argued the authenticity, greatness, superiority, and uniqueness of Christianity. Calling, like his fellow Catholics Bonald and Lamennais, on the ideology of supercession, Labouderie showed that Jesus' coming was predicted in the Jewish scriptures. He complimented the neophyte's patrons and then focused on the neophyte, telling him or her to be sure to be a good and true Christian. He then called on God and Jesus to forgive the neophyte for the sins of their ancestors and to admit him or her into the kingdom of God. Finally, he concluded by turning his attention to those

---

[36] "Baptêmes de deux juives à Strasbourg," *L'Ami de la religion et du roi, journal ecclésiastique, politique et littéraire*, 25 June 1825.

[37] "Baptême de David Drach," *L'Ami de la religion*, 2 April 1823. Drach's conversion and writings will be discussed in detail in the following chapter.

[38] Jean Labouderie, *Discours de M. l'abbé Labouderie, . . . pour le baptême de M.D.J.B. Lévy cadet, juif converti, à la métropole de Paris le 14 juin 1815* (Paris, 1815); idem, *Discours prononcé à Notre-Dame, le 7 mars 1817, à l'occasion du baptême, du mariage, de la première commission de sieur Alphonse-Jean-Sébastien-Louis Jacob, juif converti, par M. l'abbé Labouderie* (Paris, 1817); idem, *Discours pour le baptême d'Ange-Alexandre-Bernard-Jean Mayer, juif converti, prononcé à Saint-Nicholas-du-Chardonnet, le 23 avril 1818* (Paris, 1818); idem, *Discours pour le baptême de Joseph-Marie-Louis-Jean Wolf, Juif converti, prononcé à Saint-Eustache, le 23 mai 1818 par M. l'abbé Labouderie* (Paris, 1818); idem, *Discours pour le baptême de Philippe-Rigobert Vahl, juif converti, dans la chapelle du Collège royal des Écossais, le 12 novembre 1818* (n.p.n.d.); idem, *Discours pour le baptême de Anna et Louise Vahl, prononcé à Saint Germain-l'Auxerrois, le 24 mars 1819, par M. l'abbé Labouderie* (n.p.n.d.).

present, telling them that the conversion they had just witnessed should inspire them to be good Christians. Labouderie clearly placed the Jews of his own world in the historic context that Catholicism had taught him. Thus the "Jews of today" were still carrying "the fundamental deeds of Christianity, and refusing to read their destiny in them"; they were "eternal monuments to the most devastating vengeance."[39] Yet Labouderie believed, as did Lamennais, that the Jews had another vital role to play, and this was as the bearers of the promise of an ultimate redemption. In his speech to the neophyte, Labouderie would call the latter's salvation a miracle. Drawing on a traditionally Catholic notion, since coopted by the hated Revolution, Labouderie promised one neophyte that the waters of baptism would bring about their regeneration.[40]

Nonetheless, if converted Jews brought "consolation and elation" to Catholics,[41] predictably there was no hope at all for those who chose to remain Jewish. The miracle of salvation was the neophyte's alone, for they alone had been lifted out of the "exiled mass" and into redemption. Their "brothers of the flesh" – as Jewish converts called those who remained Jewish – still "blasphemed" in the synagogue, "blackening" Labouderie's God with "atrocious slander."[42] Nor was there any hope for contemporary Judaism: in the synagogue and the Talmud, Labouderie found the symbols of all its evils. Yet none of this could detract from the fact that a Jew who converted was a source of great joy. Not only was a Jewish apostate coming out of obstinate and wilful blindness into the light of truth, but the day that Catholicism taught its adherents to hope and pray for was brought just a little nearer. For centuries the continued existence of Jewish communities – and their continued refusal to convert – had posed a problem for the Church. One way the Church had sought to reconcile this problem was to focus precisely on Jewish conversion. The conversion of a Jew to Catholicism was a reminder of God's promise that Jesus would return. For Jansenists, this would signal no less than the Second Coming. For Catholics such as Labouderie, it proved the superiority of the Church at a time when his need to be reassured of this was

---

[39] Labouderie, *Anna et Louise Vahl*, 6.
[40] Labouderie, *M.D.J.B. Lévy*, 3.
[41] Ibid., 18.
[42] Labouderie, *Alphonse-Jean-Sébastien-Louis Jacob*, 4–5.

great. For despite the assured tones of his righteous outrage and religious faith, a note of uncertainty can be discerned in Labouderie's speeches. Labouderie's rhetoric might have inserted him in a long tradition of Catholic ideology, but his own world was filled with blind and blasphemous Protestants and Jews, in which the Church held out valiantly against "daily losses" caused by "insane philosophy."[43] Labouderie was not alone in targeting *philosophie* as a poison that threatened the sanctity of the Church. His words confirm him as an Ultra and place him in a conservative tradition of opposition to Enlightenment ideals, or *philosophie*, dating from before the Revolution. As one contemporary commentator put it: "The Revolution owes its origin principally to *philosophie*. The *philosophes* began it. They were the perpetrators of all the crimes, and of all the excesses that accompanied it. This impious and anti-social sect is still alive today in full vigour. [...] Let us not be mistaken. At all times, we must judge the future by the past."[44] In Labouderie's case, however, the drive by Catholics during the Restoration to remember and to expiate that has been detailed by McMahon and Kroen was extended to Judaism as well. For although Protestantism had long been associated with the Enlightenment by its conservative Catholic critics, the emancipation of the Jews was a new evil to add to the litany. It is interesting here to note that Labouderie equated one pernicious force with another. For Ultras such as he, it would seem, the emancipation of the Jews could be placed in a tradition of evil that found its roots in the Enlightenment. Moreover, Labouderie clearly did not feel that Catholicism was secure. Similarly, Bonald and Lamennais could place the Jews of their time safely in the historic context that Catholicism offered them, but both writers were also clearly uncomfortable with the visible – or at times invisible (because, for example, no longer identifiable by dress) – presence of Jews in their society. Lamennais manifestly could not bear the notion that Judaism had been placed on an equal footing before the law with Catholicism. Discussing the Sacrilege Law, Lamennais used withering tones to describe what he saw as the "touching *equality* that unites in the same protection the *faith* of the Christian who adores Jesus Christ, and the *faith* of the

---

[43] Ibid., 17.
[44] J.A.P., *De la Monarchie avec les philosophes, les révolutionnaires et les Jacobins* (1817), cited in McMahon, 153.

Jew who blasphemes him."[45] The Jew in Bonald's eyes was a fascinating mix of the lowly, degraded, and downtrodden Jew of Catholic teaching and a new Jew who, in being recognised as a French citizen, had seen all barriers to his greed lifted and was thus becoming ever more powerful in French society. Bonald saw the Jew as a "lively plant," whose growth nothing could stop and "which thrives in all climates, between the blessing of heaven and the curses of earth."[46] He was clear that no Christian government could allow its subjects to be dominated by Jews, for Judaism had a difficult and ambiguous relationship to Christianity. Although traditionally subject to the latter, Judaism nonetheless was a potentially redoubtable enemy. To give the Jews equal status in society would be to risk domination. The very nature of Judaism would mean that, if unchecked, Jews would take advantage of their power over Christians, and dependence would offend Christian dignity:

The Jews, all of whose ideas are perverted, and who despise or hate us, would find terrible examples in their history, which they could be tempted to reapply to us. In their prophecies they would find forecasts of domination that they may take literally and in the wrong way.[47]

Indeed, Bonald wondered whether Christians were not already more oppressed by the Jews, "albeit in another way," than the Jews were by the Christians.[48] In "Sur les Juifs," published in 1806, Bonald had described the Jews of Alsace as the region's true feudal "high and powerful lords,"[49] and in the same article he made more than one reference to the hunger for wealth that he saw as a trait of the Jewish character. Twelve years later, he was to return to this notion in an article written for the royalist newspaper the *Quotidienne*, probably in reaction to the impending expiry of Napoleon's Infamous Decree. In this article, he wrote of the "vile traffic in money" that Alsatian Jews supposedly practised. He painted a picture of evil Jews, taking advantage of the "superb" Alsatian population,

---

[45] Lamennais, *Mélanges religieux et philosophiques*, in *Oeuvres complètes*, 4: 444. Original emphasis.
[46] Bonald, "Sur les Juifs," 368.
[47] Ibid., 370.
[48] Ibid., 373–74.
[49] Ibid., 365.

preying on their credulity and inexperience, only releasing their unfortunate victims "once their entire fortune has been stolen away."[50]

It is hardly surprising that men such as Bonald saw threats, if not competition, around them. For under the veneer of an apparently seamless return to monarchy and Catholicism, the Church faced nothing less than the task of reassuming its right to unquestioned and legitimate authority as though this came to it naturally, and had indeed never been lost. The awkward attempts by Charles X to equate deicide and parricide under his Sacrilege Law, and the popular reaction against this, provide just one example that the Church could not merely take up where it had left off as though the twenty-two year interregnum following the execution of Louis XVI had not occurred. The years of Enlightenment, Revolution, and Napoleonic rule had left the structure of Catholicism in France severely challenged and weakened. The Revolution had thrown the legitimacy of Church and King into question, and had ultimately transferred it from a monarch who ruled by divine right to a secular nation.

The Church was not unaware of the enormity of the task that it faced. On many fronts, the Church retained none of its former glory. The material wealth it once enjoyed had been drastically reduced since its lands had been nationalised and sold during the Revolution. In terms of personnel, the Church faced a serious crisis, and this, then, severely restricted its ability to reach out to what the Church itself saw as an alarmingly blasphemous population.[51] Nonetheless, Church leaders went to great lengths to reintroduce the notion of its sacred place in French society, and the missions were to be the means to bring France back to the Church. Mission leaders undertook a full-scale effort to encourage the population in full remembering and expiation of the revolutionary years. The priests who travelled the French countryside bringing Catholic missions to the people of France targeted the symbols of the Revolution and deliberately expunged them. But in these efforts the Church stood alone, if not in direct opposition to monarchy. The latter, equally seeking to reassert its right to rule as though it were still a given, pursued a policy of compulsory forgetting, wishing to close a parenthesis around the previous twenty-five years and effectively make them illegal.[52] Nor were Church

---

[50] From *La Quotidienne*, July 1818, reproduced in *Mélanges littéraires*, 363.

[51] From *L'Ami de le religion et du roi*, cited in Kroen, 84.

[52] Kroen, 53, 41. On the "cult" of mission crosses, see Phayer.

and monarchy the only agencies who felt that they had a stake in the way the Restoration was to be played out. Over the years that had preceded the Restoration, the French had been exposed to new and different ways of imagining society. The Revolution had left French men and women of the ancien régime Third Estate with an understanding of the power of their voice and a taste for popular sovereignty. In their opposition to – and ultimate overthrow of – Charles X in 1830, they showed that they had understood the full importance of this period and that they were not willing to forget it quickly. Moreover, a group of energetic and idealistic young men born during the years of the Revolution and therefore having never known the ancien régime was adding its voice to discussions of what France could and should be.[53] Some of these men were Jews. Kroen has argued that the Restoration should be seen as a period of "extreme crisis" where legitimacy was concerned.[54] Numerous groups were negotiating the meaning of the Revolutionary and Napoleonic periods at this time: one clearly wished to efface them, another sought to expiate them, another seemingly wished to celebrate them, and an emerging generation had known only them. It would certainly appear that this process was not only ongoing, but also remained unresolved during this period.

Thus, what was at stake was legitimacy itself, and none were more aware of this than those who had lost it. The great lengths the Church went to in order to lay claim to its rightful place can be interpreted as an indication that it was aware that it had competition in the challenge to regain it. Labouderie may have had reason to fear Philosophism. Yet, contrary to his beliefs, those who aligned themselves with the Revolution and its legacy did not necessarily identify with the Jewish population. When in 1816 Charles-Joseph Bail – the man with whose pamphlet this chapter began – wrote the work that was to provoke Sacy into responding, he was inspector of troops in Paris and had served in the army for more than twenty-five years. Napoleon was in distant exile, and France – the prodigal eldest daughter of the Church – was restoring itself to the fold of Catholicism. *Des Juifs au dix-neuvième siècle* was Bail's first work on Jews. It achieved great sales and two editions in a short space of time. It attracted no small amount of attention, bringing people such as Sacy,

---

[53] Alan Spitzer, *The French Generation of 1820* (Princeton, 1987).
[54] Kroen, xi.

who had previously had nothing to say publicly about the Jews in France, into the debate. But the body of Bail's work is essentially unoriginal. From his assertion that the commonly named Jewish vices (ignorance, greed) were the result of long degradation imposed by Catholic rulers, to the conclusion that an enfranchised Jew was therefore a man, Bail was following the path set down by the most well-known "possibilists," in Sepinwall's words, and advocates of Jewish emancipation, such as Dohm and Grégoire.[55] Similarly, his suggestion that there might be a need to "modify" Jewish religious observance that "comes across as being inconsistent with the spirit of modern government,"[56] can be seen as an echo of the Enlightenment and revolutionary view of those both for and against Jewish emancipation, which argued that rabbinic Judaism was a barrier to true Jewish reform. In his desire to hurry along the process of Jewish emancipation, once again, Bail was not presenting an original idea. The emperor in whose army he had served had gone to extensive lengths to bring what was seen to be a recalcitrant Jewish community into line with the expectations that were the legacy of the Revolution. Although Bail did not state overtly here, or in his later work, *État des Juifs*, that he perceived a lack of sufficient progress in Jewish self-emancipation, he clearly felt that there was some ground left to cover. Bail believed that thirty years after emancipation, despite the best efforts of legislators (and of some Jews), "legislation that was beneficial, gentle and equitable had produced no noticeable improvement" in the Jews of Alsace.[57] Bail's primary concern was that the Jews should be good citizens. His was the world of the Revolution and of Napoleonic France, in which citizenship implied loyalty to a secular nation above all else. The tone of Bail's work is generally confident, suggesting that he had faith in Revolutionary values. In his eyes, if Jews were a problem, it was because they were not living up to the citizenship that had been bestowed upon them. However, unlike his fellow citizens who looked to Catholicism to define the place of Jews in society, Bail considered the Jews to be redeemable as Jews, as long as

---

[55] Sepinwall, 62.

[56] Bail, *Des Juifs*, 49.

[57] Charles-Joseph Bail, *Etat des Juifs en France, en Espagne et en Italie, depuis le commencement du cinquième siècle de l'ère vulgaire jusqu'à la fin du seizième, sous les divers rapports du droit civil, du commerce et de la littérature; ouvrage qui a concouru au prix décerné par l'Académie des inscriptions et belles-lettres de l'institut de France, dans le mois de juillet 1823* (Paris, 1823), 88.

they could become good citizens. The only threat they appeared to pose was that of their continued foreignness. Sacy also saw the Jews in terms of their foreignness. It is interesting that what he called religious affiliation, and Bail national affiliation, amounted to the same thing in their eyes. This is arguably symptomatic of the Restoration: while a Catholic such as Lamennais would criticise the Jews as a separate (and therefore unassimilable) nation,[58] the most republican of writers would scorn Jews who waited for a Messiah who would not come.

The impending expiry of the decree in 1818 was to provide France's Jews with a reminder that nearly thirty years of emancipation did not entail acceptance. In 1817, the Marquis de Lattier (from the department of the Drôme, where no Jews lived), petitioned the two chambers of the royal government to renew the decree. In Alsace, public demands to the same end were not settled until after 1823. None of these efforts was ultimately successful. Nonetheless, the public discussion inspired more than one writer to contribute to the debate. This may well have been what motivated Agricole Moureau. Previously a Jacobin and now a lawyer to the Royal Court, Moureau was moved to write about Jews because he felt that they were not showing themselves worthy of the trust the nation placed in them when it emancipated them.[59] This was a source of concern for Moureau because of the great love he felt for his nation. "Fatherland" (*patrie*) was for him a "dear, sublime and holy word."[60] Harking back to the Revolutionary debates, Moureau understood citizenship of France as bringing with it a strong obligation, both to the nation as a citizen and to one's fellow citizens as brothers. A true citizen loved his nation above all else.[61] Jews lived in Moureau's France, yet they did not love it or observe its laws. Moureau arrived at a conclusion of exclusivity no less harsh than that of Lamennais and Bonald: no one could be an effective member of more than one society or nation; one could no more be a *German Jew* than a *German Englishman*. Jews, Moureau argued, actively sought exclusivity, and this was the fault of Jewish law. For the Jews, religious adherence was Jewish national loyalty, and this could take precedence

---

[58] Lamennais, *Essai*, vol. 1, in *Oeuvres complètes*, 1: 48.
[59] Agricole Moureau, *De l'incompatibilité entre le judaïsme et l'exercice des droits de cité et des moyens de rendre les Juifs citoyens dans les Gouvernements représentatifs* (Paris, 1819), 80.
[60] Ibid., 83.
[61] Ibid., 13.

over – and be a barrier to – the observance of civic duties. Moreover, if Jewish law demanded exclusive observance and obedience, in return it gave a sense of superiority. Thus, for example, the Jew would not intermarry, nor would he defend the nation or help others if it interfered with his observance of Jewish law. Furthermore, Jewish law did not apply to non-Jews, and although, for example, it would be illegal for a Jew to make a usurious loan to another Jew, he could do so to a Christian. Moureau cited the lack of Jews working in "honest" professions, such as those to do with trades or the land, and a supposed distinct lack of Jews in the army, as proof that Jews did not see France as their fatherland. Moreover, it was this desire for exclusivity that had brought calamity upon the Jews over the centuries:

Obstinate blind men that they are! They look at what has been done to them, and they do not want to see what they have believed themselves to be allowed to do against others in the name of religion! They do not want to see that they are the ones who isolate themselves from humanity! It does not reject them, as its essence is to reject no one; they themselves do not wish to belong to it.[62]

Reference to Jewish blindness was not the only borrowing Moureau made from Catholic anti-Jewish rhetoric. He also scorned the Jews who still awaited a Messiah who would come "when the seventy-two weeks that began four thousand years ago" had passed. This same Messiah was to elevate the Jews "above all the nations of the earth," making the Jews their masters.[63] For like Bonald, Moureau saw powerful Jews around him who were potentially dangerous to the nation. Moureau believed that denial of citizenship to Jews was not only justifiable but also reasonable, for while humanitarian rights did not require reciprocity, civil rights did. Or as Moureau put it: "I will save a Jew from drowning but I will not allow him to sit beside me in Parliament."[64] All that was exclusive, as was Jewish law, exposed itself to exclusion. For Moureau, who believed in the importance of brotherhood, although it might be "odious, unjust and atrocious" to discriminate against Jews purely on the basis of prejudice, it was perfectly

[62] Ibid., 30.
[63] Ibid., 64.
[64] Ibid., 60.

right to discriminate against them on the basis of experience and fact.[65] There was no intolerance where there was not reciprocity. Any Jew who wished to be a citizen would have to earn trust by showing himself to be adequately deserving of citizenship. He did not advocate "burning or exile," as he put it, but rather, persuasion and surveillance. Republican that he was, he did not like laws of exception, preferring "statutes that are liberal, great, and durable."[66]

On the basis of their political and religious allegiances, the ideal world that Moureau, Bail, Labouderie, Bonald, and Lamennais envisaged should have had little or nothing in common. Yet if we look at the way they responded to Jews in Restoration society, we find striking similarities. In fact, during a period such as the Restoration, in which myriad different ideologies were competing for ascendancy, it was inevitable that there would be some exchange of ideas. Thus, both Catholics and republicans saw the Jews around them as a wilfully separate nation, "foreign," worthy of scorn and yet also of wariness. Both drew on what they knew and what was around them to express the discomfort they felt with the presence in society of a population that had for centuries been identifiable by its lowly and separate status. This variety in attitudes to Jews during this time is revealing of the intellectual framework of the Restoration. Sacy's argument for the rightful place of the Jew was based on a supreme confidence in Catholicism. Arguably, this was a reflection of the time in which he lived. Yet Bail's pamphlet, to which he was responding, showed no less confidence in the administrative procedures and beliefs set in place by revolutionary governments. In Bail and Sacy we have what may appear to be two extreme views of the way French society and the place of Jews in it was envisaged. But if in these men we have two ends of a spectrum of political belief and attitudes to the Revolution, between them and touching them there was a fertile middle ground: a criss-cross of ideas that borrowed incessantly from one another. In a time that was a crossroads of ideologies, the exchange of views on the place of Jews in the new world was no exception. Some continued to view Jews in terms of a world in which Catholicism was the only legitimate religion, others sought to place Jews in a world where Revolutionary ideology stated that

---

[65] Ibid., 61.
[66] Ibid., 76.

equality implied sameness, and yet others used Jews to illustrate the benefits of their new spirituality. They drew on one another. The Restoration was a period of such intense negotiation over the future of the nation that it is not surprising we should find such a fascinating spectrum of worldviews, reflected in discussions over what the place of the Jew in an ideal world should be, or of how the Jew messed up the ideal world. Perhaps the best example of this latter type of rhetoric comes from Labouderie, who, while preaching fire and brimstone to blasphemers from the safety of the pulpit, betrayed a sense of insecurity regarding the status of the Church. Although his religious belief told him who the blasphemers were and what their fate would be, it could not provide any explanation for their growing prosperity and confidence. For even though the power of the State under Charles X was put to work in the revival of Catholicism, ultimately Catholicism was not to regain the position of dominance it had held before the Enlightenment and the Revolution came to shake its foundations. The expropriation of the Church's wealth by the National Assembly in 1789 had made it financially dependent on the State, and Napoleon had increased this control: it had simply become another of the State's organisations. The beginning of the Restoration saw a Catholic Church that was a spiritual and financial shadow of the mighty body it had been under the ancien régime. Determined efforts by Revolutionary governments to transfer sacrality from a Christian monarchy to a secular nation meant that the return to the throne of the Bourbons saw a significant sector of the French population generally ignorant of and indifferent to the teachings and practices of Catholicism. The Church of the Restoration was a self-conscious entity, going to unprecedented lengths to form and regulate public opinion, knowingly in competition with other ways of envisaging the world.

Yet although the efforts of men such as Bonald and Sacy to revive the Church in France were ultimately to fail, the exclusive understanding of citizenship that they expounded was not without effect on some Jews. As we have seen, some Jews did choose to bridge the still-existing gap between Judaism and the French mainstream by becoming Catholic, perhaps as a way of escaping this identification and its eternal connotation of foreignness. A handful of converts took on a Catholic identity that included hatred of Judaism. It is to them that we now turn.

2

The Unyielding Wall: Christianity and Judaism

*A*LPHONSE RATISBONNE WAS THE YOUNGEST SON OF THE
Ratisbonne family, part of Alsatian Jewry's elite. Its members were
known for their wealth and acculturation. Alphonse himself had a repu-
tation as a man-about-town, a dandy, and an "ironical and blasphemous
free thinker."[1] He claimed that he was indifferent to religion. Yet in January 1842, while travelling in Italy, Alphonse saw an apparition of the
virgin at *Sant'Andrea delle Fratte*, and experienced a sudden and dramatic insight. "She didn't say a word to me," Alphonse was to note of
the apparition, "but I understood everything."[2] In the genuine account
of the conversion of Marie-Alphonse Ratisbonne – for so he was to be
known – the Abbé Dupanloup wondered at the sight "of this young man,
a few days ago an obstinate Jew, and today an impassioned Catholic."
Ratisbonne, it is recounted, "did not hesitate one moment" when it came
to the part of the ceremony where he was required to "abhor Jewish
perfidy, reject Hebraic superstition."[3]

---

[1] Antoine Compagnon, *Connaissez-vous Brunetière? Enquête sur un antidreyfusard et ses amis* (Paris, 1997), 61.

[2] Marie-Alphonse Ratisbonne, *Conversion de Monsieur M.-A. Ratisbonne, racontée par lui-même* (Le Mans, 1842), 5. This account ran to several editions and was widely translated.

[3] Horresce judaicam perfidiam, respue hebraicam superstitionem. Marie-Alphonse Ratisbonne, *Conversion de M. Marie-Alphonse Ratisbonne. Relation authentique par M. Le Baron Th. De Bussières; suivie de la lettre de M. Marie-Alphonse Ratisbonne à M. Dufriche-Desgenettes, Fondateur et Directeur de l'Archiconfrérie du Très-Saint et Immaculé Cœur de Marie, établie en l'église de Notre-Dame-des-Victoires, à Paris,* 3d ed. (Paris, 1844), 69, 50. On the Ratisbonnes, see: Kselman, 10–18; Isser and Schwarz, "Sudden Conversion," 17–30; eadem, *Conversion and Contemporary Cults,* 80–94; Katz, "Religion as a Uniting and Dividing Force," 1–18; and Compagnon, esp. 60–70.

In the previous chapter, I explored the hope with which clergy and Ultras greeted the return of the Bourbon monarchy, and the energy that was put into the restoration of a society in which the Church would enjoy absolute legitimacy and dominance. Ultimately, the efforts of men such as Bonald and Lamennais had not elevated their religion to the great heights to which they aspired. The government of Charles X was deposed over the three glorious days in 1830, and the reign of the relatively liberal and bourgeois Louis-Philippe commenced. Ultras retired to their country estates in an "internal emigration," as disappointed yet still hopeful Legitimists.[4] But despite their withdrawal from public life, Ultras did leave a legacy. The ideology of exclusivity that they had expounded had clearly not been without effect on some Jews, who chose to become Catholics. Some of these, like Marie-Alphonse Ratisbonne and his elder brother Théodore, found a truth in Catholicism that they felt had been lacking for them in the religion of their birth. They saw themselves as sincere Catholics, taking on a Catholic identity that included a complete repudiation of Judaism. They turned their focus on the community they had left behind and became active proselytes and vocal detractors of Judaism, in the hope of helping more Jews to perceive the truth that was clear to them. However, although they are perhaps the best known of such Jewish converts in early-nineteenth-century France, they were by no means the only ones.

Why did some emancipated Jews in post-Revolutionary France come to see themselves as genuine Catholics? During the Restoration, as we have seen, there remained a close identification between the Church, and state, culture and society. Jacob Katz has argued that there were limitations to the neutral nature of post-Enlightenment society, in that the "secularised" Christian symbols that permeated post-Revolutionary social and political rituals remained invested with centuries of meaning.[5] Arguably serving to reinforce this was the Romantic movement, which idealised a glorious past in which church and throne were the essence of national glory. Kselman has argued that the response among the young to the political chaos engendered by the Revolution cannot be

---

[4] Jardin and Tudesq, 236. On the transition from Ultra-Royalism to Legitimism, see also René Rémond, *The Right Wing in France from 1815 to De Gaulle*, 2d ed., trans. James Laux (Philadelphia, 1969), chap. 1 and 2 passim.

[5] Katz, "Religion as a Uniting and Dividing Force," 3.

overestimated. In the search for a philosophy that would enable them to create a new world, many found a response in the revival of religion that was Romanticism.[6] It is not inconceivable that some young and talented Jews, seeking to make their way in the world, would have experienced a continuing sense of isolation in a society still imbued with Christian significance. Historians who have examined sincere conversions such as those of the Ratisbonnes agree on the overwhelming influence of such symbolism. They suggest that Jews living in Restoration France could not but be influenced by the power that renascent Christianity wielded in the society in which they wished to participate.[7] Thus Natalie Isser and Lita Linzer Schwartz have suggested that sincere converts, who often came from among the brightest and best of the Jewish community, would have been driven by a "sense of malaise"; they were "confused, alienated, and vulnerable"[8] and felt unable to fulfil their potential or to integrate successfully into what was essentially a Christian society.[9] Newly emancipated Jews must indeed have felt deeply alienated in a society where there were few choices for Jews who sought to become more French by changing their behaviour, but not their religion.

What exactly can converts tell us? As new Catholics, some were very public in making known their new world-view, including the place that Jews should take in it. At the same time, their proselytising ensured that they remained very involved with the Jewish community. In this sense, they were both at the vanguard of relations between Catholics and Jews and representative of the Catholic voice in these relations. One scholar of the fin-de-siècle has suggested that little research has been undertaken on Jewish apostasies in nineteenth-century France because they "trouble both Jews and Catholics, reminding the former of the short-lived decline of their religion, and the latter of the fanaticism of their coreligionists of the past."[10] Nonetheless, the choices that they made, the identity they assumed, the relationships they maintained with family and community, and the place they envisaged for Judaism can offer revealing insights into the ways in which the traditional boundaries

[6] Kselman, "Bautain," 181.
[7] Berkovitz, *Shaping*, 116.
[8] Isser and Schwartz, *Conversion and Contemporary Cults*, 74.
[9] Helfand, "Passports and Piety," 65. See also Berkovitz, *Shaping*, 114–17; Piette, 125; and Katz, *From Prejudice to Destruction*, 117–18.
[10] Compagnon, 66.

between Catholicism and Judaism were being perceived – and in some cases, redrawn – by Catholics in the years following the emancipation of the Jews. In this chapter, I examine genuine conversions as neither indicators of Jewish acculturation nor of Catholic "fanaticism." Rather, I would like to place these few Jews who took on a Catholic identity that included full repudiation of Judaism and the desire to proselytise among Jews in the context of their world and its influence on the choices they made.

The subjects of this chapter were all Jews from the east of France: Nicolas L'évèque, David Drach, Ignace Morel, and the Ratisbonne brothers Théodore and Alphonse. They were all active proselytisers, through a mixture of writing and activity. But although the stories of the Ratisbonne brothers are well documented, very little has been written about the other subjects. Ignace-Xavier Morel and Nicolas L'évèque are the least known. Morel, according to his own story, was born Levy Gumpel, a native of Mutzig in the Lower Rhine region of Alsace. He was brought to Paris as a young boy. He became a military physician and converted to Catholicism in 1826, "due to Drach's edifying example."[11] Morel became a devout Catholic and was involved in missionary activity. He also became Drach's most vociferous partisan. Little more is known about Nicolas L'évèque, and what facts we have are those that he himself chose to reveal. Before his conversion, he was a rabbi and *schohet* named Israel,[12] and he lived and worked in Metz and then in Reims. It was in Reims that he was converted to Catholicism by the vicar-general, M. Macquart, in August 1826. We are given no indication of the reasons for L'évèque's conversion, other than the views he presented in his work, *Erreurs des juifs en matière de religion*, where he left somewhat surprising – one might even say dubious – hints as to his identity.

In contrast, David Drach was a well-known figure in the Jewish community. Of all the figures who are the subjects of this chapter, arguably none embraced their new religious identity more fully than Drach. Born in 1791, his early experiences were not uncommon for an Alsatian Jewish

---

[11] Ignace Xavier Morel, *Renseignements relatifs à la persécution dont M. Drach, rabbin converti, a été l'objet* (Paris, n.d. Reprinted from the *Mémorial catholique* of March 1826), 3.

[12] The *schohet* performs the ritual killing of animals for consumption according to the Jewish dietary laws.

boy. Paula Hyman has shown that well into the nineteenth century, Jews in Alsace continued largely to live in semi-rural poverty.[13] Drach's family was both poor and pious. The young David's father was a scholar, and he saw potential in his youngest son. So Drach's fate was to be decided by his father's ambition: from an early age, Drach's life was devoted to rabbinical studies, and he made rapid progress. But in early-nineteenth century France there was no shortage of rabbis, and Drach found himself to be merely one of many clever young Jewish men. In 1807, having feigned short-sightedness to avoid conscription, he went to work as a private tutor to the children of a well-to-do Jewish family. Yet Drach showed signs of interest in the world around him, and he harboured wider ambitions. In Alsace he had taught himself Latin and Greek. In 1813, against his father's wishes, he went to Paris. There he not only found work in the Jewish community as both a private tutor and secretary to the Central Consistory, but he also obtained a diploma from the Faculté de lettres and the Ecole normale in Paris and taught classical languages at the Institut des langues étrangères. In 1817, at the age of twenty-six, he married Sara Deutz, the daughter of the assistant chief rabbi (and later the chief rabbi) of France, Emmanuel Deutz. The heir apparent to his father-in-law, Drach seemed destined to become one of the rabbinic elite. But on Easter Saturday 1823, in an act that for the Jewish community was sudden and shocking, Drach was baptised by the archbishop of Paris (taking the names Paul-Louis-Bernard) and had his children – two girls aged four and three and a boy aged sixteen months – baptised along with him. Why?

Drach's conversion was nothing if not controversial. Members of both the Jewish and Christian communities alleged that his motivation was the promise of an appointment as chair of Oriental languages at the Sorbonne, a position that brought with it a good salary. One biographer of Drach has suggested that the community was still poorly equipped to offer many possibilities for one with Drach's ability and ambition, refusing in January 1823 to print his synopsis of Jewish history because of a lack of funds.[14] Another historian has argued that talented yet poor Alsatian Jews like Drach would have found Alsace "stifling" and Paris

---

[13] Hyman, *Jews of Alsace*, 34, 38–40.
[14] Paul Klein, 91.

"not yet ready" to assimilate them.[15] Indeed, caught as he was between his very traditional upbringing and the opportunities offered by post-emancipatory France, it appears that Drach felt he had no alternative but to convert. Beset by pressures from both the Jewish and non-Jewish worlds, Drach, given his background, could neither abandon his religiosity while remaining within the Jewish community nor could he satisfy his ambition in the broader Christian community of the Restoration while still remaining a Jew.[16] Yet Drach himself vehemently denied allegations of greed and maintained that his conversion was simply a matter of belief. He stated that his interest in Catholicism, as evidenced by his study of Greek and Latin, had begun many years before and that he had slowly come to realise that Judaism was corrupt and schismatic. Drach claimed that he had first begun to see the truth of Christianity when his own study of the Septuagint led him to believe that the traditional text of the Pentateuch had been falsified. Using the Aramean version of Onkelos, a work especially valued by Christians because it illuminated the Old Testament text in a version supposedly free of the rabbinic obliterations of any prophetic reference to the coming of Christ, he had reconstructed what he believed was the original. The result of this was his *Sancti Pentateche textus hebraicus quem Alexandrinæ versionis LXX auctories secuti sunt*, a work that was approved by none other than Silvestre de Sacy, who presented it to Corbière, then minister for the interior. An examination of his last publications before his conversion tends to support his claims. In June 1822, he gave the eulogy at the funeral of a woman whose family had befriended Drach when he had lived in Colmar. He spoke of Judaism as the "enlightened religion of our fathers" and "our holy religion."[17] But at a eulogy given in January 1823 – two months before he was baptised – although the departed was an "estimable Israelite," not one mention was made of Judaism itself.[18] Drach's writings after he became a Catholic

---

[15] Helfand, "Passports and Piety," 66.

[16] Berkovitz, *Shaping*, 114. Drach was later to state that in his eyes, assimilated Jews occupied a sort of purgatory in which they had yet to prove their worth; they had "ceased to be Jews, and [were] still far from being Christians; they [were] in effect none other than French Israelites." Paul Drach, *Lettre d'un Rabbin converti aux Israélites, ses frères, sur les motifs de sa conversion* (Paris, 1825), 33.

[17] David Drach, *Discours prononcé aux obsèques de Mme Claire Javal aînée, qui ont eu lieu le 10 juin 1822, par le rabbi Drach* (Paris, 1822), 5–6.

[18] David Drach, *Discours prononcé aux obsèques de M. Lan (Léon), célébrées à Paris le 14 janvier 1823, par D. Drach* (Paris, 1823).

offer yet another clue to the way in which, as a young and talented Jewish scholar, he perceived his world. Writing twenty years after his conversion, Drach noted that at that time, he had seen "an unyielding wall that still stood between the Israelites and Christian society, which saw them literally as a race of pariahs."[19]

While Drach came from an observant home, the opposite was the case for the Ratisbonne brothers, Théodore and Alphonse. The two were the grandsons of Naphtali Cerf Berr, the most prominent of the Jews of Alsace before the Revolution and a strong advocate for his coreligionists. A wealthy army purveyor and merchant, Cerf Berr, as he was known, was officer general of the Jewish Nation in Alsace from 1760 to 1788, commissioner for food supplies to the garrison in Strasbourg, an industrialist, and a property owner. He was the only Jew under Louis XVI to receive letters of naturalisation and to obtain the right to own property and to live permanently in Strasbourg. This was significant because Jews had been barred from residing in Strasbourg since 1349. On the fourteenth of February in that year, the people of Strasbourg, motivated as much – if not more – by resentment of the Jews as economic competitors, as by fear of the plague and religious prejudice, burnt some 2,000 Strasbourg Jews at the stake. (It is telling that all debts owing to those Jews who were murdered in this way were then cancelled, and their belongings were divided up among the population.) For almost 450 years, the city held to its policy, and while Jews were allowed into Strasbourg during the day to trade, they were all obliged to leave the city by nightfall. It is in this context that we should understand the prominence of Cerf Berr and the extent to which he was perceived to be useful to authorities. But Cerf Berr also sought to use his position to ameliorate that of his coreligionists in Alsace. He was known for his philanthropy in the Jewish community. It was Cerf Berr, in contact with leaders of the Jewish community in Berlin, who asked Moses Mendelssohn to come to his aid in 1777 when Joseph Hell's false receipts to Jewish loans were circulating widely throughout Alsace. Mendelssohn forwarded this request to Christian Wilhelm Dohm, whose *Über die bürgerliche Verbesserung der Juden* (Regarding the Civic Improvement of the Jews) was the work that opened consideration of

---

[19]   Paul Drach, *De l'Harmonie entre l'église et la synagogue, ou Perpétuité et catholicité de la religion chrétienne, par le chevalier P.-L.-B. Drach*, 2 vols. (Paris, 1844), 36, cited in Jonathan Helfand, "Passports and Piety," 63.

the status of the Jews in ancien régime France. In 1789, he took the title of Syndic of the Jews of the three provinces in order to make the voice of the Jews heard in the Estates General. He died in 1793. By the 1820s, the extended Cerf-Berr-Ratisbonne family was still very involved in the Strasbourg Jewish community, playing an active role as leaders and philanthropists. But some had discarded religious observance. For example, Alphonse, the son of Auguste Ratisbonne and grandson of Naphtali Cerf Berr, declared that religious traditions were "completely wiped out" in his family.[20] Alphonse himself saw himself as a Jew "in name only."[21]

Both Alphonse and his older brother Théodore studied law in Paris. They were both destined for careers in banking. When Théodore returned to Strasbourg in 1823, he enrolled in courses in the law faculty of the University. For most Jews – and Strasbourgeois non-Jews – the presence of a Jewish community in this city was a phenomenon that dated only from 1791. The Jewish community had grown rapidly, and by 1810, it numbered approximately 1500. In 1823, when we pick up the story of Théodore Ratisbonne, the atmosphere in Strasbourg was what Thomas Kselman has called one of "religious pluralism and confessional tension,"[22] with Catholics, Protestants, and Jews living newly, and not entirely comfortably, side by side. Protestants had been fearful since 1815 of the possibility of Catholic violence against them. Rumours to this effect were still circulating in the early 1820s.[23] In 1819, Jews in Strasbourg had felt the heat of the so-called Hep Hep riots, the mob attacks on Jews that took place in nearby southern and central Germany.

It was in this atmosphere that Théodore was introduced by a Jewish friend and fellow law student, Jules Lewel, to the private courses in moral theology being run at the home of the devout Catholic, Mlle Humann, by Louis Bautain. Bautain had been a prodigy, a brilliant and charismatic student of Victor Cousin at the École normale. On his graduation in 1816, he was appointed to teach philosophy at the Collège royal in Strasbourg, and shortly after, at twenty-one, he also began to teach at the university. But by early 1819, in the clutches of depression, he had stopped

---

[20] Compagnon, 62.
[21] Marie-Alphonse Ratisbonne, *Conversion de Monsieur M.-A. Ratisbonne, racontée par lui-même*, 7.
[22] Thomas Kselman, "The Bautain Circle and Catholic-Jewish Relations in Modern France," *The Catholic Historical Review* XCII.3 (July 2006), 180.
[23] Ibid. I have drawn on Kselman's work in the discussion that follows, on Louis Bautain.

teaching. Despairing of ever returning to his profession, he happened to meet Louise Humann, and, as Kselman has described it, it was her piety and intelligence that led Bautain to what we might call the typically Romantic conviction that his search for truth had to begin from his heart rather than his head. Under her influence, he returned to the Catholicism in which he had been raised. Shortly afterwards, the study circle was formed. Ratisbonne attended these classes, bringing along another law student, and member of the Strasbourg Jewish elite: Isidore Goschler. Lewel accompanied them. Théodore Ratisbonne and his friends were influenced by Bautain's charismatic teaching, and they began to live a double life. Bautain did not encourage his students to cut themselves off from the Jewish community; on the contrary, he told them that in improving themselves, they could be useful to their fellow Jews, degenerate and vegetating in misery. Bautain instructed them to love these Jews, the "leftovers of a royal and degenerate race," as they loved themselves, and to do all that was in their power to improve them.[24] Thus encouraged, Theodore went to work to promote the regeneration of the still largely poor and observant Alsatian Jewish community. He became a prominent figure in educational and charitable initiatives, taking over the direction of the Consistory Jewish School in Strasbourg and teaching and preaching there. Yet all the while Théodore was evidently becoming increasingly attached to Catholicism and convinced of its truth, and, along with Goschler and Lewel, he was secretly baptised in 1827, going, as he put it, "from death to life."[25] Goschler portrayed his conversion as a "Christian liberation"; Lewel described the "innermost happiness" of feeling that his conversion had lifted him out of the "deep degradation" in which he had suffered. In converting, he felt, he had been bound to the "great tree of life," and he "finally belonged to humanity's elite."[26]

Eventually, Théodore's apostasy became a matter of public knowledge, and under outraged pressure from the Jewish community, he resigned

[24]   Louis-Eugène-Marie (Abbé) Bautain, *Philosophie du christianisme*, 2 vols. (Paris, 1835), 24.

[25]   Ratisbonne, Goschler, and Lewel all published accounts of the process of their conversion in the introduction to Bautain's *Philosophie du Christianisme*, which took the form of letters between him and his three Jewish disciples. Théodore Ratisbonne also published his own works. Ratisbonne in Bautain, xlvii.

[26]   Goschler in ibid., lxxii; Lewel in ibid., cx.

as school director to devote himself to his studies for the priesthood. He went on to found the Congregation of Notre Dame de Sion, an organisation of Catholic sisters dedicated primarily to the conversion of Jews. He maintained a high and controversial profile in the Jewish community for this work, which included several disputed apostasies.[27] For several years, Théodore's younger brother Alphonse was hostile to his brother. When Theodore had converted, Alphonse, then thirteen, described how he was "revolted" by his brother's behaviour and "came to hate his dress and his character."[28] Nonetheless, Alphonse was to follow his brother into Catholicism, as we have seen, and in a manner that was even more dramatic. He went to work with Théodore, saving Jewish souls by making them Catholic.

Although the Ratisbonne brothers are perhaps best known for the very active role they played in proselytising among the Jewish community, they, along with Drach, also left a more enduring testament to their sentiments, in the form of writings. Drach was by far the most prolific. He had already published several pamphlets before he converted, and he continued publishing thereafter. Ignace Morel and Nicolas L'évêque also left writings; however, little or nothing has been written about them. In fact, their very origins are doubtful. Morel has left no trace of himself in the records, and his two published works are vociferous defences of Drach, leading one scholar to surmise that Morel is most probably an alter ego of Drach himself.[29] Similarly, the only facts we can ascertain regarding Nicolas L'évêque are those that he himself chose to reveal. The date of publication of his sole work, *Erreurs des juifs en matière de religion*, coincides with the 1828 conversion of Simon Deutz, brother of Sara Drach. Among his apparently more outrageous claims, he states that his father "was once chief rabbi of the Jews."[30] It is not impossible that L'évêque was indeed Deutz.

In choosing to direct writings at the Jewish community, these converts were inserting themselves in a long tradition that had its roots in the

---

[27] For examples of the Ratisbonnes' aggressive proselytism, see Helfand, "Passports and Piety," 66–67.

[28] Marie-Alphonse Ratisbonne, *Conversion de Monsieur M.-A. Ratisbonne, racontée par lui-même*, 5.

[29] Philippe-E. Landau, "Le cas étrange de Simon Deutz (1802–1844)," *Revue des études juives*, 164 no. 1–2 (janvier-juin 2005): 213–34.

[30] Nicolas L'évêque, *Erreurs des Juifs en matière de religion* (Paris, 1828), 53.

thirteenth century.[31] At that time, it was Jewish converts who led the push to convert other Jews, using their knowledge of Jewish sources and understanding of Jewish thought. Drach and his fellow converts drew to a great extent on the themes of Christian rhetoric regarding Jews, which had been established around this time. With the exception of Morel, the converts, and especially Drach, all wrote of their experiences with the stated hope that they could persuade the "blind" Jews to see the truth as they had. Drach and L'évèque in particular appeared to feel an urgent need to communicate to the Jewish community a truth of which they were aware but to which the Jews remained blind. L'évèque focused very much on an imminent judgement day, with all its attendant horrors and which, predictably, could only be avoided by conversion. Drach beseeched his Jewish readers, promising never to stop "engaging," "asking," and "begging" them to *choose life*," that is, to choose the sublime and holy doctrine of the gospel,[32] and he called on God more than once to relieve their blindness. However, unlike L'évèque, Drach did not undertake to achieve his aim by pleading, or even threatening. Rather, he drew once again on a tradition, this time the ideology of supercession. He set out to prove this truth to the Jewish community. Thus he wrote that the Old Testament was an authentic record of mankind's early years but that the main importance of the prophetic books of the Hebrews was that they foretold the coming of a messiah who would be the son of God, who would end all suffering, and whom the Christians clearly recognised as Jesus. Christian Hebraists of the late Middle Ages had undertaken long studies of ancient Hebrew and Aramaic, as well as Rabbinic Hebrew and the Talmud, to cleanse the Old Testament of the muddying layers of rabbinic exegesis: "to separate the true metal from the dross" and ultimately to use this as a tool to persuade the Jews to convert.[33] By the end of the seventeenth century, the study of Jewish texts as a form of Christian scholarship had declined and become marginal, at best, as the view of the texts changed. The stance of commentators such as the prominent Protestant intellectual Henri Basnage was typical of this time,

---

[31] See Robert Chazan, *Daggers of Faith: Thirteenth Century Christian Missionizing and Jewish Response* (Berkeley, 1989), and Frank Manuel, *The Broken Staff: Judaism Through Christian Eyes* (Cambridge, MA: 1992), 24.

[32] Drach, *Deuxième lettre*, 161.

[33] Manuel, 128.

in that he viewed the Talmud and the Gemara as ridiculous, tedious, absurd, and excessive.[34] Drach, formerly a rabbi and celebrated within the Jewish community for his Talmudic learning, set himself no less a task than that of returning the Jewish texts to centrestage in Christian-Jewish relations. He was to turn his intimate knowledge of the Talmud against the Jews with a fury that did not fall far short of fanaticism.

In fact, the basic premise of much of Drach's scholarly work was not original, nor was it terribly scholarly. He set out to prove the legitimacy of Christianity by showing that ancient Jewish scripture prophesied the coming of Jesus and that the Catholic Church was therefore the true continuation of Judaism as the Jews themselves had foreseen it.[35] Thus, he distinguished between the ancient synagogue, whose doctrines provided the foundation for the Church, and the modern synagogue, made up of those Jews who had turned away from God at the time of Jesus' coming. For L'évèque, too, Judaism had no place in the world; it was an anachronism, the forerunner to Christianity that had ceased to have meaning when Jesus came to signal its end and the Church's beginning. Still vainly awaiting their Messiah, the Jews were "hapless blind men who ask when the dawn will come; while the sun is already halfway to having run its course."[36] Marie-Alphonse Ratisbonne was in agreement. In his eyes, the Jews had no religion at all: they had left the ancient temple eighteen centuries before, but they had not yet chosen to enter into the new one.[37] However, Jews went far beyond merely passively awaiting the Messiah's coming; they also harboured an active and bitter hatred of all that Christianity embodied.

Jewish enmity towards Christianity and Christians, an extension of the original Jewish hatred and killing of Jesus, had long been a dominant

---

[34] Sutcliffe, 32–4.

[35] For example, see Drach, *Harmonie*, 1: 452; or idem, *Lettre*, 8. According to Langmuir, there were three reactions to Judaism that constituted the core of Christian anti-Judaism: belief in the deficiency of Jewish understanding ("Jewish blindness"), the deicide accusation, and the belief that historical events demonstrated that God was punishing the Jews for their deicide (Langmuir, *History, Religion, and Antisemitism*, 285). Langmuir also notes that James Parkes demonstrated how, over time, Christians gradually revised their early history and reinterpreted Hebrew Scriptures to conform with Christian belief. The work of Drach certainly bears this out (ibid., 287).

[36] L'évèque, 2.

[37] Marie-Alphonse Ratisbonne, *Conversion de Monsieur M.-A. Ratisbonne, racontée par lui-même*, 11.

feature of the Christian understanding of Jews.[38] Both Drach and L'évèque interpreted the history of Jewish-Catholic relations as one in which intolerant and hateful Jews nurtured animosity through the centuries towards Catholics, who either behaved with tolerant goodwill towards them or sought merely to help them see the error of their ways. This was a hatred that Drach and L'évèque took personally. L'évèque set a scene where he was the victim of Jewish fury and revenge, accusing the Jews of returning his goodness (that is, having interceded with God on their behalf) with evil. He alluded to persecution from the Jewish community, claiming that he was "constrained against his will" by the Jews when he made public his desire to leave Judaism, "to the point where [he] was obliged to call on the law." Then, he claimed, he was pursued for two weeks by Jews as they sought to kill him.[39] Drach described his conversion by comparing himself to Saint Paul, whose name he shared: "like him, my conversion earned me the hatred and persecution of the Jews, my brothers."[40] Drach also noted the "atrocious intolerance" of the Talmud and its followers towards Christians, which stated that "all those children of Adam who [were] not part of the Jewish nation" were classed *as less than human.*" This hatred, he took care to point out, was especially directed at converted Israelites.[41] Morel called this hatred "Pharisaic intolerance." In his eyes, it was responsible for preventing a large number of baptised French Israelites from openly declaring their conversion.[42]

How did the Jewish community respond to news of apostasies? In his investigation into the Terquem family, Kselman has found that there was a sharp increase in conversions of Jews to Catholicism in the 1840s. This was certainly noted by some converts. Cerfberr de Medelsheim, a cousin of the Ratisbonne brothers whose father converted to Catholicism, noted in 1843, with some glee, that Jews were converting in large numbers, that Judaism was "weakening each day" and its ranks "thinning

---

[38] See, for example, Robert Chazan, *Medieval Stereotypes and Modern Antisemitism* (Berkeley, 1997); Joshua Trachtenberg, *The Devil and the Jews: The Medieval Conception of the Jew and Its Relation to Modern Antisemitism* (New Haven, CT, 1943), and Pagels.

[39] Ibid., 57.

[40] Drach, *Lettre*, 28.

[41] Drach, *Usure*, 19. Original emphasis.

[42] Morel, *Renseignements*, 12.

more and more."[43] In the early part of the 1840s, the *Archives israélites*, the major periodical for the French Jewish community, tended in fact to ignore apostasies (including that of Alphonse Ratisbonne in 1842). However, by 1843, when Medelsheim made his observations, the Jewish community perceived itself as being well and truly under threat. This was compounded by various events: for example, the Damascus Blood Libel of 1840 had been followed by further accusations over the first years of that decade. By 1842, Théodore Ratisbonne had come to Paris and was working to convert Jews, in concert with the Congregation of Notre Dame de Sion. He established a school for young Jewish girls from poor families, and there were conversions among the student body. In 1844, there was a public quarrel between Jewish and Catholic leaders over the activities of Catholic chaplains in hospitals. Jews felt that these latter were putting "inappropriate and illegal pressure" on patients.[44] The *Archives* now began to respond to each case of conversion. And the community took action beyond the pages of its mouthpiece. Kselman has detailed the "public discussion" that took place around the 1845 sickbed conversion of Dr Lazare Terquem, by Théodore Ratisbonne.[45] Terquem was a physician, a well-known and equally well-respected member of the Jewish community. His wife and daughters had converted to Catholicism, and it was on the invitation of his wife that Ratisbonne was present in the dying man's home. The events of his baptism by Ratisbonne are the subject of conflicting reports and became grounds for conflict between the Catholic and Jewish communities. Deprived of Terquem's body for burial, the Central Jewish Consistory made an official complaint to the Minister of Justice and Religion about the actions of Ratisbonne, and the Church in general. The community clearly felt that the government had a part to play on its behalf in what was essentially a religious dispute, as did the minister himself: he forwarded the complaint to Archbishop Affre, although he chose not to pass on to the Consistory the haughty and dismissive letter he received in response.[46]

---

[43] Cerfberr, *Ce que sont les Juifs de France* (Strasbourg, 1843), viii.

[44] Kselman, "Turbulent Souls," 95.

[45] Ibid., 100.

[46] Affre stated that no Catholic priest would baptise someone who had not expressed a clear desire to convert. He concluded his letter by making clear his view of Judaism, placing the disputed baptism in the broader context of Jewish insults against the Church: "While the Isralites denounce a chimerical attack with regard to M. Terquem,

But not all Jews saw themselves as being in opposition to Catholics on this issue. In the case of the Ratisbonnes, Théodore was not disowned by his father and in fact was present at the latter's deathbed. The father of Simon Deutz responded similarly to his son's apostasy, as we shall see in the following chapter. Kselman argues that stories such as that of Lazare Terquem highlight a less than clear-cut relationship between Catholicism and Judaism – or Catholics and Jews – in nineteenth-century France. Rather, he suggests that we borrow the term "interweaving," to better characterise such relationships.[47] Does the apparent hatefulness of one such as Drach bear this out?

Drach was perhaps at his most hateful when he turned his attention to rabbis – and to their organ, the Talmud. The allegedly widespread practice of usury among Jews was of great use to those Catholics – such as Drach – who sought to assert the moral superiority of Christianity, and, by comparison, the moral inferiority of Judaism. According to Drach, for example, it provided a good example of Jewish malevolence, because it was condemned by the Talmud, but rabbis distinguished between Jewish and non-Jewish borrowers, the latter not being covered by Jewish law. In fact, all that was evil in Judaism after Jesus could be attributed to rabbis or their predecessors, the proud, ambitious, and intolerant Pharisees who had founded the "schismatic synagogue," "opposed to the synagogue of Jesus Christ."[48] Drach argued that according to rabbis, "the commandments of equity and charity towards one's brother or neighbour that can be found in the sacred texts, only apply between Jews."[49] He set himself up in opposition to this rabbi/Pharisee, and the latter came to constitute the focus of much of his anti-Jewish fury. Even though he repeatedly referred to the Jews as his "dear brothers" or his "brothers in the flesh," when the discussion centred on rabbis, he separated himself from the community, calling them "your doctors." To L'évêque, they were arrogant, self-interested "hardened and obstinate hypocrites" who, with

---

I am assured that they are themselves guilty of a serious insult against Catholicism in giving public masked balls on Holy Saturday, which are authorized by the police." Archives of the Archdiocese of Paris, 4r F7 (Correspondence of Affre), 1: 147–48, letter dated 22 March 1845. Quoted in Thomas Kselman, "Turbulent Souls," 100.

[47] This is taken from Gauri Viswanathan, *Outside the Fold: Conversion, Modernity and Belief* (Princeton, 1998), 4, quoted in ibid., 104.

[48] Drach, *Harmonie*, 1: 126; idem, *Deuxième lettre*, 54.

[49] Drach, *Usure*, 19.

illogic, insanity, and absurdity, had deliberately disfigured and covered up the prophecies to deceive their flock. With a seemingly well-defined idea of what would appeal to the public taste for scandal, Drach warned his readers that to fight the rabbis "with their own weapons," he would be obliged to cite passages from the Talmud that might offend some modesties. He promised to use "as much tact as the French language will allow,"[50] pointing out, but not quoting from the more 'offensive' passages of the Talmud. In fact, in attacking rabbis, Drach was again on safe territory, taking on a long-standing and ongoing discourse. A figure such as Grégoire, for example, although known for his sympathetic position towards Jews, attacked what he called "Rabbinism" right throughout his life.[51] Drach was equally not alone in railing against the Talmud. It was on the initiative of Nicholas Donin, a Jewish convert in the twelfth century, that Catholic authorities became aware of the Talmud. Another convert, Friar Paul Christian, was a significant contributor to the development of the use of the Talmud in proselytising to Jews. Langmuir argues that Catholic opposition to the Talmud was inspired by the realisation that "Jews were teaching their children to understand their Bible according to the Talmudic interpretation, not according to the Christian interpretation, and that interpretation would make it harder to persuade Jews to acknowledge the superiority of Christian beliefs."[52] Thus, if rabbis personified the corruption of contemporary Judaism, their tool was the Talmud, the rabbinic authority to which the synagogue accorded a greater authority than to the word of God. "Between evangelical morality and the immorality of the Talmud, there [was] all the distance that separated heaven, not only from the earth, but also from the depths of hell."[53] Drach did take care to make his distance from his subject clear to the reader: "we who, through the grace of the most high, have renounced the false doctrines that it preaches, we will speak of it with knowledge of cause, and with impartiality. If on the one hand we devoted our best years to it, on the other, it no longer means anything to us."[54] And indeed, Drach made use of his lifelong rabbinic training to launch an attack on

---

[50] Drach, *Troisième lettre*, 129.
[51] Sepinwall, 205.
[52] Langmuir, *History, Religion, and Antisemitism*, 296.
[53] Morel, *vérité*, 132. Drach, *Divorce*, 145.
[54] Drach, *Harmonie*, 1: 122.

the Talmud that was breathtaking – not only in the force of its acrimony but also in its thoroughness and attention to detail:

This voluminous compilation contains a heap of stories and assertions that are so extravagant and occasionally so licentious, that one can be surprised that the human mind can lose itself to such an extent, and that the imagination can let itself go to such turpitude. [...] In its interpretation, the Talmud uses reasoning that is so specious and subtle, and at the same time so grotesque, that it is quite difficult to understand it completely: its logic is unique. [...] Its style, its way of splitting hairs, makes it inaccessible to even the most capable non-Jewish orientalists.[55]

As a former "Jewish orientalist," this was where Drach came into his own. His attack on the Talmud was three-pronged. First, he declared the Talmud blasphemous: Drach wrote that the Talmud encouraged Jews to hate Christians and contained "horrible blasphemies against all that Christianity holds most sacred and dear."[56] Second, the Talmud was nonsensical: it was a "deluge of nonsense and lies," containing "fantastical musings, vain subtleties of the rabbis and their fairy tales."[57] Its "daydreams" encouraged the minute and superstitious observances that characterized Judaism. Finally, and perhaps most important, the Talmud was dangerous. It contained "revolting indecencies"; it was "impious, hateful and atrociously intolerant."[58] It is perhaps not surprising to find that Drach concluded that "there is no morality more pernicious, nor more subversive to social order."[59]

In the eyes of these converts, therefore, this was contemporary Judaism: an edifice "that the Lord had only meant to be temporary, awaiting the hour to build another, more perfect and more durable edifice." The Judaism that they described was represented by a Talmud full of "errors, and palpable absurdities"[60] and upheld by thoroughly despicable rabbis. This was the ritual – "not even worthy of man" – to which Théodore Ratisbonne reacted with "deep boredom and insurmountable disgust," discovering in it "the visible mark of great degradation."[61] Ratisbonne

---

[55]   Drach, *Lettre*, 32.
[56]   Drach, *Harmonie*, 1: 163.
[57]   Drach, *Harmonie*, 2: xxvii.
[58]   Drach, *Harmonie*, 1: 166.
[59]   Drach, *Croix*, 15.
[60]   L'évêque, 37.
[61]   Ratisbonne in Bautain, 8.

saw Jews around him living in guilt, ignorance, and disgrace, their degradation both a consequence and a part of their punishment for the deicide. In a mute comparison with the religion he had left behind, he declared that "if you wish to make men who are not only reasonable, skilful, learned, fair-minded, but also truly moral and thoroughly virtuous, make Christians."[62] For Théodore Ratisbonne, the Talmud was symptomatic of all that was wrong with Judaism, from its "deplorable outcomes," to the "disgusting idiocy of those who make it their main occupation, and by the imbecility of zealous Jews who place their own perfection in its practices."[63]

Yet it was these very "imbeciles" that the converts sought to reach. How did they do so? As we have seen, Drach, L'évêque, and the Ratisbonne brothers generally placed Jews within the context of Judaism and its falsity as a religion. However, they had a link with their former coreligionists. After all, as Jews who had accepted what they saw as the natural progression of Judaism into Christianity, they still called themselves Israelites in the flesh and descendants of Abraham, and they saw themselves as "brothers in the flesh" of the members of the modern synagogue. For the most part they addressed the Jews as their "dear brothers." At times they turned on their "brothers" with all the pettiness one would expect to encounter in the bitterest of sibling rivalries. And the most consistent in this inconsistency was Drach. In most of the works published after his conversion, the prolific Drach took care to address his Jewish readers, stating that while he hoped they would not be offended by his words, he had to tell the truth:

I pray that those Israelites into whose hands this work falls will understand that my intention is in no way to offend my dear brothers of the flesh. Nonetheless, I cannot betray the truth, and those among them whose heart is upright will experience a healthy distancing from a belief that is founded on an antisocial and monstrous morality.[64]

When Drach directed his writing at Jews – whom he hoped to convert – he would address them as his brothers, or even his "dear brothers," or his "brothers in the flesh." Yet when Drach was not addressing his

---

[62] Ibid., 47.
[63] Ratisbonne in Bautain, 36.
[64] Drach, *Usure*, 36.

"Israelite brothers" directly, he would distance himself from the latter entirely. For example, in 1831 when he was writing to a fellow convert, the Abbé François Marie Paul (formerly Jacob) Libermann, his tone was notably more hateful.[65] Here "our Jews" were no longer brothers; they were corrupt, hateful and "fanatical".[66]

In becoming a sincere Catholic, Drach had left what Bautain called the "cadaver," the "withered trunk" that was contemporary Judaism, to join the religion that had absorbed Judaism's "living sap."[67] It would appear that once Drach became a Catholic, any expression of solidarity with his former religious community was at best insincere. His works contain a multitude of negative and vilifying references. Writing in 1840, Drach drew on what Alain Corbin has shown to be common rhetoric of the time, to describe the Parisian Jewish community, living in the Marais, and its inherent dirtiness and corruption. "This area," according to Drach, was "like the cesspit of the dregs of the Jewish population." Those who lived there were often without papers "to present to the civil officers, or if they do have some, it is better for them not to show them because of their *quarrels* with justice."[68] The corruption of Jews who had ongoing "quarrels with justice" was a reflection of the corrupt nature of Judaism. It could be discerned even in their languages: Drach noted that the Jews of Alsace spoke "a Germanic jargon mixed with corrupted Hebrew words," and the Sephardic Jews of the South and South-west spoke "a highly corrupted Espano-Portuguese, also mixed with distorted Hebrew."[69] Similarly, "Talmudic Hebrew" was synonymous with "extremely bad" writing.[70] Drach also belittled his former coreligionists with ridicule:

[65] This is Drach, *Croix*.
[66] Ibid., 12.
[67] Bautain, 100.
[68] Drach, *Divorce*, 7. Original emphasis. In Louis Chevalier's well-known work on the perception of the working classes as 'dangerous,' 'degraded,' and 'criminal,' there is no mention of this rhetoric being applied specifically to Jews. Louis Chevalier, *Labouring Classes and Dangerous Classes in Paris during the First Half of the Nineteenth Century*, trans. Frank Jellinek (London, 1973). In *The Foul and the Fragrant: Odor and the French Social Imagination* (Leamington Spa, 1986), p. 145, Alain Corbin does make direct reference to the notion of Jews as having their own odour.
[69] Drach, *Harmonie*, 1: 96. Drach's criticism of the Sephardic Jews was unusual.
[70] Drach, *Lettre*, 25.

The *Jew* of whom we speak is a different *species* from that which is currently called a *French Israelite*. [. . .] If a new Zerubbabel led his nation to the holy land, the French Israelites would come along as a part of the Babylonian captives, speaking all sorts of *barbaric languages*, and bringing with them *infidel* women of more than one nation, French women, Germans, English; perhaps there would also be, who knows? in this curious collection, Hottentots and other *savagesses*. [. . .] After this small digression, we ask pardon of the Mrs Hottentot and other *savagesses*.[71]

Moreover, in a distinct echo of the writings of Bonald, both Drach and Morel depicted the Jews as powerful and wilfully separate. Indeed, in Drach's eyes, the secret of their very existence was "the close fraternity that united them."[72] Morel described a malevolent network of Jews who understood one another "from one end of the earth to the other."[73] They were a "compact body," with a national spirit that made them "the enemy of Christian society."[74] Indeed, it was Morel who went further than the other converts in his depiction of a Jewish community that bore nothing but ill will towards its supposed fellow citizens. Seemingly driven by a sense of outrage at the way the community had treated Drach following his conversion, Morel portrayed a community which disposed of extraordinary means, and that formed a "vast and permanent conspiracy scattered over the entire globe." They had at their disposition "the couriers of a great house that criss-cross Europe in all directions" [the Rothschilds]. When it was in the interest of their religion, they would "stick together like a battalion in square formation." These "hard" and cruel Jews joyfully persecuted the newly Catholic Drach.[75]

But why did Drach himself attack his former coreligionists with such force? Perhaps Drach's bitterness towards Judaism was a reflection of this "persecution." In its report of his baptism, the *Ami* had observed that "the synagogue," having learned of Drach's act, "had shut him out from its bosom."[76] Behind this one line lay much acrimony. When she learned

[71] Drach, *Harmonie*, 1: 197–198.
[72] Drach, *Divorce*, 141.
[73] Morel, *Renseignements*, 9.
[74] Morel, *Vérité*, 102.
[75] Ibid., 41–44.
[76] "Baptême de David Drach," *L'Ami de la religion*, 2 April 1823.

of his act, his wife Sara, who had not converted, immediately took the children and fled with them to London, where they went into hiding. The police took an interest, and following claims by Drach that one of Rothschild's messengers had "played a very active role in the kidnapping of my children," they undertook close surveillance of Rothschild, along with Simon Drach, and Olry Worms de Romilly and Jacques Javal, both of whom were members of the Consistory.[77] However, despite the préfet's conviction that Sara's brother and father, at the least, were both involved, no concrete evidence of this was uncovered. Drach spent more than a year searching, including several trips to Mainz, where his father-in-law had studied. Eventually he found Sara in London and established himself there, maintaining contact with his wife and children. (According to some sources, he feigned a return to Judaism to regain her confidence.[78] There is also evidence to suggest that Drach and Sara had a fourth child.[79]) All the while, however, he was plotting to kidnap the children and return them to France and Catholicism, and he ultimately succeeded in carrying out this scheme with the help of some French nobles – the carriage of the Princess Mazzinghi was used to transport the children to the English coast. Once on French soil, the children were hidden in a convent and a monastery, all three of them apparently taking to their new life: the girls became nuns and the son a priest. They wrote plaintive letters to their mother, begging her to convert so that the family could be reunited. Their hopes were never to be realised. Twenty years after these events, Drach wrote that his wife, who remained in London "in spite of my repeated invitations that are all that is urgent and tender, still clings stubbornly, I will not say *to Judaism*, but to her aversion to Christianity, renouncing her husband and children."[80] It is impossible to know what ties bound Drach and his wife Sara. Yet his unusually negative depictions of Jewish women, such as the acerbity with which he tore into "Hottentots and other *savagesses*" are perhaps a sign of lasting bitterness

---

[77] AN F⁷ 9430 14314a: La disparition de Mme Drach.

[78] Paul Klein, 94. See also Simon Deutz, *Arrestation de Madame* (Paris, 1835). In a letter to the chief of police, the then minister for the interior, Chateaubriand, stated that Drach, then in Prussia, was known to have returned to Judaism. (Drach, initially believing his wife and children to be in Prussia, spent a year there.) Letter dated 20 January 1824; AN, F⁷ 9430, 14314a.

[79] See the detailed discussion on this matter in Landau, *Cas étrange*, 221.

[80] Drach, *Harmonie*, 1: 85.

towards the mother of his children who would not help him to justify his choice by acknowledging it.

The central players in this story were not the only ones with a stake in the proceedings. The kidnap and counter-kidnap of Drach's children became a symbol for the evils of the religion that Drach had assumed, or the one he had left behind, depending on who was writing the account of it. Apart from Drach's own testimony, there are two versions of this tale and they differ dramatically. The first was that of Ignace Morel. Morel's story of the fate of the Drach children, written in 1826, was highly coloured by what was clearly his own sense of bitterness and anger towards the Jewish community.[81] (When Morel told his own story, he noted that his own mother, a widow, "left the capital following my conversion due to the intolerance of the Israelites of Paris."[82]) He used highly emotive language to describe the affair, referring to the Jews as "abductors" and Drach's children as "prey," and his portrayal of Drach as an innocent victim was equally evocative:

Imagine the position of this unhappy family man. Rejected and persecuted by those to whom he belongs by blood, there is no cruelty that will not be directed against him in order to do violence to his conscience. His moans and prayers, which would have touched tigers, fail against the Judaic hardness of those from whom he begged only for one reassuring word on the fate of his children. Jews, even his brothers-in-law, insult him in his unhappiness even in his dwelling, and enjoy the suffering of their victim.[83]

His sense of the unjust way the Deutz family had treated Drach with regard to the children led him to tamper with the facts, claiming, for example, that Sara's inhuman treatment of her children had resulted in the death of the youngest boy.[84] In fact, Paul-Auguste Drach became a priest and died in 1895, canon of Notre-Dame cathedral.

The second account of the fate of the Drach children was written in 1835 by Drach's brother-in-law, Simon Deutz.[85] The son of the chief

---

[81] Morel, *Renseignements*.
[82] Morel, *Vérité*, 23.
[83] Ibid., 7.
[84] Morel, *Renseignements*, 9.
[85] Deutz, *Arrestation*. A comprehensive discussion of Simon Deutz is the focus of the following chapter.

rabbi of France, Deutz had in 1828 become another of Drach's protégés. In Morel's version of the story, the innocent Drach had been persecuted by the Jewish community. According to Deutz, however, it was Sara who was the unfortunate victim of Drach's cold ambition. Reliance on these two tales as sources would leave the researcher no wiser regarding certain intricacies of the story. (For example, Morel made the claim that Drach supported Sara and the children while in London, but Deutz maintained that he kept them, and at great expense to himself.) Nonetheless, the message that comes through very clearly from these two works is that this was a story involving two sides, and moreover, that each side sought to discredit the other and to place as much ground as possible between them.

Is this a true reflection of the way in which these converts generally viewed Christianity and Judaism? It is undeniable that although all these men had ostensibly left the Jewish community behind them, in making Jews the subject and the object of their writings and their activities, they were arguably still inextricably involved with them. L'évêque wrote to family members in intimate terms, even asking his mother to send him money. Drach had a close – if ultimately bitter – involvement with his wife and brother-in-law. As we have seen, Thomas Kselman has suggested that the "complex religious identity" of Théodore Ratisbonne challenges the idea that there were cleanly defined boundaries between Catholicism and Judaism.[86] Their situation may well have been one of confessional "interweaving", but what comes through from the writings of men such as L'évêque and Drach, is a strong desire for distance. The converts sought to take on a Catholic identity so completely that even though many of the allusions they made to Jewish power, malevolence, greed, corruption, and inhumanity were placed in the context of contemporary France, their criticisms of Jews were based on rhetoric that in many cases was as old as Christianity. Reflected in all of the writings discussed in this chapter is a clear understanding of Catholicism and Judaism separated by an unyielding wall, which could only be crossed through conversion. In general, these men clung to the Catholicism that had brought them "from darkness to light" and defined their world by it. In this world, there was no place for Judaism.

---

[86]   Kselman, "Social Reform," 15.

We can only conjecture as to the reasons why these men chose to proselytise and to vilify Judaism. Perhaps this was a way for them to prove their sincerity and to publicly announce their new allegiance. Perhaps this was a way to dispel any lingering doubts about the choice they had made. Perhaps, as they themselves maintained, their actions were simply an expression of their deep commitment to the truth that they had discovered. In their world, frustrated young Jewish men such as they may well have been could have identified Judaism as a burden and a cause of suffering, and from here it would perhaps not have been such a great step to take on a Catholic identity that included hostility towards Judaism. Their writings reveal a strong desire to maintain distance between themselves and the community, if not to promote and encourage a return to a world in which Jews had their traditional foreign status. Nowhere is this clearer than in the voice and the story of Drach and his constant vilification and belittling of Jews. Yet even the Ratisbonnes, although they were undeniably redrawing bonds between the Catholic and Jewish communities, were also, in their tireless and often controversial proselytising in the Jewish community, taking on the Catholic ultraroyalist/ Legitimist view of France – what we might call "absolutist conditionalism" – that stated that the only acceptable condition for the entry of Jews into society was their conversion. In the eyes of conservative Catholics such as these, there was no common ground on which Jews and Catholics could interact as equals, for there was only one truly satisfactory solution to the continued existence of Jews in France, just as there had only ever been one truly satisfactory solution to the continued existence of Jews.

We cannot assume that these men felt secure in their Catholicism. In fact, their actions suggest the opposite. What his works show is that Drach wrote about Jews as though he sought to reinforce the foundations of the "wall" that he perceived. Indeed, the ongoing and strenuous efforts of Drach, L'évèque, the Ratisbonne brothers, and, to some extent, Morel, to proclaim themselves publicly as good Catholics suggest that they could not truly leave their origins behind them. In the 1830s, Louis Bautain came under attack from the Church hierarchy. In 1834, the local bishop, Le Pappe de Trévern, put out an official warning against Bautain's teachings. Théodore Ratisbonne and his fellow Jewish converts Isidore Goschler and Jules Lewel were also regarded with suspicion at this time as less than fully committed Catholics. Ratisbonne wrote that his Catholic "colleagues" could not forgive his origins and the "religion of [his] father."[87] In this sense, it is surprising that Drach continued to see the wall as unyielding. Once on the other side of it, it must have seemed all too fragile.

[87] Bautain, *Philosophie du christianisme*, I:lix, quoted in ibid. On Bautain's feud with the Church in Strasbourg, see Kselman, "Bautain," 186–7.

3

࿇

The Eternal Jew

*I*N 1839, THE COMPOSER GIACOMO MEYERBEER – A JEW – WROTE to former fellow Jew Heinrich Heine who, through his conversion to Christianity, had famously bought his ticket to European society:

No *pommade de lion* or bear blubber, nor even baptism can grow back the foreskin of which we were robbed on the eighth day of life: those who, on the ninth day, do not bleed to death from this operation shall continue to bleed an entire lifetime, even after death.[1]

Meyerbeer was the eldest of three sons of the Beer family, wealthy and high-profile Berlin Jews. He was born Jacob Beer but over the course of his life became first Jacob Meyerbeer, and then later, Giacomo. (Deborah Hertz has detailed how the changing of names to sound less Jewish and more German was a way to move more definitely into mainstream society in Germany.[2]) Meyerbeer was enormously successful in France, its most popular composer of opera in the nineteenth century. In 1834, he became a permanent associate member of the Académie des Beaux-Arts. In the middle of that century, Jewish composers nearly dominated the Paris Opéra, an interesting contrast with Germany, where, for example, in 1832 Felix Mendelssohn was turned down for the post of director of

---

[1] Heinz and Gudrun Becker, *Giacomo Meyerbeer: A Life in Letters*, ed. Richard G. Pauly, trans. Mark Violette (London, 1989), 82. I am grateful to Professor Kerry Murphy of the Faculty of Music at the University of Melbourne for bringing this quote to my attention. Sander Gilman has discussed circumcision as a marker of Jewish identity, and Jewish difference, in the context of nineteenth-century Germany. See Gilman, *The Jew's Body* (New York, 1991), 18, 91, 119.

[2] Deborah Hertz, *How Jews Became Germans: The History of Conversion and Assimilation in Berlin* (New Haven, CT, 2007), 104.

the Choral Society in Berlin, on the basis that this Christian institution could not possibly be directed by a Jew.[3] Mendelssohn, of course, had been baptised on the wish of his parents in 1816, when he was seven. All of this suggests that success as a composer in France did not require conversion. Yet Meyerbeer, who was famously sensitive to reviews and public opinion, clearly felt that his religion was as inescapable as the mark of his ritual circumcision. Was Judaism truly so rooted in the body? And what was it about French society that made the composer feel that he was condemned to bleed for a lifetime?

We saw in the previous chapter how Drach, Morel, L'évèque, and the Ratisbonnes immersed themselves wholly in Catholicism, to the extent that they could be viewed as voices for this religion. The way in which they all chose to publicly show their allegiance to their new religion, ensuring the foundations of the "unyielding wall" that separated Judaism and Catholicism were as strong as possible, may well indicate a deep religious conviction. It may also suggest insecurity in their new identity, springing perhaps from a sense that their origins were not sufficiently far behind them. Were Drach's outpourings and the Ratisbonnes' aggressive proselytism part of a need to prove themselves to their fellow Catholics? One way to answer this question is to look at how Jewish converts were received by their fellow Catholics. What can their experiences tell us about the place envisaged in society for Jews, forty years after their emancipation and in a period when the nation was leaving behind it a failed attempt to re-establish Catholic absolutism, while embarking on an experiment in controlled liberalism? Did Meyerbeer have cause for his pessimism? The interweaving stories of David Drach and of his brother-in-law, Simon Deutz, provide a good starting point.

Drach's conversion was announced in triumphant tones in early April 1823 in the leading Catholic periodical of the era, the *Ami de la religion et du roi*. Indeed, for this conservative journal, this new convert to Catholicism was "an important and glorious conquest" – not only because it was expected that Drach's erudition would be of great benefit to the Church but also because, as the author of the article stressed, it was Drach's own reading and reflection that had led this learned Jew to embrace Catholicism. "He did not know any clergy," we are told; it was

---

[3] Ibid., 214.

he "who discerned the truth, and who was disposed to pay homage to it as soon as it was known to him." The journal had "no doubt" that Drach, with his knowledge, would be a useful addition to Catholicism.[4] Indeed, this paper was to become Drach's champion, for it greeted each new publication from Drach with a laudatory review. In one review the journal took the opportunity to note that the honourable sentiments expressed by Drach in his *Deuxième lettre* demonstrated "how worthy he was of becoming a Christian."[5] The publication of Drach's first *Lettre* was greeted with a glowing review and the hope that Drach would soon finish the two additional promised volumes, as the completed work would "bring to light the links between the two Testaments and the solidity of the base on which Christianity rests."[6] Drach did not disappoint, publishing two further letters in 1827 and 1833. The attention and praise showered on Drach by the Catholic press suggest that through his highly specific and, in the Catholic context, unusual knowledge, he was able to carve out a niche for himself in the Church. Indeed, Drach's work was seemingly received with enthusiasm and seriousness throughout the Church hierarchy. Drach himself told readers that the first volume of his *De l'Harmonie entre l'église et la synagogue*:

was honoured with august encouragement, as well as some most flattering approval from several people, eminent in doctrine and highly placed in the hierarchy of the Church, including some members of the Holy College; and the Propaganda [council for the propagation of the faith] deigned to authorise a supply in its own bookshop. It has already been cited with high praise by ecclesiastical writers whose names are dear to religion. Letters of great goodwill that were addressed to us from Rome on the occasion of this publication, expressed a desire to soon see a sequel appear, and engaged us to persevere in our work for the greater glory of God.[7]

"Encouragement" and "approval" in fact came from those highest placed in the world of Christendom. In its review of his *Deuxième lettre*, the *Ami* informed its readers that the minister to the King's Palace had twice ordered several copies of the work.[8] And in its issue of 11 August 1827,

---

[4] "Baptême de David Drach," *L'Ami de la religion*, 2 April 1823.
[5] "Deuxième lettre de M. Drach," *L'Ami de la religion*, 6 June 1827.
[6] "Lettre aux Israélites de M. Drach," *L'Ami de la religion*, 6 August 1825.
[7] Drach, *Harmonie*, 2: preface.
[8] "Deuxième lettre de M. Drach."

the *Ami* announced that Drach had received a precious expression of satisfaction from the Pope, in the form of a brief note addressed to him "in highly flattering terms" and a gold medal "of large dimensions." The author of the article hoped that this gesture would be "a powerful encouragement to Mr. Drach to devote his days to the good of the religion, and to continue along the same path that he has followed until now, endeavouring to turn the knowledge he has of rabbinic traditions to the defence of Christian truths."[9] Drach's vilifying asides were noted by the *Ami* with indulgence. To one reviewer these were "unexpected witticisms with which the caustic mind of the author has sought to temper the gravity of the topic."[10] Another saw them as "pathetic exhortation[s] to his brothers," and found that Drach's "candour" added "new value to his knowledge:"

The previous studies by the author are of great benefit to him; he combats the Jews according to their own traditions. Brought up in Judaism, he learnt to understand the Talmud well, and to know all the Rabbis' secrets. [. . .] We can only applaud Mr. Drach's zeal, and it is a consolation to see that this zeal has already shown good results and promises further ones. [. . .] His *Letters* will be a useful source of information for those who wish to get up to date on the controversy with the Jews.

Thus, it was that those writing in the *Ami* were able to approach Drach's criticisms of Judaism with absolute seriousness, noting, for example, in the review of his *Deuxième lettre* that Drach revealed "the feelings of hatred and intolerance" that rabbis were supposed to hold towards Christians, and mentioned "the nonsense and the revolting things that can be found in the Talmud."[11]

---

[9]   "M. Drach," *L'Ami de la religion*, 11 August 1827.

[10]   *L'Ami de la religion*, 17 November 1842.

[11]   "Deuxième lettre de M. Drach." In fact, Drach's authority was to be enduring. During the Second Republic and the Second Empire, Louis Veuillot, then editor of the Catholic paper *L'Univers*, mounted a sustained attack on Jews in response to episodes such as the Mortara Affair in 1858. Indeed, Veuillot, who strongly defended the Vatican's position on the Jewish child Edgardo Mortara, baptised in secret and kidnapped by Vatican authorities to be brought up a Catholic in 1858, had been guided by none other than Drach in his denunciation of the Talmud. Veuillot even cited the kidnapping of the Drach children as evidence that Jews also stole Catholic children and acknowledged his debt to Drach's "excellent work." (Cited in Catrice, *L'Harmonie*, 636. It is perhaps worth noting that Catrice entitled the relevant chapter "Paul Drach exploited by antisemites" (Catrice, 756). On the Mortara affair, see David Kertzer, *The Kidnapping of Edgardo Mortara* (New York, 1997).) In 1869, Henri de Gougenot des Mousseaux, one of those

It would seem, then, that Drach was the ideal prodigal son for the Church: the one who, in returning to the fold, brought the greatest possible joy and satisfaction to his new family. We have seen how the continued existence of Jews had long been an irritant to those Christians – such as the protagonists of the first chapter – who wished for no such challenges to the foundation of their faith. The self-motivated conversion of Drach, a learned rabbi, was as great a vindication of their position as such Catholics could hope to see. Moreover, having converted in such spectacular fashion, Drach then went on to further make himself useful by proving age-old supercessionist claims and encouraging other Jews to follow his example. His brother-in-law Simon Deutz did so in 1828, and an exultant Drach published an account of this conversion.[12] Drach, then working at the Sorbonne, had every reason to feel secure in his Catholic identity. Yet in 1832, when the attention of those most important to Drach came to focus on Deutz and to vilify him, Drach's public repudiation of his erstwhile protégé was rapid and thorough. Why?

Drach and Deutz were not always distant. The relationship between the brothers-in-law vacillated between cordiality and bitter hatred. After Drach and Sara Deutz were married in 1817, Deutz spent much time at the home of his sister and her husband. When Drach converted in 1823, Deutz reacted with anger and violence, threatening Drach and smashing his windowpanes with stones. On 27 November 1824, after he had retrieved his children, Drach wrote to the police complaining that Deutz was following and threatening him.[13] But the two were reconciled in 1828 when Deutz joined Drach in Catholicism. Drach went so far as to undertake to acquit Deutz's debts and to ensure his good reception into the Catholic world. He even persuaded Lamennais to write a letter in

Legitimists who had 'migrated' to his country home following the revolution of 1830, published the Catholic antisemitic work, *Le Juif, le judaïsme et la judaïsation des peuples chrétiens*, in which, like Veuillot, he drew heavily on Drach's writings on the Talmud. Gougenot des Mousseaux attributed his knowledge of "this treasure-chest of hideous absurdities and at times, of sublime science and notions" to Drach. (Gougenot des Mousseaux, quoted in ibid., 516.) Gougenot des Mousseaux's work was revived by Drumont who encouraged its republication in the 1880s, and beyond that, well into the 1930s.

12 Drach, *M. Hyacinthe Deutz.* On his conversion, Deutz took the name Hyacinthe Gonzague. Given that he ultimately reverted to his given name, I will continue to refer to him as Deutz.

13 AN F⁷ 9430, 14314a.

Deutz's favour.[14] However, this reconciliation was to last only four years. Two years after Deutz's conversion, the events of July 1830 brought an end to the attempt to re-establish royal absolutism in France under the Ultra Charles X. When Charles's reign came to an end, so did Ultras' hopes of a lasting return to their ideal France. Under the Restoration, Jews may have been recognised under the Charter, but, as we have seen, their acceptance into all sectors of society did not necessarily follow. The Charter of 1830 apparently renewed this commitment to religious freedom: very soon after the July revolution, in 1831, parliament voted to pay the salaries of rabbis. And in 1832, a law provided dispensation from military service for rabbinic students.[15] For Ultras, such acts spelled the death of their aspirations. They were unable to reconcile themselves with the regime and, in particular, with its king, who was not only a usurper from the house of Orléans and the son of a regicide, but also, apparently, a determined liberal. They "migrated" to their country homes and became "intransigent" Legitimists, so influenced by Romanticism, and perhaps by the nature of Restoration Catholicism, that they preferred to turn away from an importune present to dwell in an illustrious past. In 1820, the Duke de Berry, son of the Count d'Artois (later Charles X) had been assassinated by Louvel. Berry's son, the only possible direct heir to the Bourbon throne, was born to his wife, Marie-Caroline, after his death. After the 1830 revolution, cloistered Legitimists awaited the moment for the miracle son, the Count de Chambord, or "Henri V," to make his claim to the throne.[16] An answer to their hopes seemed to arrive in 1832, when the mother of the Bourbon pretender, the Duchess de Berry, landed in Provence with the express purpose of inciting an insurrection. The duchess travelled through the South, making her way to the Legitimist heartland of the Vendée. The government was on her trail, but she was able to elude its agents, moving from one safe house to another disguised as a peasant. It was Simon Deutz who revealed

---

[14] *Correspondance générale de Lamennais,* t. IV, *juillet 1828 à juin 1831,* Paris, 1973, lettre du Père Ventura du 1er mars 1830, p. 253. Quoted in Landau, 223.

[15] Phyllis Cohen Albert has argued that it is not unreasonable to assume that the placing of Judaism on the "state payroll" was in fact in order to more tightly control the rabbinate. She notes that a law of 15 October, 1832 spelled out "very detailed requirements for the rabbinate." Albert, *Modernization,* 61.

[16] Jardin and Tudesq, 189.

the duchess' whereabouts, leading to her arrest in November 1832 and dashing the hopes of Legitimists forever.

The task of unravelling Deutz's story, like that of Drach, is complicated by the fact that almost all those who have published works about him have been strongly – and unashamedly – influenced by their own subjectivity. Legitimist works allude to him in their accounts of the "tragic" arrest of the "heroic" Duchess de Berry.[17] Deutz published his own version of his story, and two works, one of them by Morel, were written purely in reaction to this version.[18] These different stories often stand in stark contradiction to one another. Morel, as noted earlier, often sacrificed fact for dramatic effect and went to great lengths to defame and discredit Deutz. For example, in 1831, Deutz travelled from England to Italy, accompanying the Misses de Bourmont. In his work, the Legitimist General Dermoncourt, who had no reason to praise Deutz, noted that the latter had left them "edified by his behaviour and his delicate attentions."[19] In contrast to this, Morel claimed that Deutz became so unbearable over the course of the journey that they left him in Geneva, when they had originally planned to go with him to Italy.[20] Nonetheless, some details can be established with certainty. For example, Deutz's early failures, first in rabbinical school and then as a printer's apprentice, would seem to indicate that his was a somewhat unstable youth. Yet the reasons for his conversion remain unclear. In his memoir, Deutz – whose testimony must be taken with a grain of salt – stated that in 1827 he went to Rome to find Drach, moved by "a strong desire to know the mysteries of Christianity and the organisations and institution of the Jesuits, [and] perhaps also a hope of avenging myself on a scoundrel who had betrayed my sister's affection."[21]

It was in 1831 in London, then a centre of Legitimist intrigue, that Deutz – now a Catholic – met exiled French Legitimists. Through them,

---

[17] See, for example, Théodore Anne, *La prisonnière de Blaye* (Paris, 1832); P.F.S. (Général) Dermoncourt and Alexandre Dumas (père), *La Vendée et Madame*, 2d ed. (Paris, 1833); and Duke de Guibourg, *La Relation fidèle et détaillée de l'arrestation de S. A. R. Madame, duchesse de Berry* (Nantes, 1832).

[18] Deutz, *Arrestation de Madame*; P.F.S. (Général) Dermoncourt, *Deutz ou Imposture, ingratitude et trahison par l'auteur de "La Vendée et Madame"* (Paris, 1836); Morel, *Vérité*.

[19] Dermoncourt, *Deutz*, 20

[20] Morel, *Vérité*, 114–16.

[21] Deutz, *Arrestation*, 7.

he was recommended to the Duchess of Berry. He took up the Legitimist cause, and the duchess entrusted him with missions which, by all
accounts – including that of a somewhat begrudging Morel – he fulfilled
with intelligence and ability. Yet Deutz claimed that he soon began to
feel doubts about the Legitimists and their goal of reinstating the sole
heir to the Bourbon dynasty to the throne, a prospect which evoked a
potential civil war in France, or even foreign involvement. He realised
his power: "Without letting one drop of blood flow, I could, with the
arrest of one woman, prevent these rifts and these miseries."[22] Thus, he
continued to play faithful servant to the duchess, all the while undertaking negotiations with the then Minister for the Interior Montalivet
(soon to be replaced by Adolphe Thiers), to deliver up the Duchess
de Berry. Deutz travelled to Nantes where he knew the duchess to be
hiding, and on 6 November 1832, he led soldiers to the house. They
entered and began a search. But the duchess was not found immediately.
Alerted to the soldiers' presence, she managed to reach a pre-arranged
hiding place behind a fireplace, which she shared with three other people, the elderly M. de Menars, her companion Mlle de Kersabiec, and the
Duke de Guibourg, who was to write an account of the episode.[23] The
search continued through the evening and resumed again the following
morning until the duchess and her three companions were forced to
reveal themselves or be asphyxiated or burned by a fire the gendarmes
had lit to keep out the cold. The duchess was taken away and imprisoned in the fortress of Blaye, north of Bordeaux. This episode brought
to an end what Jardin and Tudesq have called "the last hurrah of the
Vendée."[24]

The news of the duchess' arrest exploded in the press on 9 November
1832. Details of Deutz's role were at first vague: on 11 November, the
royalist *Quotidienne* reported that "happily" he was not French but rather
the son of an Italian, and his name was given as Hyacinthe Gonzalve.

---

[22] Ibid., 32.
[23] Guibourg, *Relation fidèle*. Interestingly, Guibourg painted Deutz almost more as a
victim of the government than as a perpetrator. This was an unusual stance, where the
more common position was that of Théodore Anne, who, in his work, depicted Deutz
as calculating, and driven by a greed so strong that his religion was no more than an
"obstacle" in the realisation of his desires (Anne, 197).
[24] Jardin and Tudesq, 229.

(Deutz was in fact born in Koblenz in 1802. He and his family moved to Paris in 1806 when his father Emmanuel was summoned to be a member of Napoleon's Sanhedrin.) Two days later, a letter from the Duke de Guibourg was reprinted, with complete – and more-or-less accurate – details regarding Deutz. Deutz was cast as public enemy, and key themes quickly became evident in the way in which he was portrayed. First, the sincerity of his conversion was thrown into doubt. In his letter, printed in all the papers, Guibourg charged Deutz with having "converted to the Catholic faith superficially."[25] The *Ami de la religion* went even further: "After a true or feigned study of the Christian religion, [Deutz] requested baptism."[26] For most, however, Deutz's conversion was not an issue. It soon became clear that even though Deutz had converted almost five years earlier and remained a Catholic all that time, with his betrayal of the duchess, in the eyes of his critics, he had reverted to Judaism, and he was identified with the most infamous of Jews in the Catholic tradition: Judas.[27]

Moreover, much was made of the fact that Deutz was not only a Jew but also a foreigner. The duchess herself was reported to have said "Happily he was not a Frenchman!"[28] Others specifically pointed out that he was German. Some journals made a heroine of Marie Bossy, a servant in the Duguin home where the Duchess was staying, who refused to reveal the duchess' hiding place to the police even when offered a reward for the information. The Toulousain *Gazette du Languedoc* found the coincidence of Ms Bossy's first name too much to resist. The journal opened a subscription for Marie Bossy, with the following preface: "You honour us, you protect us, you show with one stroke the distance that separates Judas from Marie, the German Jew from the French Christian! [. . .] Let us pray for her, this woman who rejected the thirty deniers of the Pharisees."[29] Morel also pointed out Deutz's Teutonic origins, and indeed made much of them. Deutz was the "Prussian apostate, who like

[25] *La Gazette de France*, 13 November 1832.
[26] "Arrestation de la duchesse de Berry," *L'Ami de la religion*, 15 November 1832.
[27] "Judas-Deutz," *La Quotidienne*, 15 December 1832. Modern sources also generally refer to Deutz as a Jew. Jardin and Tudesq make no allusion to Deutz's conversion whatsoever, calling him simply "the Jew Deutz" (Jardin and Tudesq, 229).
[28] Guibourg's letter, *La Gazette de France*, 13 November 1832.
[29] *La Gazette du Languedoc*, 23 November 1832.

a coward, betrayed a French princess."[30] One poem, printed in several newspapers, united these themes:

> This gold marks the traitor's brow
> For him, neither family nor homeland
> No country will have witnessed his birth
> And this Judas is of no God.[31]

Deutz's story even became a theme of popular songs and theatrical performances. Reporting on a vaudeville performance held on the "traitor Deutz" the previous evening at the Palais-Royal, the *Gazette du Languedoc* described its enthusiastic reception: "a torrent of applause echoed throughout the hall; the entire audience demanded a repeat performance of the couplet, which condemns one of the greatest acts of cowardice of modern history:"

> For the gold that he was given
> A traitor said: there she is
> Who is this new Judas?
> Is it a Frenchman? Certainly not.
> It means nothing (repeat)
> He is not a fellow citizen
> It means nothing (repeat)
> Our honour is doing fine [*se porte bien*].[32]

The allusion to gold was widespread in these poems and songs. Deutz's Jewishness was generally linked to the widely held conviction that he had received a large sum of money – variously thought to be between half a million and one million francs – for his act.[33] One letter printed in the

---

[30]   Morel, *Vérité*, 170.

[31]   "Cet or marque le front du traître/ Pour lui, ni famille ni lieu/ Nul pays ne l'aura vu naître/ Et ce Judas n'est d'aucun Dieu." *La Gazette du Languedoc*, 9 December 1832.

[32]   *La Gazette du Languedoc*, 25 November 1832.

[33]   Modern sources often report this as fact. See, for example, Collingham, 127; and J. Lucas-Dubreton, *Aspects de Monsieur Thiers* (Paris, 1948), 57. John Allison claimed to have found proof of the transaction in a receipt from Deutz to Thiers for the amount. John M. S. Allison, *Thiers and the French Monarchy* (New York, 1926), 173–4. (Allison referred to a receipt from Deutz [Bibliothèque nationale, 20,601, Part II., 18–27], as well as to *Le Correspondant* of 25 September 1832, and the records of Madame Dosne, and of Thiers). The only one to actively refute this claim was Deutz himself. Zosa Szajkowski, who took on the role of Deutz's champion, did not refute the claim but stated that no archival proof had been found of it. ("Simon Deutz: Traitor or French Patriot?" in *The Jews and the French Revolutions of 1789, 1830 and 1848*, 1043–57).

Quotidienne described the duchess' captivity as having been "bought at such a high cost by the cleverness of M. Thiers from the ignoble avidity of a Jew."[34] The transaction was similarly described in a book on the duchess' arrest. The Legitimist Théodore Anne was a former garde-du-corps of Charles X. Like many Legitimists under the July Monarchy, he was influenced by Romanticism. In this case, it was a refuge from his inability to act. Thus, he romanticised the duchess that he had been unable to help, calling her *La prisonnière de Blaye*.[35] In his work, the "vile minister" counted out his gold to the "Jewish turncoat."[36] In case the link was not sufficiently clear in the minds of its readers, the *Ami de la religion* spelled it out for them: "The man who delivered Madame the Duchess of Berry for a sum of money is a Jew by nation."[37]

Moreover, if Deutz was a Jew "by nation," then this national adherence was set up in opposition to the people of France. The *Quotidienne* printed a letter from a town in the Bouches-du-Rhône, in which it was noted that at least "the people" had played no role in the "ignominious pact" which had taken place "between the Jew who sold the princess, and the Frenchman who bought her."[38] Bonald also pitted Deutz against "the people" of France in his letter to the press: "It is the minister of a royal cabinet who concluded this shameful deal with a Jew, and who seals it with money stolen from the needs and the sweat of the people."[39] For vital in this transaction was the fact that, if Deutz had betrayed honour, that of the French was still intact. After all, this was a society preoccupied with a code of honour, which required that men show themselves to be capable of – among other things – loyalty.[40] Indeed, the rhetoric of honour comes through clearly in the attacks on Deutz. For example,

---

34 "Lettre à Madame de M. le Vicomte de Suleau," *La Quotidienne*, 10 December 1832.
35 Jardin and Tudesq, 189. Jo Burr Margadant has discussed a similar romanticisation by Legitimists of the duchess in her idealisation as imprisoned royal mother. Jo Burr Margadant, "The Duchesse de Berry and Royalist Political Culture in Postrevolutionary France," *History Workshop Journal* 43 (1997): 43.
36 Anne, *La prisonnière de Blaye* (Paris, 1832). Extracts reprinted in *La Quotidienne* on 11 December 1832.
37 "Arrestation de la duchesse de Berry," *L'Ami de la religion*, 17 November 1832.
38 *La Quotidienne*, 14 December 1832. This was a reference to the interior minister, Adolphe Thiers.
39 *La Quotidienne*, 21 December 1832.
40 On the bourgeois concern with honour during the July Monarchy and its feudal roots, see Robert Nye, *Masculinity and Male Codes of Honor in Modern France* (New York, 1993), esp. chap. 3, passim. See also William Reddy, "Marriage, Honor, and the Public

those conservatives who criticised Deutz drew on the feudal tradition of honour that they valued so highly and which had grown out of an ideology that stated that nobles who served militarily were supposed to do so with courage, gallantry, and loyalty.[41] In the 1790s, loyalty had shifted from being a duty that bound noble to king, or foot soldier to lord, to one that bound the citizen to the nation. The bourgeoisie of the 1830s and 1840s, very much concerned with controlling reproduction and sex in such a way as to ensure the perpetuation of family lines, took on these notions, developing a combination of honourable qualities that were expected from the bourgeois male in public life.[42] Attacks on Deutz drew on all of these traditions. Thus, in his betrayal of the duchess, he had not only shown himself to be dishonourable, he was also "un-French." Such sentiments were echoed in the left-wing press, ensuring that, as the poems predicted, Deutz found friends nowhere. Even liberal journals such as the *National* and the *Constitutionnel*, which regarded the duchess' capture as good news for the nation, portrayed Deutz as foreign and described his betrayal as an "un-French" act.[43]

Moreover, Deutz's act of *ignominie* made him unmanly. As medical scientists from the 1790s onwards had come to focus their gaze on men and women (or men as opposed to women), the bourgeois preoccupation with the perpetuation of the male line, together with discourses of separate public (male) and private (female) spheres of existence and influence were enshrined in male and female bodies. Man and woman were considered to be different "in every aspect of their physical organisations."[44] Complementarity of the sexes was necessary to ensure attraction and fertility. The ideal male, therefore, was masculine – the ideal counterpart to a feminine woman. Effeminacy in a man was evidence of "demasculinisation."[45] This was the new medical language that embedded a man's honour, as Nye puts it, "deep in the blood and bone of his

---

Sphere in Postrevolutionary France: *Séparations de Corps, 1815–1848*," *Journal of Modern History* 65 (1993): 437–72.

[41] Nye, 15.

[42] Peter McPhee, "The Changing Contours of 1848," in *The Sphinx in the Tuileries, and Other Essays in Modern French History, Papers Presented at the Eleventh George Rudé Seminar Held at the University of Sydney, 4–6 July 1998*, ed. Robert Aldrich and Martyn Lyons (Sydney, 1999), 115.

[43] See, for example, *Le Constitutionnel*, 9 November 1832.

[44] Nye, 57.

[45] Ibid., 66.

sex."[46] Deutz, who had betrayed all that went to the very core of honour –
and thus manliness – was described in the press as:

a man of medium height, with a swarthy complexion; he has black and
frizzy hair; his sharp eyes are small and deep-set, he has a large mouth and
extremely thick lips, his nose is ordinary, he has beautiful hands, perhaps
too beautiful for a man, and he shows it with affectation.[47]

As a burgeoning metaphor for all that was unacceptable for the age,
Deutz captured the attention, and the imagination, of figures such as
Victor Hugo. Hugo, whose ideas at this time were evolving from staunch
royalism to liberalism, was perhaps driven to write about the betrayed
duchess either by his own sense of betrayal resulting from his wife's
affair with Sainte-Beuve or by his ongoing attachment to the concept
of royalism and to the person of Louis-Philippe. Hugo differed from
the Legitimists in that his work on Deutz, entitled "To the man who
delivered up a woman," did not seek to make any political statement.[48]
Nonetheless, the title of this piece and the anger and indignation of its
tone, leave no room for doubt as to Hugo's stance on the matter. Nor
does the writer's virulent use of the word "Jew" in addressing Deutz. Yet
in Hugo's eyes, Deutz was not merely a Jew. He was also a foreigner who
had sold honour ("honour, his word, pity, his oath") – by implication
an un-French act – for a "bag full of gold that was vomited over you!"
This honour was something that Deutz himself would never be able to
acquire, even if he managed to accumulate all the riches in the world,
for it "[could] not be bought"; presumably, particularly not by a Jew and
a foreigner such as he. Nonetheless, for Hugo, Deutz's worst crime was
neither his betrayal, nor the price he had exacted for it but, rather, his
conversion, as though his apostasy was a forerunner to his later betrayal:

> He is not even a Jew!
> He is a vile heathen,
> A turncoat, the world's disgrace and its dregs,
> A fetid apostate, an aberrant foreigner[49]

---

[46] Ibid., 71.

[47] *La Quotidienne*, 14 November 1832; also in *Le Constitutionnel*, 14 November 1832.

[48] Victor Hugo, *Œuvres poétiques* vol. 1, *Avant l'exil, 1802–1851* (Paris, 1964), 848–50. For
the full text of the poem, see appendix A.

[49] Hugo, 848.

Other prominent Catholics echoed Hugo's antipathy. Like the assimilated Jews who earned the disdain of the Baron Silvestre de Sacy, Deutz, as a convert, had endeavoured to leave his Jewishness behind him. Yet although he was no longer necessarily identifiable as a Jew, for Hugo and many like him, this seemed to be his most telling characteristic.

Figures such as Deutz illustrated that the once-clear boundary between Jews and Catholics that had helped the latter to explain their world was no longer reliable. Yet having attempted to leave Judaism behind him, Deutz, seemingly, belonged nowhere: "no country had seen his birth"; he was a foreigner, a turncoat, and an apostate. Apparently, the one thing Deutz could not escape was his Jewishness, any more than he could escape his own body. Thus, it was not only sex that was marked on the body. Chevalier has shown that in early-nineteenth-century French society, physical appearance came to denote class in both popular and bourgeois thought.[50] The case of Deutz suggests that bodily difference could also be seen as an indicator of religion or, specifically, of Jewishness. The belief that Jews had certain bodily characteristics that distinguished them from others had been a feature of medieval anti-Jewish sentiment. This included the belief that Jews had horns and a tail (and were thus linked with Satan) and that they emitted a particular smell, the *foetor judaicus*.[51] By constantly addressing him as "Jew," Hugo suggested that whatever Deutz did, his Jewishness would always remain with him, as though it were an immutable quality, anchored in his body. What was this Jewishness? It was greed, cowardliness, dishonour, and, above all, eternal difference and separateness.

It followed that other Jews could be just as guilty as Deutz. In his attempt to redress what he saw as the imbalance in writing about Deutz, Zosa Szajkowski makes the claim that from the first moments of news of the duchess' arrest, an anti-Jewish campaign was started. The *Gazette du Languedoc* extended its criticism of Deutz to include all Jews. In its section entitled "Various," it was noted that a ruling from 9 November, countersigned by Thiers, opened a special credit to the Minister for the Interior of "*one million* for *secret spending*. [. . .] it is up to France to pay as *secretly* as possible the Jew Gonzagues, and his cronies the other Jews, the

---

[50] Chevalier, esp. book 3, part II, chap. 4.
[51] See Trachtenberg, chap. 3.

little million that these gentlemen have earned so loyally."[52] But then, of all the Legitimist papers, the Toulousain *Gazette du Languedoc*, printed in one of France's Legitimist strongholds, stands out because of the force of the language and imagery it used. The *Gazette* variously described Deutz as a "traitor," the "traitor Deutz," the "infamous foreigner," the "foreign Jew," the "Jew Deutz," and the "villainous Jew."[53] Yet even this paper distinguished between "Jews" like the "traitor Deutz" and honourable "Israelites." This may have had to do with the rapid and public repudiation of Deutz by Adolphe Crémieux, the high-profile Jewish lawyer. When Deutz asked the talented nîmois for legal aid, Crémieux wrote back to him in no uncertain terms:

You counted on me as a fellow Jew, let your error cease. You now belong to no religion, you renounced the faith of your fathers, and you are no longer Catholic; *no religion* wants you.[54]

This letter found its way into several newspapers. In its introduction to the letter, the *Gazette du Languedoc* described Crémieux as an "Israelite lawyer."[55] The *Quotidienne* also distinguished between Deutz and other Jews, assuring its readers that "Deutz's fellow Jews were no less indignant than other French men at his betrayal."[56] And once again reinforcing the separation between "Jews" such as Deutz, and Frenchmen, Morel observed that it was "right to recognise that a good many Israelites, whose hearts are true, whose sentiments are French, shower Deutz with their contempt, just as much as do Christians."[57]

In fact, the Central Consistory, the ruling administrative body of the Jewish community, did seek to distance itself publicly from Deutz by censoring Deutz's father – still the chief rabbi of France – for his refusal to repudiate his son. Szajkowski claims that the Consistory was motivated to do this through its wish to stem the tide of anti-Jewish sentiment that the affair unleashed.[58] In the *Quotidienne* of November 17, it was noted

[52] "Variétés," *La Gazette du Languedoc*, 1 December 1832.
[53] *La Gazette du Languedoc*, 19 November 1832–17 December 1832.
[54] See, for example, *La Gazette du Languedoc*, 27 November 1832; *La Quotidienne*, 23 November 1832.
[55] *La Gazette du Languedoc*, 17 November 1832.
[56] *La Quotidienne*, 17 November 1832.
[57] Morel, *vérité*, 117.
[58] Szajkowski, "Simon Deutz," 1050.

that the Consistory was forcing Emmanuel Deutz to resign. In reality, as Phyllis Albert has shown, the Consistory did not have this power, and in the face of this inability to physically remove Rabbi Deutz, the Consistory chose rather to ignore him, excluding him from meetings for two years.[59] In fact, police agents were keeping a close watch on the Jewish community as it divided. Thus, for example, they reported on incidents such as that in which members of a synagogue violently protested against the chief rabbi's presence. On this occasion, the police commissioner of the Saint-Martin-des-Champs district assured the prefect of police that these occurrences did not betray any Legitimist sentiments among the Jews. Rather, the report stated, in general, it could be said that all the Jews were aware of the advantages offered by the July government.[60] To the Jewish community, conversion was anathema, and perhaps we can best understand the Consistory's response to Deutz's actions as an extension of this abhorrence. Or perhaps, as Szajkowski argued, the Consistory's response suggests that they felt vulnerable in the face of attacks on Deutz as Jew. Or, like Crémieux, were they as horrified as anyone else by Deutz's betrayal of honour?

"Deutz's fellow Jews" were not alone in seeking to cut off any associations with him. When news of his role became public and the Legitimist and conservative press turned on him, Deutz's relationship with Drach was also revealed. The *Ami* leapt to Drach's defence:

We are happy to be able to say today that Mr Drach has nothing to do with this horrible and shameful affair. Since his conversion, Mr Drach has always behaved perfectly; he has shown a great deal of zealousness in enlightening his coreligionists, he has published several works on the controversy with the Jews. [. . .] We are certain that Mr Drach will be dismayed at this dreadful act.[61]

Drach was indeed dismayed, and he was quick to add his voice to the chorus of condemnation. Barely a month after its own article appeared, the *Ami* had cause to write, with pleasure, that Drach had confirmed "the opinion that we had expressed."[62] In an open letter to the press, addressed

---

[59]   Albert, *Modernization*, 310.
[60]   AN, F¹⁹11038.
[61]   *L'Ami de la religion*, 17 November 1832.
[62]   *L'Ami de la religion*, 13 December 1832.

to the duchess, Drach dissociated himself not only from Simon Deutz, but indeed from the entire Deutz family:

All of Europe shuddered with indignation at the news of [...] the terrible act of which Judas has made himself guilty. I was even more dismayed by it than many other good Frenchmen. [...] The man who has become the execration of all time has never known honour, and even less the spirit of the holy religion that he claims to profess. He belongs to a family that separated itself from me several years go, breaking all the ties of nature, because it detests the principles of the Gospel. I will legally renounce any inheritance that could fall to me from the head of that family. The gold that has enriched it makes me shudder with horror.[63]

In later works, Drach continued to condemn his brother-in-law and to seek to distance himself from Deutz's betrayal. Indeed, Drach linked Deutz's dishonour directly to his Judaism: Deutz had "forsaken honour" and Drach could hear "repeated from all quarters, like opprobrium, the name of Jew."[64] In a handwritten letter contained in the preface of his Troisième lettre and dated 16 January 1833, Drach took advantage of the fact that he was sending a copy of his third letter to the publisher of a journal to thank him "for having so charitably defended me in your journal at the time of the betrayal by the unhappy Deutz." He also made reference to Deutz in the preface of this work:

Alas, the one new convert who should have given me the most consolation has become an object of compassion! He only ever wavered when he walked before Jehovah, and he was not perfect. His affections had remained with perfidious Agar, and he has finally married the impure Egyptian woman.[65]

The fact that Drach chose to repudiate his brother-in-law so swiftly and so publicly is striking. Perhaps the speed and certainty with which Deutz

---

[63] L'Ami de la religion, 28 December 1832.
[64] L'Ami de la religion, 13 December 1832.
[65] Drach, Troisième lettre, x. Eleven years on, Drach was still writing about Deutz:

Thus, in punishment of his stunning crime, the hand of the Lord weighed upon him: he has been cut off from the commerce of men. Thus the moderator of the world, making a healthy example, never avoids manifesting his providence through terrible punishments for public scandals. Let us pity this new Cain, a wanderer and a vagabond on the earth, and let us pray for his enrichment. May the stigmata printed on his forehead, and which he is condemned to carry from land to land, tear this repairing cry from his conscience: "Lord, my sin is too great to carry, see, I repent, cover it with the coat of your misericord!" (Drach, Harmonie, 1: 4.)

had been branded a "Jew" made Drach feel the insecurity of his own position. The rapidity with which he wrote to the press, defiant and proud, yet careful to separate himself from Deutz and other "Jews," could be interpreted as an attempt to emphasise the gulf between his world, and the Judaism to which Deutz truly belonged. After all, General Dermoncourt, in his response to Deutz's attempt to set the record straight, saw fit to comment that Deutz, having decided to convert, approached Drach, "who, still a little Jewish, was doubly enchanted, both by Deutz's conversion and by the fact that demands for frequent contributions would no longer be made on his purse."[66]

Despite the extensive publicity surrounding them, the stories of Drach and Deutz, so rich in clues and emotions, have been met either with resounding silence or with unabashed bias on the part of historians. Of three works about the brothers-in-law, only one can lay any claim to impartiality.[67] Another is an apologetic doctoral thesis dedicated to Drach's life as a Catholic, and the third, written in reaction to the Legitimist pamphlets published immediately after the duchess' arrest, openly paints Deutz as a patriot rather than as a traitor.[68] Perhaps the historiography suggests that the wall between Catholics and Jews still exists for those who have had a stake in the story: the only interest in it is as a celebration of Drach the Catholic or a defence of Deutz the Jew. Yet the stories of Drach and Deutz can tell us much about how conservative Catholics – or in this case, Legitimists – were adapting their centuries-old view of Jews to a changing world. They reveal to us that some Catholics were still profoundly uncomfortable with a new world in which Jews were present and nominally equal, and in which traditional hierarchies and boundaries between Catholicism and Judaism were being challenged. The angry and unwavering identification of Deutz as Jew by Legitimists who saw a great hope dashed by his act of betrayal, the certainty with which the Legitimist press identified Deutz as a Jew and the association of Deutz's name with greed and dishonour suggest that conservative Catholics still held on to the notion of Jews as a foreign and separate

---

[66] Dermoncourt, *Deutz*, 6.

[67] Paul Klein, "Mauvais juif, mauvais chrétien." In this article, the stories of the two men were told as "striking" examples of the *déséquilibre* of some Jews following the Revolution (and presumably the emancipation).

[68] Paul Catrice, *L'Harmonie entre l'église et le judaïsme d'après la vie de Paul Drach* (Lille, 1978); Szajkowski, "Simon Deutz."

entity. It is telling that Deutz's conversion was a particular point of focus, because this precisely challenged those boundaries.

In 1835, the Abbé Bautain, the mentor of Théodore Ratisbonne, remarked on how difficult Christians found it to see Jews in any other way:

There are few Christians, even among the least religious, who dare to show publicly that they are the friend of a Jew. They fear sharing the disgrace of the name; it is like a reflected disgrace that they avoid. Some (Jews) try to circumvent the obstacle: [. . .] They manage only to buy a little condescension and tolerance. Non-Jews consent to see them, they receive them, they will even go to their home, if the table is laid; and when they have enjoyed themselves at the Jews' expense, they say: they are good people, it's a pity that they are Jews. If they meet a Jew who is rich, learned, commendable for some moral virtue: politeness, sociability, trueness to his word, somewhat disinterested, all at the same time, the world is surprised by him, and it cries naively: he is a right honest man for a Jew![69]

Conservative Catholics in early-nineteenth-century France – such as the Legitimists in this story – were caught between trying to reimpose the place of the Jews in traditional Catholicism and attempting to adapt this to what was clearly a new world, particularly after 1830. One way in which they reconciled what to them was apparently a chameleon-like Jew was to envelop him in the rhetoric of physical difference. They encased him not in a ghetto but within his origins, and thereby prevented him from truly escaping them. In other words, they made Judaism an immutable quality. The strength of this physical identification was such that, in the eyes of the highly successful Meyerbeer, the Jew would spend his life "bleeding" for the ritual when he, as an eight-day-old boy, was consecrated to Judaism. "Good people" and "right honest men" they may have been but, above all, the Jews of Bautain's story were still just that. For as Simon Deutz's story shows, even conversion was not a guarantee of respectability. One could revert to one's inherent Judaism simply by one's acts. Jewishness, it would seem, had become eternal.

[69] Bautain, 68–9.

4

ော

Sensuality, Depravity, and Ritual Murder: Jews in the Orient, and Jews at Home?

*I*IN JUNE 1798, NAPOLEON SET FORTH WITH AN ARMY MORE THAN thirty-six thousand strong to conquer Egypt and the Holy Land. He was stirred by a desire to challenge British interests and ambitions in the region, but Napoleon's expedition was also inspired by Enlightenment and Revolutionary rhetoric that saw the modern French republic as a continuation of the ancient Mediterranean civilisations of Rome and Greece. In ancient times, the great republics of the Mediterranean had given birth to empires in the Middle East and northern Europe. But now, the path of civilisation was to be reversed, and those who had inherited this tradition were returning to its birthplace, now sadly only a relic of its former greatness, to once again establish new empires. Thus, the purpose of the expedition was not merely military conquest. Napoleon's soldiers were accompanied by 150 scholars, chosen for the mission of establishing a new Académie des sciences in Cairo, to be modeled on the French Académie in Paris – as intrinsic to this project of renewal as was the military conquest. These scholars were to inaugurate the field of study that was to become known as Orientalism. Following Napoleon's initial campaign, the work of his intellectual army gained momentum, and through the first half of the nineteenth century, the great scholar of the Orient Silvestre de Sacy – who was to train a generation of Orientalists – led the charge of academics, writers, artists, and adventurers, who served as mediators for those in France, interpreting and packaging an Orient for French consumption.

In France itself, the term *orientalisme* was recognised by the Académie in 1835. It reflected this growing interest in all varieties of oriental matters, including the more established meaning of oriental studies, the scholarly studies of the languages, cultures and customs of Asiatic peoples from the Mediterranean to Japan. Of course, the Académie could not be accused of being ahead of the times. Those in the world of the arts were well and truly *orientalistes* by this time, following the path laid down by Victor Hugo. His collection of poems, *Orientales*, had been published in 1829, and it was this work that earned him the title, among his fellows, of the father of Orientalism. This so-called Orientalism was largely a projection: romanticism and biblical themes were made use of, as artists sought to explore ideas of masculinity and femininity that went beyond the bounds of the permissible in the bourgeois world of July Monarchy France. It is precisely this aspect of Orientalism that I would like to explore here. I undertake this in a strictly historical sense; that is, I will attempt to read Hugo and his contemporaries in the spirit of their times, rather than of ours.[1] Because by the middle of the nineteenth century, the fascination with the Orient had fully permeated the arts in France. What was the attraction of these lands, so foreign to French society? In part, it was precisely their foreignness. The Orient as it was depicted for those in France, was a place that could contain all that France, and particularly bourgeois French society, could not. Sex, for example, had become encumbered with expectations and obligations in a society where the perpetuation of the family line was of paramount importance.[2] In contrast, in the Orient, it could be perceived as unbounded by limitations; the Orient was a place of sensuality that revelled in its own glory.

It is hardly surprising that this prospect should have been so attractive to artists and writers. Desire was projected onto the Orient, and in this context, so were romanticism and sensuality. Thus, it was that in this

---

[1] On the politicization of Orientalism, see James Pasto, "Islam's 'Strange Secret Sharer': Orientalism, Judaism, and the Jewish Question," *Comparative Studies in Society and History* 40, no. 3 (July 1998), 472–3. On the writing of Jews into Orientalism, see Ivan Davidson Kalmar and Derek J. Penslar, eds, *Orientalism and the Jews* (Waltham, MA, 2005). In contrast to the French approach, Jonathan Hess and Susannah Heschel have both documented how, during the same period in Germany, the Orient became the battle terrain on which Christians sought to write a definitive historical account of Christianity's relation to Judaism – in the context of debates over Jewish emancipation – and where, from the middle of the nineteenth century, Jews sought, in riposte, to unsettle this monolithic theological discourse, by constructing their own representations of early Judaism and Islam. Susannah Heschel, *Abraham Geiger and the Jewish Jesus* (Chicago, 1998), 20–2; Jonathan M. Hess, *Germans, Jews, and the Claims of Modernity* (New Haven, CT, 2002), 51–89.

[2] Nye, 62.

realm, unbound by societal expectations, Oriental women were to be defined by their sensuality.[3] In the preface to his collection of poems entitled *Orientales*, Victor Hugo claims to have obeyed – "perhaps without knowing it"[4] – a general preoccupation with the Orient, the place that for Hugo is a spring at which he has long desired to quench his thirst. In Hugo's Orient, all is great, rich, fertile; it is a sea of poetry, of colours that insinuate themselves into his thoughts and dreams. Hugo, who was seen by other nineteenth-century artists as having created Orientalism, dreamed of an Orient that was "Hebraic, Turkish, Greek, Persian, [and] Arab," all at once.[5] His writing reflects this failure to make distinctions. In his melting pot of exoticism, Hugo's depictions of Jewish and Muslim women are at times one and the same. Hugo was literally creating; he never travelled to the places he described. In contrast, Hugo's friend, the artist Eugène Delacroix, travelled extensively through North Africa in 1832. Similar to Hugo's creations, in his images of Oriental women, at times it is simply not possible to see what differentiates a Jewish from a Muslim woman, if not perhaps for the greater detail with which the faces of the former are drawn. Hugo, Delacroix, and others like them were influenced by a desire to create a space where sensations not permissible within the bounds of bourgeois *moeurs* could be explored fully. Their interest was in colour, texture, and suggestion. Jewesses could serve as subjects, but so could Muslim women. The "belle juive" of Hugo's poem "La Sultane favorite" has an "ebony breast,"[6] but so do the virgins of "Le feu du ciel."[7] "Sara la baigneuse" is observed while taking a prolonged and dreamy bath, and Hugo recommends to the observer that they, too, like the poet, stay, for in an hour they will see "the ingénue" emerge from her bath, naked, arms crossed:

> Car c'est un astre qui brille
> Qu'une fille
> Qui sort d'un bain au flot clair[8]

---

[3] For an argument that Orientalism and "the Jewish" are equally feminine in the European Christian imagination, see Hess, *Germans*, 20.

[4] Victor Hugo, *Les Orientales* (Paris, 1829), 4.

[5] Ibid.

[6] Hugo, *Les Orientales*, 93. For the full text of the poem see Appendix B.

[7] Ibid., 13.

[8] Ibid., 126. For the full text of the poem, see Appendix B.

Similarly, the regretted mistress in "Les Tronçons du serpent" was "like an angel" when she crossed her arms over her naked chest.[9]

Nonetheless, from this generic Oriental woman there did emerge a very specific notion of the Jewess. For just as Jews themselves were both exotic and familiar, what better vehicle to make the Oriental woman accessible than to make her Jewish? The Jewess lived in the Orient, so that it was possible to imagine her. Yet at the same time, she was an approachable subject because she was also familiar; as one of the group condemned to eternal wandering, she was very much present in French society.[10] And it was all the more possible to imagine her, for she still existed on the periphery of this same society. Men from disparate fields such as Hugo and Delacroix – as well as the lesser known writer, Charles Didier – all found in the Orient and its Jewesses something sufficiently distant to be idealised and made mysterious, and yet which still had elements of familiarity. All contributed to the ambiguous image of the Jewess who was both spiritual and carnal: beautiful, sensual, and knowing.[11] Thus, for example, the beautiful Jewesses of Hugo's creation are not merely objects of desire; they insinuate themselves into man's consciousness, participating knowingly in the act of seduction, and thus possessing a certain power. In "Sara la baigneuse," the Jewess Sara dreams in her bath of a life of indolence and power, where men would have to "risk their head" to see her.[12] The "belle juive" of the sultan's seraglio in "La Sultane favorite" cruelly demands the death of her competitors and dominates the sultan with her beauty and her heart of steel. Delacroix, who was received by the Jewish communities in the places he visited, painted Jewesses that echo Hugo's depictions. In his paintings, the subjects are dressed sumptuously in multicoloured clothing. They look directly at the artist, seated with a casual arm thrown over the back of a couch,

[9] Ibid., 160.

[10] Schechter, 206.

[11] The word "Jewess" is the most accurate translation of the French *juive*, and indeed, it is an equally accurate reflection of the general sense in which the Jewish woman was constructed. As Sartre put it, behind the words *belle juive* is a very specific notion of sexuality (Sartre, 56). However, it is precisely for this reason that I hesitate for my own descriptive purposes to employ a word that tends towards objectification, although I use it deliberately to reflect the goals of those whose work I discuss.

[12] Luce Klein, *Portrait de la juive*, 128. See also Suzy Badia-Evzline, "Histoire d'une beauté idéale ou un certain reflet de la femme juive à travers la littérature française du XIXe siècle," *Combat pour la Diaspora* 8 (1982), 54.

4.1. Eugène Delacroix, *Jeune femme juive assise*, 1832. Musée du Louvre. By permission of the Réunion des musées nationaux Agence Photographique.

indicating an open attitude (Figure 4.1); or they turn their back to show a long, luxurious plait, and almost suggest that the observer follow them (Figure 4.2).

Examples of such depictions by artists and writers of the age could be multiplied to create a broad and repetitive portrait.[13] However, it was a relatively obscure Swiss-born writer named Charles Didier who furnished the clearest and most distinctive picture of the Oriental Jewess, perhaps because he linked her with the Jew. Charles Didier was born in

[13] For example, Madame Emile de Girardin wrote the plays *Judith* (1843) and *Cléopâtre* (1847), set in the Orient, for the Jewish actress Rachel. See also, for example, Alfred de Vigny, "Le bain," in *Poèmes antiques et modernes* (Paris, 1826); and Théophile Gauthier, *Le voyage en Italie* (Paris, 1860).

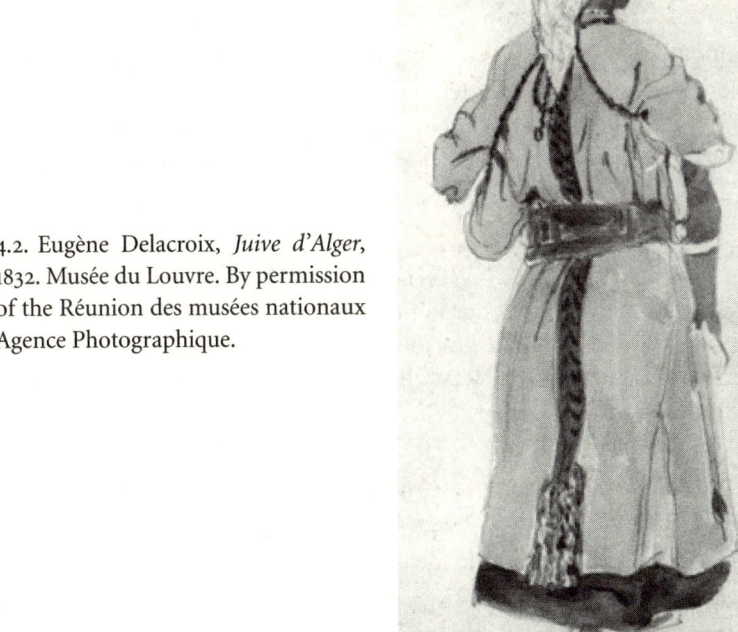

4.2. Eugène Delacroix, *Juive d'Alger*,
1832. Musée du Louvre. By permission
of the Réunion des musées nationaux
Agence Photographique.

Geneva in 1805, and went to Paris as a young man to make his way as
a writer. He mixed with literary figures who are among the best-known
of mid-nineteenth-century France, although he himself only achieved
moderate success. His sole biographer, John Sellards, has argued that
Didier deserves to be written into the history of nineteenth-century
Paris, although at the same time Sellards has chosen to describe Didier,
in the work's title, as having lived "in the wake of Romanticism."[14] Didier
travelled extensively through the Orient, and contributed travel articles
regularly to *La Revue des deux mondes* between 1820 and 1845. His contributions can be understood as part of the increase of articles on the Orient
that were published in this journal following the conquest of Algeria in
1830. But Didier found his own niche; in his writings, he provided close

---

[14] Charles Didier, "Le Maroc," *La Revue des deux mondes*, 1 November 1836, 241–69. John
Sellards, *Dans le sillage du romantisme. Charles Didier (1805–1864)* (Paris, 1933).

descriptions of the Jewish and Muslim populations he encountered. And in his work, there is a clearly defined division between Jewish and Muslim women; indeed, the world he describes is one in which Jews lived separately from the Muslim population and in fear of it.[15] Like his contemporaries, Didier dwelt enthusiastically on the beauty of the Jewess. "Nowhere," he told the reader, "could be seen faces that are more perfect, more ideal." Reflecting their combination of accessibility and exoticism, the beauty of Jewesses was original – "oriental splendour united with European finesse, the point where the two types meet and merge:"

The delicacy of the traits is especially remarkable, and the line of the face, while being neither Greek nor Roman, has something of both; it is less pure than the former, and more gracious than latter. All Jewesses have beautiful black eyes full of fire, and very white skin, and are of medium height, but svelte and shapely.[16]

Yet it was her very beauty that was the Jewess' Achilles' heel. For where her biblical ancestors had been spiritual creatures, she was defined by her physicality, and thus she was imprisoned by it. Like the Jew, defined by his overwhelming (and degrading) desire to possess lucre, she was ultimately a creature of carnality and matter, and this was what linked her to her fellow – in Didier's eyes, equally original, but in hideousness.[17] When a Jewess married a Jew, they became linked in their physicality, and it was his that prevailed. A Jewess of thirteen, according to Didier, was:

a woman; as a rule she is married at fourteen; at fifteen, she is a mother and a wet-nurse; at twenty, she is withered; she is stout at twenty-five; marriage seems to be their ruin; barely married, they are absorbed by their husbands, that is to say that they become ugly and degraded. [. . .] nothing is as charming as a young Jewess, nothing is more hideous than an old one.[18]

---

[15] Didier, 261.
[16] Ibid., 260.
[17] Ibid. Sander Gilman has written about a similar stereotyping of the *belle juive*, particularly in the person of Sarah Bernhardt, in *fin de siècle* France and Germany. Sander L. Gilman, "Salome, Syphilis, Sarah Bernhardt and the Modern Jewess," in *The Jew in the Text: Modernity and the Construction of Identity*, ed. Linda Nochlin and Tamar Garb (London, 1995), 97–120. See also Carol Ockman, "When is a Jewish Star Just a Star? Interpreting Images of Sarah Bernhardt," in ibid., 121–39.
[18] Didier, 262.

The Jewess as created by Didier, Hugo, and others like them was an article to be desired and owned, so it is hardly surprising that they saw her relationship with her fellow Jew in such terms. Imagining the Jew's possession of the Jewess, Didier could not avoid feeling "repulsion and disgust at the thought of the hands that pluck the flower of this rapid beauty."[19] Describing a widow of eighteen, Didier observed, "a Jew had possessed her. Who would wish to accept such an inheritance?"[20] For where the Jewess's body expressed all her sensuality in fullness, on the Jew's body could be read all his misery and degradation:

The lowest passions of humanity, avarice and fear, are the two distinctive traits of the modern children of Israel; they wear its indelible mark on their face and in their entire person. They look at you with a sidelong and worried expression, and they mask the terror that possesses their heart under a syrupy smile that is painful to look at when studied. The Jew does not speak; he whispers like a prisoner who fears waking his sleeping executioner. The Jew does not walk; he glides along the walls, his eye on the lookout, his ear pricked, and he turns corners closely, like a thief under pursuit. [...] The Jew's ugliness is a highly specific ugliness and it belongs only to him. There is no deformity in his traits; yet, faithful mirror to his interior life, his physiognomy has an ignobility and a brutality about it that cannot be defined, which is striking at the first glance, and which is invincibly repulsive. It is a moral ugliness; it is the soul that is deformed, and which is reproduced in each of the features.[21]

Perhaps Didier chose to write about Jews in the Orient because he could indulge in criticisms of these exotic creatures that would have been met with strong protests had he attempted to apply the same criticisms to the Jews at home. For Didier was clearly a critic of the materialistic nature of his own world. For a period, he and the novelist George Sand were lovers. In her work *Les Mississipiens*, Sand had created a Shylock; a Jew named Samuel Bourset. She situated him squarely in July Monarchy society, and called capitalism a Jewish invention. Sand was also friends with Pierre Leroux, a strident critic of early capitalism, and it is not inconceivable that he was the source of this notion. In any case (as I discuss in the next chapter), the idea that Jews were linked to the rise of capitalism

[19] Ibid.
[20] Ibid.
[21] Ibid., 259–260.

had currency in France at the time. Didier took the notion further. He painted the Jewish men he encountered in North Africa as metaphors for his own society and its evils. Thus, the Oriental Jew's supposed desire for lucre was what best characterised him. Money was both god and religion to these Jews, and their greed was the "perfect personification of material society."[22] Yet this lust for the golden calf had not gone unpunished. In the eyes of Didier, the Jews' pitiable situation was entirely of their own making: the Jewish people had become a pariah among the nations because of the deicide, and their separation and exclusion from greater society meant that the greatest and most base evils had been able to fester and grow in their bosom. The Jews were an example of

what a long system of intimidation can do to men. Intelligent life has been extinguished for centuries in these miserable beings; all that remains of their humanity is inferior instincts and base appetites; no superior thought could germinate in these petrified brains; no generous sentiment makes these bronze chests palpitate.[23]

The Jew lived indifferent to the catastrophes and prosperities of nations, and to the pains and joys of men. His only attachment to them was by way of the stock exchange, his only interest in the world around him was in the prospects it offered for speculation. Without feeling, "without grace or greatness," he had no need for exchanges of knowledge or affection.[24]

Nonetheless, although he was undoubtedly miserable, the Jew inspired no pity, for although he suffered humiliation at the hands of Muslims and Christians, he knew "how to make them pay."[25] The trafficking and ruse in which he engaged were his consolation for the insults and misery he had to bear, and when he returned home from the "affronts, terrors and dissimulations of the day," the Jew indulged in "transports of hatred and greed. It is then, under the protection of his triple locks, that he weighs down his oppressors with curses that they cannot hear, and counts the quadruples that they cannot see; that is the hour that consoles him for everything."[26] Money was the Jew's comfort. And the richer a Jew was, the more energy he devoted to playing poor. This was the

[22] Ibid., 260.
[23] Ibid.
[24] Ibid., 268.
[25] Ibid., 365.
[26] Ibid., 266.

Jew who dissembled, who had nothing in common with humanity and who could not be trusted. This was the Jew who, along with his fellow, the Jewess, was rooted in base carnality. From the liberal bourgeoisie, fascinated with exoticism, who hung Delacroix's paintings on the walls of their homes, to the bourgeoise who would read tales of exotic lands in her women's magazine, to conservative Catholics, steeped in centuries of Church teachings about the evils of Judaism, Jews in the Orient became objects: images and clichés. Is it so surprising, then, that so many French could find it entirely plausible that these same Jews would brutally kill a Catholic priest and his assistant, and use their blood to make unleavened bread? Such was the reaction to what has become known as the Damascus Blood Libel.

On 5 February 1840, a monk named Father Thomas, who was living in Damascus, disappeared along with his servant.[27] As a member of the Capuchin Order, Father Thomas was protected by the French government, and thus by the French consul, who was directly responsible for the safety of French nationals. The Count de Ratti-Menton was the serving consul at the time of Father Thomas's disappearance, and he approached his role in the investigations with great seriousness. He was closely involved from the outset in finding and prosecuting Father Thomas's killers. Father Thomas had last been seen in the Jewish quarter where he had gone to put up some posters, and so suspicion quickly came to settle on the Jews. One of the first to be arrested was a Jewish barber, whose shop was situated near where the posters had been placed. He confessed after torture and inculpated several other Jews. Disparities in social rank seemed to have played a part in his choice, because most of those he named were members of the community's most prominent and wealthy families. Those of the accused who had not hidden or sought refuge in a foreign consulate were arrested and held for questioning. At the alleged scene of the crime – revealed under torture by one of the accused men to be the home of another of those arrested – fragments of bone and

---

[27] Jonathan Frankel covered the Damascus Blood Libel thoroughly in his *The Damascus Affair;"Ritual Murder," Politics, and the Jews in 1840* (Cambridge, 1997). The historical veracity of the ritual-murder charge has been dealt with in works such as Alan Dundes, ed. *The Blood Libel Legend: A Casebook in Anti-Semitic Folklore* (Madison, 1991). Frankel based his study on the premise that the charge has been discredited, an approach that I will also take. Neither the bodies of Father Thomas and his assistant nor the true murderers were ever discovered.

bloodstains were discovered.[28] Ratti-Menton, increasingly certain of the Jews' guilt, became convinced that the chief rabbi of the community – who was subsequently arrested – had in fact ordered the killing of a Christian to mix his blood for the unleavened bread for the Jewish Passover. He pursued this theory assiduously. All of those arrested were tortured; four died. Ten remained in prison for some months while the case dragged on. One of the dead – killed in prison by flogging – was a Jewish witness who had come forward to state that he had seen Father Thomas outside the Jewish quarter on the night he disappeared. However, by the time he presented his testimony, the authorities were certain of the truth of the ritual murder story and were doing all in their power to prove it.[29]

The pattern of accusations of ritual murder can be said to have begun with the case of William of Norwich in England in 1144.[30] The victim was nearly always a young boy who, as an innocent and pure Christian, was to sacrifice his blood to the Jews for their use. In the thirteenth century, various popes issued bulls that cast doubt on the accusation against the Jews of ritual murder, or blood libel. However, at the same time, the most prominent pope of the thirteenth century, Gregory IX, authorised

---

[28] The bone fragments were later found to be those of an animal.

[29] Why did Ratti-Menton pursue the prosecution so actively? In Frankel's narration Ratti-Menton does not emerge creditably. He encouraged the execution of the accused, and requested that particular members of the Jewish community, including women, be tortured. He wrote about the Jews of Damascus in hateful terms and clearly became frustrated when the Austrian consul, Merlato, challenged his investigations. Nonetheless, ultimately his beliefs and motivations remain unclear, and Frankel has suggested that his actions indicate more an unwillingness to go against the tide of anger directed at the Jews (the day after Father Thomas's disappearance, angry crowds gathered outside the Capuchin monastery) than any particular malice (Frankel, 56). Historians of the affair, such as Heinrich Graetz, have tended to depict Ratti-Menton as an antisemite, and the sole driving force behind the arrest and torture of the Jews of Damascus. On the basis of previously unexamined correspondence, Yaron Harel has suggested an alternative interpretation of Ratti-Menton's actions. Harel argues that Ratti-Menton was not motivated by hatred towards the Jews. He portrays Ratti-Menton rather as a man desirous of proving himself a faithful and capable representative of France's interests. Yaron Harel, "Le Consul de France et l'affaire de Damas à la lumière de nouveaux documents," *Revue d'Histoire diplomatique* 113, no. 2 (1999): 143–70. If this is the case, it would certainly appear that the torture and death of some Jews was seen by him to be an acceptable price to pay for his own success.

[30] See Gavin Langmuir, "Thomas of Monmouth: Detector of Ritual Murder," in Dundes, 3–40. On the history of the ritual murder charge, see, as well as Dundes, R. Po-Chia Hsia, *The Myth of Ritual Murder: Jews and Magic in Reformation Germany* (New Haven, CT, 1988), and Trachtenberg.

a Christian-Jewish disputation that led to the decision to ban and destroy
the Talmud. Thus, ambiguity regarding Jews existed in the higher levels
of the Church, and its edicts had little influence on the credulous general
population. Nonetheless, due to changes in legal systems, by the eighteenth century, cases were reaching the courts less often, particularly in
Central Europe. At the same time, claims of ritual murder were becoming
less uniform, so that as well as boys, Jews were accused of killing girls, and
adult men and women. Even so, the Damascus case was unusual, both
in that it involved two adult men, one of them sixty-two years old, and
that it was the first of its kind to occur in a Muslim country. Jonathan
Frankel's examination of testimony and transcripts of the interrogations
lead him to conclude that the reasons behind this lay in the presence in
Damascus of a Christian population, made up of Marronites, Greeks,
and Armenians, and foreign Christians, including Catholic priests and
European diplomats and businessmen. He saw two issues as being
vital: first, he found no record of anyone among the Christian population opposing the charges, and second, once the motive for Father
Thomas's death was supposedly discovered, the details of the case were
largely invented. Thus, he argued, what occurred was "not the invention
of a tradition, but rather its reinvention or reinvigoration" in the collec-
tive memory of Damascus' Christian population.[31]

Whatever its origins, this affair was rapidly to assume greater proportions than the mere question of the veracity or plausibility of the
accusations. It took on international importance, becoming one facet
of the tussle between the European powers for influence in the Middle
East. In the region, Egypt was fighting Turkey for control of Syria and
Lebanon. Damascus was occupied by the Egyptians and under their de
facto rule. The English, Austrians, and Russians had formed a loose coalition to back the Turks. The French, motivated perhaps by their original
links with Egypt through Napoleon, had decided to stand alone and
back the Egyptian ruler Muhammad Ali. The blood libel accusation in
Damascus took place as Ali was building up his armies in Syria, and the
ensuing tension that this caused between France and other European
powers played out in the affair. Father Thomas was a French national,
but some of the accused held Austrian or British citizenship. Yet despite

---

[31] Frankel, 30, 52.

the protestations and efforts of other European governments, the French were the only ones to have any real influence over Ali and the fate of the Jews. Thus the affair was of great importance and interest for France, in more than one respect, and it certainly caused a stir in the French press, eager for news.[32] We have seen that for France's conservative Catholics, Judaism was an eternal quality. Was Jewish infamy, such as ritual murder, equally eternal? For many newspapers, the question of whether Jews still committed ritual killings was as burning as that of France's role as a power in the region. Perhaps sensing a story, centrist and conservative papers set out to "to penetrate the horrible secret of this drama."[33] They spared the reader no detail and no theory in their quest for the truth. Graphic details were given of the supposed manner of Father Thomas's death, and the case was backed up with details of other such blood libels throughout history.

The four major newspapers on which this review of contemporary journalistic opinion is based – the *Constitutionnel*, the *Quotidienne*, the *Univers*, and the *Ami de la religion* – represented some of the many different voices of the right, ranging from Legitimism to broad support of Thiers. Yet from this wide range of outlooks, there was uniformity in the assumption of Jewish guilt where the question of ritual murder was concerned. To be sure, at times the approach taken differed slightly. In the *Constitutionnel*, reports appeared to be printed as they arrived with little or no vetting, so that both extremes of points of view were presented. At the same time, the wish "that the truth will out" was repeatedly expressed. In its first analysis of the affair on March 29, the *Constitutionnel* reported in terms of what "people claim," that is, that the human sacrifice was one of the "mysteries of Judaism," "whose atrocity and barbarism

---

[32] Damascus was isolated from Europe in terms of the amount of time it took mail to travel, and it was those journals with the most rapid access to the Middle East, such as the *Sémaphore de Marseille* and the *Sud*, also printed in Marseille, that tended to feed the national and regional press. Aside from the four major papers that form the basis of this review (*Le Constitutionnel*, *La Quotidienne*, *L'Univers*, and *L'Ami de la religion*), many others picked up the story, and their articles were at times reprinted in the national press. Some of these were: *Le Commerce*, *La Presse*, *La Gazette des tribunaux*, *le Toulonnais*, *Le Réparateur de Lyon*, *Le Journal général*, *La Gazette du Midi*, *La Gazette du Languedoc*, and *Le Journal de Toulouse*. Some newspapers, such as *Le National* and *Le Charivari*, chose not to report or speculate on the question of who had killed Father Thomas and why.

[33] *La Quotidienne*, 7 May 1840.

resembles the sacrifices of the Druids." The author of the article went on to note that "popular prejudice can be blind" and to express his hope that the truth would out. The article ended with the expression of fear of "extremely serious consequences" for the Jews in Damascus. However, by 6 April (perhaps in response to popular sentiment), the apparently undiscerning *Constitutionnel* was quoting directly from an anonymous letter received from the Middle East in which the Jews were described as "fanatics" and "monsters."[34] This author had so little doubt of the Jews' guilt that he extended it to other crimes. "People are realising that other disappearances in the past may also be the fault of the Jews. It was always a rumour but no one wanted to believe it; now there can be no doubt."[35] Ultimately, following the publication on 7 April of a letter of protest from Crémieux, the *Constitutionnel* was to virtually silence itself on the question of ritual murder, presumably on instructions from Thiers.

While the *Constitutionnel* looked at the case in terms of its plausibility, the *Univers*, Montalembert's voice of Catholics, with its unique combination of Catholic Orleanism, French nationalism, and support for Thiers' government, was perfectly placed to believe the charge of Jewish ritual murder. The newspaper took a great interest in the affair and reported every facet of it in great detail with the help of its "special correspondent" in Alexandria.[36] The *Univers* accepted the facts as they were sent without question, and even went to some trouble to find examples to support its belief in the guilt of the Jews.

The *Ami* claimed to be disinterested in the affair and to be "sincerely seeking the truth."[37] Indeed, all of these newspapers prided themselves on their impartiality, although ultimately this signified different things. The *Ami* self-consciously noted its impartiality by printing a letter of complaint from a Jew regarding the inclusion in the previous edition of the *Ami* of "extracts from the Talmud (that) show the hatred of Jews for the Christian name."[38] The *Ami* firmly believed in Jewish guilt, finding it difficult to understand "how the crime could be more easily explained

---

[34] This anonymous letter was likely penned by Ratti-Menton himself. In the first few weeks after news of Father Thomas's disappearance broke, Ratti-Menton, and another consular official, Beaudin, were almost the unique source of news from Damascus.

[35] Quoted in Frankel, 115.

[36] Possibly the consular official in Alexandria, Adrien-Louis Cochelet.

[37] *L'Ami de la religion*, 19 May 1840.

[38] *L'Ami de la religion*, 25 August 1840.

by an unknown cause that no one has found, than by the characteristic hatred of Jews for the Christian name."[39] The newspaper used emotive language to entrench this notion. Thus, the Jews were described as having been accused of "traitorously killing the venerable monk known as Father Thomas."[40] For the editors of the *Univers*, impartiality meant that, as it proudly pointed out, it was the only newspaper "not to have contented itself with publishing only documents provided by Jews"[41] (in fact this meant that the *Univers*, like the *Ami*, published only material that assumed the guilt of the Jews of Damascus).

The *Quotidienne* also prided itself on its impartial stance, stating that "in this affair, as in all affairs enveloped in mystery, the first duty of the press is to abstain from taking sides."[42] The *Quotidienne* criticised Crémieux for maintaining his position that the Jews must be innocent of the murder of Father Thomas. For what were the alternatives? "If one wishes to show that the Jews are innocent of the refined strangling of Father Thomas," the *Quotidienne* pointed out, "it will be necessary to accuse either the Muslims or the Christians. That is a sad alternative. Mr Crémieux will permit us to say that the Christians did not strangle Father Thomas."[43] Nonetheless, impartiality for the legitimist *Quotidienne*, still awaiting the return of the Bourbons, was not quite the same as it was for the *Univers*, and, indeed, both papers lost no opportunity to point out one another's weaknesses. When those behind the *Quotidienne* were denounced by their colleagues at the *Univers* as "bad Christians," the *Quotidienne* responded to this accusation with the comment that "[the *Univers*] had better not denounce us as Jews, because we would seek to avoid violence or reprisals."[44]

But the *Univers* and the *Quotidienne* were more consistent in their approach than either paper would perhaps have liked to admit. For both newspapers, a vital element in the supposed plausibility of the charges was the region in which the murders had taken place. It would most probably have been challenging – even for the most hardened Legitimist – to find French Jews, emancipated for nearly fifty years and, in the words

---

[39]   *L'Ami de la religion*, 11 June 1840.
[40]   *L'Ami de la religion*, 1 September 1840.
[41]   *L'Univers*, 21 July 1840.
[42]   *La Quotidienne*, 7 May 1840.
[43]   *La Quotidienne*, 9 April 1840.
[44]   *La Quotidienne*, 11 May 1840.

of one observer, "mixed in with Europeans,"[45] guilty of the brutal murder of a priest and his assistant. Even a highly conservative newspaper such as the *Ami* allowed that the Jews of France had benefited from their long exposure to European culture, and that this had "softened their morals."[46] Ritual murder might have become defunct in civilised Europe. Nonetheless, many French were clearly prepared to believe that such an act could still take place in the backward and still-mysterious East. This was, after all, the region where, as the *Univers* reported, all religions were practised "with the greatest fanaticism," and the Jews of Damascus, "five hundred years behind [their fellow Jews in Europe] in all knowledge and all moral notions," still had "the morals and all the barbarism of their ancestors."[47] For the *Quotidienne*, this was a drama that took the reader "back to the Middle Ages"[48] and its protagonists "surpassed all their coreligionists with their fanaticism."[49]

Another element lent strength to the belief in Jewish guilt. Conservative French Catholics could draw on a long tradition that taught that the Talmud was full of violent hatred and blasphemy. These charges were confirmed for them by men such as the apostate Drach. Indeed, in the first volume of his *Harmonie*, Drach compared his suffering during the kidnapping of his children with that of Father Thomas, and hinted at a Jewish conspiracy: "The assassins of Father Thomas in Damascus, convicted of their crime, were shielded from the vengeance of the law by the united efforts of Jews of all nations. [. . .] Money played the main role in this affair."[50] Any number of solemn oaths from rabbis was not enough to counter such words from one Christian, all the more so one who was once a learned Jew. And while the opinion of Drach added weight to any argument, apostates who challenged the Church, or who expressed sympathy for Jews, were greeted with at best mistrust, but more generally, derision and disdain. Thus, for example, Pieritz, a Jewish convert to Protestantism who went to Damascus to speak out in support of the accused Jews, was referred to by Ratti-Menton as "a false apostate, an avowed slanderer," who belonged "*in petto* to the sect of

---

45 M. P.-N. Hamont, *L'Egypte sous Méhémet-Ali*, 2 vols. (Paris, 1843), 2: 364.
46 *L'Ami de la religion*, 11 June 1840.
47 *L'Univers*, 5 July 1840; 29 May 1840.
48 *La Quotidienne*, 28 March, and 7 May 1840.
49 Letter published in *La Quotidienne*, 6 June 1840.
50 Cited in Catrice, 219.

dissembling Jews."[51] Another writer described him as "another ex-Jew, currently a Protestant missionary, a man worthy of no esteem, and who is described in letters from respectable personages with these two words: *banker-missionary*; did he not receive a banknote from the grateful Jews of Alexandria for a letter he had had placed in a Levantine newspaper?"[52] Thus, predictably, conservative papers found proof in the Talmud that Judaism authorised – or even encouraged – crimes such as ritual murder. In an article entitled "Translations of the Talmud that authorise the murder of Christians by Jews," the *Univers* published a letter from their special correspondent in which it was alleged that the Jews of Damascus were trying to hide a translation of the Talmud that would reveal to the non-Jewish world "the horrible blasphemies that the Jews vomit against the Saviour."[53] For, as Frankel has shown, the most popular theory of those who supported the accusation stated that only a small minority of Jews, such as certain rabbinical families, closed sects, or isolated communities, was still party to this particular tradition. The *Univers* concluded that if one considered all circumstances of this case, it was not impossible to conceive "that a fanatical rabbi could have preserved the former traditions, and that he wanted to put them into practice."[54] Certainly, the Damascus case seemed to reach a new level of momentum with the incrimination and arrest of the chief rabbi. Thus, it was easy to counter the protestations of French Jews with the claim that they could quite possibly know nothing of such practices.[55] Such claims also tended to exonerate the Jews of France, although, as we shall see, through their involvement they were to become guilty of what was just as great a crime.

At the news of the accusations, prominent Jews in France sought to come to the aid of their co-religionists in Damascus, undertaking a well-publicised letter-writing campaign in the press and, at the same time, lobbying those in power. Lisa Leff has shown how French Jewish leaders, sensitive to the delicacy of their own position in publicly stating

---

[51] *L'Univers*, 6 July 1840.
[52] Achille Laurent, *Relation historique des affaires de Syrie depuis 1840 jusqu'en 1842: statistique générale du Mont-Liban et procédure complète dirigée en 1840 contre des juifs de Damas à la suite de la disparition du Père Thomas*, 2 vols. (Paris, 1846), 2: 366.
[53] *L'Univers*, 23 July 1840.
[54] *L'Univers*, 5 July 1840.
[55] Frankel, 256.

their allegiance to foreign Jews, felt constrained to choose their response carefully.[56] Sure enough, their actions made them targets for criticism. To those who ranged themselves against the notion of liberal materialism, the Jews were using their wealth and influence in an attempt to wield power, and this was an example of the evils of the new regime. For many, it was a crime simply that French Jews should publicly show sympathy for the accused Jews of Damascus. The identification by French Jews with other Jews in a foreign country was seen to be a public statement of affiliation: France's Jews were choosing publicly to be Jews before they were Frenchmen. Conservative newspapers criticised these men, both for their inappropriate use of their power and wealth, and their equally inappropriate identification with men who were not French. The *Ami* had warned the Jews of France to recognise their good fortune in not being judged by the French population on the behaviour of the Jews in Damascus and to restrict themselves to enjoying this advantage.[57] The same newspaper stated that "several Parisian and departmental newspapers rightly note that the defenders of the Jews of Damascus make their speeches with much too much fervour and passion for them to do any great good in the cause of their clients."[58]

Perhaps the most eloquent defender was Adolphe Crémieux. As a young lawyer in Nîmes, Crémieux had become known for his fight against the *more judaïco*, the specific oath for Jews that they were required to take in instances where they had to give testimony or take an oath.[59] In 1817, at his own swearing-in, Crémieux had refused to wait for a Bible to be brought to him, so that he might swear *more judaïco*. He was sworn into his profession with the general oath. It was he who, a decade later, challenged the use of the oath in Nîmes and achieved a ruling from the court there that Jews might swear no oath other than that in general usage. At this time, he argued, on the basis of Republican ideology, that equality consisted of "the absence of all official distinctions among men."[60] When he took on the cause of the Jews of Damascus with his customary energy, Crémieux chose to frame his commentary on

---

[56] Leff, 121.
[57] *L'Ami de la religion*, 11 June 1840.
[58] Ibid.
[59] On the *more judaico*, see Phyllis Cohen Albert, "The Jewish Oath in Nineteenth-Century France," *Spiegel Lectures in European Jewish History* (Tel Aviv, 1982).
[60] Albert, "Jewish Oath," 25.

the affair in similar terms. In his eyes, the Jews of Damascus were the innocent victims of oriental barbarism, and they were in need of the enlightened protection of the French State.[61] Crémieux saw himself as the eldest child of a France in which "the sublime words 'honour' and 'dignity' resound in every soul."[62] He tied his Jewishness to the Republic that he held so dear and defended Jewish causes in the name of this civilised France.[63] His response to the Damascus Affair, as well as his fight against the *more judaïco*, can be understood in this context. Indeed, once he was elected to parliament in 1842, Crémieux would regularly call on his own Jewishness, in what Leff has suggested could be seen as "a means to emphasise his credentials before others similarly committed to the revolutionary tradition."[64] What Crémieux's response suggests is that many French Jews did indeed take great comfort from the State. And with good reason, it would appear: Crémieux's success can be seen as a reminder of the open nature of mid-nineteenth-century French society. His utter confidence in the Republicanism and civilisation that he saw going hand-in-hand enabled Crémieux to take up publicly the cause of the Jews of Damascus. If, as we have seen, voices on the right saw the Damascus Affair as a chance to criticise Judaism legitimately, Crémieux and other Jews felt their cause was equally legitimate: it was their right to defend the Jews of Damascus on the grounds of what France stood for. And we have seen that, in the thick of the controversy surrounding Simon Deutz, the *Gazette du Languedoc*, not normally well-disposed towards Jews, saved a measure of respect for Crémieux, denoting him an "Israelite."[65] But on this particular occasion, its sister journals in Paris were not so kind.

For the choices French Jews made during the affair did mean that they were singled out in the public eye. When Crémieux and other prominent Jews in France criticised their government's actions, they were not joined by a chorus of similar complaints. The sole Jewish deputy, Benoit Fould,

---

[61] See Leff, 122–23.

[62] *En 1848. Discours et Lettres de M. Adolphe Crémieux, membre du Gouvernement provisoire* (Paris, 1883), 10; cited in Daniel Amson, *Adolphe Crémieux. L'Oublié de la gloire* (Paris, 1988), 115.

[63] Leff, 155.

[64] Ibid., 126.

[65] This was opposed to the word "Jew," which this paper used in this instance as an epithet.

rose (reluctantly) to censure Ratti-Menton in the French parliament and was severely castigated by the *Ami* for "complaining bitterly" not about Father Thomas's murder, but rather, about the treatment of the accused.[66] Indeed, not only the newspapers, but Adolphe Thiers himself, defended the servant of the nation. Why did Thiers choose to take this path? Well aware, as he put it, that the Damascus Affair had "ostracised the Jews from the Christian world,"[67] Thiers nonetheless sought to use the affair as a way to win political support – or at the least, minimise opposition – from French Catholics, and in particular Legitimists, who so hated Thiers since his role in the arrest of the Duchess of Berry. Thiers also wished to make a dramatic gesture in the arena of foreign policy. He therefore chose to play the nationalist card; he vigorously protected Ratti-Menton as a public servant and the representative of France's interests in the region.[68] To the very end, Thiers, when questioned on the affair, stated that he believed Ratti-Menton to be doing his job properly.[69]

Thiers's policy certainly appears to have worked where the Catholic press was concerned. Even the *Quotidienne* congratulated Thiers on his declaration that Ratti-Menton "would be energetically defended against all the interests and passions, political or not, that are stirring around him. Until proof to the contrary," the *Quotidienne* maintained, "the cause of this agent is the cause of justice; the cause of France."[70] And, as France's representative, Ratti-Menton could do no wrong. Some claimed that it was only the zeal of Ratti-Menton that brought the Jews to justice.[71] Ratti-Menton, the incorruptible representative of an incorruptible nation that was under attack, was almost to become a martyr. In June, the *Quotidienne* reported that the fanaticism of the Jews had been excited against Ratti-Menton to such a point that his very life was threatened. Ratti-Menton was alone against the other European consuls, themselves

---

[66] *L'Ami de la religion*, 6 June 1840.
[67] Archives, Ministère des affaires étrangères, Correspondance politique, Rome, 1840, vol. 982, p. 108, draft letter by Thiers to Rayvenal, 8 July 1840, quoted in David Kertzer, "The Montel Affair: Vatican Jewish Policy and French Diplomacy under the July Monarchy," *French Historical Studies* 25, no. 2 (2002): 280.
[68] On Thiers' policy regarding the Middle East, see, for example, Allison, 278–87, and J. P. T. Bury and R. P. Tombs, *Thiers 1797–1877: A Political Life* (London, 1986), although Bury and Tombs make no mention of the Damascus Affair.
[69] Reported for example in *L'Univers*, 11 July 1840.
[70] *La Quotidienne*, 6 June 1840.
[71] *La Quotidienne*, 7 April 1840. See also *L'Univers*, 1 July 1840.

"almost all Jewish." However, the *Quotidienne* trusted that any manoeu-vres directed against the French consul "would doubtlessly be the subject of an active and energetic intervention on the part of our government."[72] Thiers was not to disappoint. In the battle that ranged France against all other powers save that of Muhammad Ali, the Jews of France became Thiers' fifth column. Once again, the newspapers agreed. In the *Quotidienne*, it was claimed that the Jews had tried to "stifle" the affair with money, making offers to Ratti-Menton.[73] However, it was the *Univers* that observed that although the Jews were "powerful" and "enormously wealthy," "in the authorities of Damascus, the French consul and his secretary they have found honest men that no offer has been able to corrupt."[74] For once, those at the *Univers* and Thiers were in agreement, and it was Jewish power that united them. For in the eyes of Thiers, "the Jews" were "more powerful than they wish to appear."[75]

Jewish power: this was the new danger that Jews in French society presented. If the Jews in faraway Damascus could be found guilty of a medieval crime, those in France were found to be practising an evil that ultimately threatened to do much more damage. And it was Thiers' reference to the Jewish desire to dissemble that was most significant, for if power was potentially dangerous, in the hands of untrustworthy and manipulative figures such as Jews it became a tool for evildoing. Men on both the right and left of the political spectrum began to see the hidden hand of the powerful Jew behind all that was wrong in the world around them. In the case of the Damascus Affair, this was the ultimate release of the accused. With three years' hindsight, one writer could reduce the affair to its fundamental elements: where "the Jew [had] imposed silence on the Christian."[76]

Jewish power also manifested itself in the coverage of the affair in France. Jews were supposedly active in influencing newspapers, partic-ularly the moderate *Journal des débats*. This paper published without comment the initial report that came out of Damascus, in which it was stated that "a number of Jewish families are suspected" in Father

---

[72] *La Quotidienne*, 12 June 1840.
[73] *La Quotidienne*, 7 June 1840.
[74] *L'Univers*, 1 July 1840.
[75] Reported in *L'Ami de la religion*, 6 June 1840.
[76] Hamont, 2: 377.

Thomas's disappearance. However, once it became clear that this was to be seen as a case of ritual murder, those at the *Journal des débats* made the cause of the Jews of Damascus their own. Readers of the conservative Catholic newspapers were outraged "at the shameful connivance of certain Paris newspapers, and especially of the *Journal des débats*, with the Jewish intrigues and ranting."[77] For the *Univers*, the *Journal des débats* made itself the "*Moniteur* of Judaism," outraging both Christian and national honour in its championing of the Jews.[78] Ratti-Menton himself connected the *Journal des débats* with what he called "la haute banque juive."[79]

Nonetheless, in a system where wealth could translate into power, none was potentially more powerful than the fabulously wealthy Baron James de Rothschild, and it was Rothschild who became the main focus of the press' attentions. In the government's "regrettable" initial silence on the affair, the *Ami* saw "the influence of an all-powerful man, who protects the Jews with his immense credit, and whom the cabinets treat with consideration because he has considerable funds at his disposition, and they often have need of him."[80] This "opulent individual" was seconded by the "clever" Crémieux.[81] Indeed, Crémieux was quickly cast as Rothschild's henchman. The *Ami de la religion* alleged that Crémieux admitted to using his "energy and activity" to buy space in the French and English newspapers.[82] In reference to Jewish efforts to obtain a full pardon for the accused, the *Ami* noted that "the Jewish side brought out all its heavy artillery,"[83] perhaps a reference to the "high Jewish bank" of Ratti-Menton's letter. The *Quotidienne* contrasted Rothschild's alleged efforts to stifle the case by offering money to Ratti-Menton with the disinterest of the nation:

The spending of this enormous amount of money which the Jews are not in the habit of doing, builds up an enormous assumption against the accused; and we must say, what tends to strengthen it even more in our mind is the

---

[77] *L'Univers*, 3 July 1840.
[78] *L'Univers*, 8 October 1840. See also *La Quotidienne*, 13 May 1840.
[79] Letter printed in *L'Ami de la religion*, 25 July 1840.
[80] *L'Ami de la religion*, 19 May 1840.
[81] Hamont, 2: 369.
[82] "Facts," *L'Ami de la religion*, 12 November 1840.
[83] *L'Ami de la religion*, 12 November 1840.

incredible pretension of Mr Rothschild to have Mr de Ratti Menton sacked. Is this an attempt to intimidate French agents in Egypt?

We must warn Mr Rothschild, that by his incredible insistence, not only does he not vindicate his coreligionists in Damascus, but he also compromises himself and perhaps with him his coreligionists in France. Let him take warning: We do not know if it is possible to buy the connivance of some government employees, more or less highly placed; but we are certain that the complicity of public opinion will not be bought.[84]

The Damascus Affair, rekindling as it did an age-old religious charge against the Jews, gave journalists such as those at the *Univers* a strong platform from which to criticise the Jews of Damascus, and traditional Christian criticism of the Jews was a major theme in their coverage of the affair. However, while it was possible to level such accusations at Jews in a far-flung and little-known country, the issues surrounding the Jews in France were much more immediate. Thus, it was that the affair took on yet another dimension. It was not only an issue in the political power play in the Middle East; not just another instalment in the long saga of Jewish-Catholic relations. For newspapers such as these, it was also an occasion to return to an important question: what was the place of the Jew – and indeed, the Church – supposed to be in this new France? By mid-1840, tensions in Europe over Ali's actions in the Middle East had risen to the point where war was expected. On July 15, Britain, Russia, Austria, and Prussia signed the Treaty of London, in which they agreed to mediate in the Turco-Egyptian conflict militarily. This threat of war ultimately drove the Affair from the papers. But the *Univers* and the *Ami de la religion* still saw fit to inform their readers of the accused Jews' eventual release. It is not surprising that the conservative journals such as the *Univers* continued to return to the Damascus Affair as it thought through this question in the 1840s. These efforts would only have been fuelled by the fact that further ritual murder accusations surfaced in the Ottoman Empire throughout the decade. Indeed, well after the affair had disappeared from its front page, the *Univers* took advantage of a book review of a translation of the Talmud to remind its readers of the eternal foreignness of Judaism:

---

[84] *La Quotidienne*, 7 June 1840.

The adoption by the Jews of the political opinions and social customs of the nations that have received them into their bosom is not in any way a proof of complete identification. Even though one people may follow another in its exterior habits, as long as it professes a secret religion and the mystery of its beliefs cannot be penetrated, it will be a foreign people, and it will be natural to be suspicious of its tendencies.[85]

The actions of French Jews in the Damascus Affair may have raised new questions regarding their position in France. But it was also inevitable that the prominence of the affair would link them to their coreligionists in the Orient. And indeed, coinciding with the affair, echoes of descriptions of the carnal Jew and the sensual Jewess of the Orient can be found in descriptions of French Jewry, all the way up to its most elite members. Criticisms of Rothschild's separateness, and his reliance on his wealth both to protect himself and to see his wishes carried out, are reminiscent of Didier's descriptions of his coreligionists in the Orient. And Rothschild's wife Betty was depicted as having all the physicality – suitably muted for a woman of her rank – of her Oriental sisters.

The Baroness Betty de Rothschild was almost universally praised, even by those authors who had little or nothing positive to say about French Jewry. The journalist Maximilien Cerfberr de Medelsheim described the Baroness as "noble and beneficent," he saw her piety and charity as "worthy of a Christian woman" – high praise indeed from a devout Catholic.[86] Over the course of the 1840s, Jean-Auguste-Dominique Ingres painted a commissioned portrait of Betty de Rothschild, completing it in 1848 (Figure 4.3). In it, while she displays the dress and the bearing of a respectable wife whose husband is one of society's elite, there is an undeniable undercurrent of sensuality. The baroness is seated. She gazes attentively at the viewer, her chin resting on her left hand, and her right hand seemingly carelessly thrown across her lap, and holding

---

[85] *L'Univers*, 10 October 1840. In its edition of 14 June, the front page of *La Gazette du Languedoc* had the title "Of Modern Jews and the Assassination of Father Thomas." The article continued: "The abuse hurled at the Christians of Syria, the threats from lawyers and Jewish bankers have proven the truth that between the partisans of the Talmud and Christians, there is no possible peace, and the deicide people are the irreconcilable enemy of Christians and Muslims" (Quoted in Tudesq, 1: 228). Tudesq himself described the Damascus Affair as "the murder of a Catholic priest, Father Thomas, assassinated by Jews in Damascus in the Spring of 1840." Ibid.

[86] Cerfberr, *Ce que sont les juifs de France*, 72.

4.3. Jean-Auguste-Dominique Ingres, *Baronne de Rothschild*, 1848. Reproduced with the permission of The Rothschild Archive. The image can be viewed in colour at: http//www.rothschildarchive.org/research/?doc=/research/articles/kalman

a fan. Significantly, her legs are crossed so that she is leaning slightly forward. The exposed left forearm gives the viewer a chance to admire the whiteness of her skin, as do her exposed shoulders. She is dressed richly, in vivid reds and sumptuous fabrics. In her analysis of this particular portrait, art historian Carol Ockman argues that it contains a checklist that could be entitled "features not usually found in Ingres's portraits of women,"[87] from the curled fingers, to the crossed legs, to the warm tones of the baroness's skin, to the fact that she is leaning forward. The pose, the colours and fabric were all redolent of the Orient for at least one critic, who waxed lyrical about the richness and luxuriousness of textures and materials, and wrote of the sitter's "large eyebrows à l'Orientale."[88] The portrait of Madame Moitessier, painted shortly after that of the baroness was completed, provides a striking contrast (Figure 4.4).

Arguably no woman could spell Jewess more clearly to the French observer than the wife of Baron James de Rothschild, and in the rich colours of the portrait, as in her pose, there are echoes of the overwhelming sexuality of her fellow Jewesses in the Orient. Even in France, the Jewess was so much less visible than the Jew, unheard and unknown, that it was possible to re-create her in idealised form, where romanticised Bible and exotic Orient were combined, ultimately making her – even when respectable – available and desirable. The baroness' availability, suggested by the unusual nature of her pose, as well as the richness of the fabrics that surround her, all anchor her in physicality and materialism. Like Didier's Jewesses, she is both the sensual foil to her husband, and his equal in carnality. Works by Ingres and Delacroix in which the Orient is depicted, although stylistically different, both used, in Ockman's words, "the materiality of flesh and fabrics, languorous poses, and light and dark to ground the myth of the exotic woman as sexually available."[89] Delacroix and Ingres – when the latter was not producing portraits of

---

[87] Carol Ockman, "Two Large Eyebrows à l'orientale: Ethnic Stereotyping in Ingres's *Baronne de Rothschild*," *Art History* 14, no. 4 (1991), 523.

[88] L. de Geffroy, "Le Portrait de Madame de Rothschild, par M. Ingres," *La Revue des deux mondes*, 1 August 1848. Quoted in Ockman, 523. Ockman also points out phrases used by the reviewer, such as "a most seductive jumble of shimmering fabrics," and "jewels of a thousand colours." Ibid. Ockman claims to know of "no other society portraits of respectable women whose legs are crossed." Ibid., 535.

[89] Ockman, 527.

4.4. Jean-Auguste-Dominique Ingres, *Madame Moitessier*, 1856. The National Gallery, London. By permission of the National Gallery.

society women – both painted Jewish women at a safe distance, be it geographical or temporal. Both men painted biblical figures, uniting an idealised spiritual biblical beauty with the physical beauty of Oriental women in a seeming contradiction, much as the respectability of the baroness was combined with a less respectable sensuality. Delacroix was inspired by Walter Scott's novel *Ivanhoe*, which enjoyed enormous popularity in France, when he depicted, at a further remove, the abduction of Rebecca. While Scott set *Ivanhoe* in England, the beauty of his heroine, the Jewess Rebecca, was that of the Orient; she was dark and sensual, as well as being intelligent and confident and thus, powerful. She was arguably as much a product of the Orient as were Hugo's heroines, or even Delacroix's Oriental subjects. *Ivanhoe* appeared in ten French editions and inspired stage versions. However, while these Jewesses were the result of some projection on the part of their creators, the Baroness was no fictional character. How was it, then, that Ingres could translate these ideas to a member of respectable French society? Ockman argues that "The Baroness' Jewishness, with all that it implied in contemporary consciousness, enabled Ingres to push sensuality further than he could in any other society portrait."[90]

What did "Jewishness," and specifically, female Jewishness, imply? In the eighteenth century, the Jewish woman was almost invisible to commentators on Judaism and the Jews. Part of the Republican project involved the definition of the perfect woman, and such definition then required the delineation of the boundary between what was perfect, and what was not. We have seen how the Jew served to define the qualities of *citoyenneté*. Perhaps the Jewish woman also served to help define the perfect *citoyenne*. And perhaps it is that the physicality of these definitions can be seen as underscoring the influence of the *Physiologies*, and the move in society towards defining groups in terms of physical delineation. What can be said with certainty, is that it was a commonplace of the nineteenth century for Jewish women to be considered beautiful. For Ingres was not alone in his assumption of the permissibility of sensuality in the case of the Jewess. Didier had idealised the beauty of the Jewess as being the meeting point of "oriental splendour" and "European finesse."[91] If Ingres's baroness was the very personification of this combination, others such as the novelist Honoré de Balzac and the journalist Cerfberr de Medelsheim also saw Didier's beautiful Jewess mirrored in Jewish women of their own society. Medelsheim described the Jewess in France as the like of her Oriental sister. She was "as beautiful as Rachel

[90] Ockman, 534.
[91] Didier, 260.

and as fertile as Leah," and her beauty was "completely Raphaelesque; the gracious and somewhat proud carriage, the gentle and melancholy expression, the slightly olive skin, the smooth whole that makes the virgins of the painter Urbin the very type of feminine beauty and majesty." Cerfberr went so far as to echo Didier's description of the downfall of the Oriental Jewess. Once married, he noted, the French Jewess "faded away very quickly," returning "to the common state of uncleanliness normal to the caste."[92] Balzac was equally influenced by biblical beauty, and perhaps by the paintings of his friend Delacroix. Balzac's Jewesses (often courtesans) were, predictably, representative of that which fell outside bourgeois society. Fascinated with notions of different types, such as those expounded in the *Physiologies*, Balzac attributed the Jewess' beauty to the Oriental origins of her race. Of one character, he wrote, "She is beautiful as are all Jewesses when the Asiatic type reappears pure and noble in them."[93] In *Splendeurs et misères des courtisanes*, Balzac created Esther, who was beautiful because she

came from the cradle of mankind, the homeland of beauty: her mother was Jewish. [...] The Jews, although so often degraded by their contact with other people, offer among their numerous tribes veins where the sublime type of Asiatic beauties still survives... Esther would have won the prize in the harem.[94]

The Orientalised identity was one that Jews themselves chose to own, as well. Leff has discussed the way in which the Jews of the 'Generation of 1820', moving in and familiar with liberal circles, fashioned a Jewish identity that was based on liberalist fears and aspirations. Thus, they saw themselves as utterly French, understanding this Frenchness to be predicated on the values instilled by the Revolution. And at the same time, like Crémieux, they could be foreign enough to underscore the universality of the codes that they embraced. Encapsulated within them were the strong foundations of the recent past, and the promise of a glorious future for the liberalist ideal. Thus, for example, in a fascinating echo of

[92] Cerfberr, 70, 71.
[93] Honoré de Balzac, *Cousin Pons* (Paris, 1848), 635.
[94] Honoré de Balzac, *Splendeurs et misères des courtisanes*, cited in Charles Lehrmann, *The Jewish Element in French Literature*, trans. George Klin (Cranbury, NJ, 1971), 166.

Balzacian notions of race, Jewish Saint-Simonians appropriated physiol-
ogy and early race theory to describe themselves. In their eyes, they were
legitimating their difference in a way that circumvented the theological
paradigm.[95] The Jewish writer Eugénie Foa portrayed her protagonists –
and by extension, herself – as exotic and oriental. And within this identity, there was none of the tension between the unknown and the familiar
described at the beginning of this chapter. For in their eyes, Jews could
maintain this ancient, unchanging identity, and be "French and modern," as Leff puts it, as well.[96] While she was not alone as a Jew rising
to prominence in the arts, Eugénie Foa was the first Jewish woman to
support herself fully from her writing. Among her writings, she created
exotic Jewish heroines. In fact, it is fascinating to note that while Charles
Didier was describing a world of hidden riches and beauty in Morocco,
in Foa's 1835 work La Juive, she was doing the same, only her protagonists
were Parisian Jews. And while Foa sought to go beyond the stereotypical
notions of Judaism, she nonetheless drew on stereotypical qualities, so
that La Juive contains a fanatical, tyrannical (Jewish) father who stifles
his beautiful daughter. If, as Leff believes, the book was written with
an eye to sales, then we can only assume that Foa was making choices
based on what she knew would resonate with the reading audience – and
perhaps it was calculated to titillate as well. Or perhaps Foa was truly
driven by the belief that, in line with standard liberal philosophy, using
such stereotypes would underscore intolerance.[97] This was certainly the
purpose of the opera with which Foa's novel shared a title. La Juive,
with libretto by Scribe and music by Fromenthal Halévy, premiered in
the same year as the novel. Like this work, the opera was intended to
highlight the injustices of religious intolerance. Yet while the heroine's
beauty, and her role as a Jewess desired by a Christian lover, may have
subverted the stereotype of the "belle juive," it also reinforced it. Foa's
creation of Midiane, the subjugated and ultimate tragic heroine, would
surely have had much the same effect. In fact, Foa was not alone in
making use of exoticism in casting the Jewess. The characterisation of
the opera heroine, Rachel, involved elements of orientalism, much as
did Scott's characterisation of the beautiful Jewess Rebecca in his highly

[95] Leff, 98–9.
[96] Ibid., 82.
[97] Ibid., 108–9.

successful and influential *Ivanhoe*.[98] In certain scenes, Rachel was dressed in a richly coloured Eastern-style costume. Equally, the celebrated actress of the same name, who was universally recognised as a Jew, was known for roles that evoked not only the Orient but also biblical figures.[99] In the mid-nineteenth century, the Jewess was the model of choice for the artist, valued for what Marie Lathers has described as her "exotic beauty and a supposedly inherent shamelessness."[100] Ingres's portrait of the baronness was positively received not only by Geoffroy for his article in *La Revue des deux mondes*, but also, it must be assumed, by the Rothschild family themselves, because the portrait remains in their possession. Their enthusiasm for the baroness' portrait can perhaps be understood in this context, where the exotic was in vogue.

We can see, then, that examples of Jewish beauties whose looks recall the Orient abounded. And whether it be Balzac, Delacroix, Hugo, or Scribe and Halévy's *La Juive*, each portrait takes its cue from one and influences another. Halévy borrowed liberally from Delacroix's paintings of Algeria and Morocco that resulted from his 1832 trip in the design of costumes for his opera. Balzac's passages conjure up the Jewesses in the same paintings who gaze at the observer, their stance open and inviting, or Ingres's images of the languid poses of women in the Turkish bath. The linking of European Jewesses with the Orient was not new (*Ivanhoe* had been published in French in 1820). Yet the growing interest in Orientalism that meant that bourgeois consumers in France were fed with images such as those described here, facilitated the development of a French Jewess who was a close if not exact copy of her coreligionists in the Orient. And just as Oriental Jewesses were ultimately imprisoned within the very physicality of their beauty, so the effect of descriptions such as these was also to root its subjects in carnality. One scholar of Balzacian myth and reality has noted that Balzac's Jewesses were "all from the family of flowers that, be they lilies, grow on manure."[101] And the depiction of their male counterparts followed a similar pattern.

[98] Diana Hallman, *Opera, Liberalism, and Antisemitism in Nineteenth-Century France; the Politics of Halévy's* La Juive (Cambridge, 2002), 211.

[99] Magy Hamache, "Regards croisés sur la tragédienne Rachel (1821–1858)," *Revue historique* 293, no. 1 (1995): 128–9.

[100] Marie Lathers, "Posing the "Belle Juive" – Jewish Models in 19th-Century Paris," *Womans Art Journal* 21, no. 1 (2000), 27.

[101] Luce Klein, 174.

Balzac often juxtaposed his beautiful Jewess against an older male (father) figure. In doing so, he was drawing on a tradition arguably begun by Marlowe in *The Jew of Malta* and developed by others such as Shakespeare in his creation of Shylock and his daughter, and Scott in his portrayal of Rebecca and her father Isaac. (Marlowe's *Jew of Malta* was published in 1590.) Thus, in the vast documenting of society that is *La Comédie humaine*, Balzac invariably cast his Jews as men of business, and their carnality in their link with money was a contrast and complement to the very physical sensuality of the Jewess. Under the guise of his realism, Balzac would revisit old Jewish myths, such as the father-daughter relationship, and also create new mythical characters. André Maurois argues that in a three-stage process, Balzac metamorphosed his characters from copies of reality to "the incarnation of an idea," so that, for example, the Baron Gobseck could become the Power of Money.[102] Nonetheless, Balzac's portraits of Jews were not one-sided. Balzac, who himself was not immune to the attractions of wealth, depicted with admiration the financial genius of the Baron Nucingen. Gobseck, the stereotypical usurer, could also display generosity and insight. Nucingen was also capable of sentiment, such as in his love for Esther. Yet Balzac also knew that he himself was no bourgeois, and this sense of distance is clear in his work. Thus Nucingen's awkward German accent was a constant reminder for readers not only of his foreignness but also of his physicality. He could not escape his accent any more than he could escape the association with wealth, and gold. Ultimately, the latter was his strongest link to the beautiful Esther.[103]

Similarly, Jewish origin appears to have been an indicator of social mobility for Balzac (both within the social hierarchy and from the Jewish community outward).[104] However, although he depicted Nucingen's modest beginnings and meteoric rise sympathetically, even perhaps admiringly, at the same time, Balzac subscribed to theories that saw beings encased within their origins. His description of Esther's "stubborn" links to her origins was illuminated with an example pertaining to animals:

Uproot two species of sheep from their habitat, and transport them to Switzerland or France; the mountain sheep will graze alone, be it in a low

---

[102] Maurois, cited in Luce Klein, 155.
[103] Luce Klein, 186.
[104] Ibid., 151.

prairie with dense vegetation; the plains sheep will graze one by the other, be they on an Alp. Several generations will barely reform acquired and transmitted instincts. At a hundred years' distance, the spirit of the mountains reappears in a stubborn lamb, as, after eighteen centuries of banishment, the Orient shone in Esther's eyes and in her face.[105]

Thus, ultimately, Balzac's pictures of the Jewish man of business could, to a greater or lesser degree, be traced back to Shylock, Shakespeare's usurer, with all his malicious cleverness and with much more power. This stereotype of the miserly, avaricious Jew appears to have resonated with the French public. In her study of *La Juive*, Diana Hallman notes that Scribe's creation of a similar figure for the opera in Eléazar, Rachel's father, was recognised by several critics as a Shylock stereotype.[106] The same imagery was used by the sculptor Jean-Pierre Dantan *jeune*, in his caricature of Nathan Rothschild, James's London-based brother.[107] George Sand's character Bourset was equally modelled on Shylock. And Thiers made use of the stereotype in his appeals to nationalism.

Yet if characters such as Nucingen and Gobseck possessed or personified the power of money, ultimately this power was greater than they. Evil and dangerous, when it possessed them they were driven to do evil (such as when Nucingen, in *La Maison Nucingen*, ruined the Aldrigger family). Thus if the Jewess was an easy object of desire because she could be controlled and dominated, the Jewish male inspired fear and outrage because he represented a system that ordinary French could not control: wealth as power. The Orient was arguably so attractive because its exoticism inspired not only fascination but also fear. What better figures in France to personify this duality than the Jewess and the Jew? And what better figure to focus the public's indignation in response to this system than the very man on whom Nucingen was allegedly based – the fabulously wealthy and powerful, yet clearly foreign, Baron James

---

[105] Honoré de Balzac, *Splendeurs et misères des courtisanes*, cited in Lehrmann, 166.

[106] Hallman, 234–52.

[107] A full description and the image of this sculpture can be found on pp. 145–6 of this text. In her biography of James de Rothschild, Anka Muhlstein writes that all the Rothschild brothers save James – who was sensitive to such portrayals – reportedly "pinned [caricatures] to the wall, as signs of Rothschild success." Anka Muhlstein, *Baron James: The Rise of the French Rothschilds* (New York, 1987), 73.

de Rothschild?[108] Rothschild united the left and the right in their condemnation of a system that allowed Jews who were not French – and
thus doubly foreign – to determine the fate of ordinary French men and
women by virtue of their wealth. By the 1830s, the name of Rothschild
was already becoming synonymous with enormous wealth. In 1835, the
Univers was complaining of "this era of money," and "all the authority
of the Rothschild name."[109] However, while mentions of Rothschild's
wealth can be found before 1840, it was the Damascus Affair that brought
together not only his wealth but also his ethnicity, and his power, to plant
the seed of the figure that was to become much greater than the sum of
these parts: the Rothschild-Jew.

The Damascus Affair, in the midst of Orientalist depictions of Jews,
captured the public's attention and catapulted French Jews into the public
arena, perhaps more prominently than in the fifty years since emancipation. The extent to which the affair resonated through society can be seen
in continuing responses to it. In 1842, a contributor to the Jewish paper,
the *Archives israélites*, complained bitterly of "friends," during the "sad
episode in Damascus" who would say, "with the laugh that offends the
soul: 'I do not wish to lunch with you, for fear that you would serve me
a Father Thomas cutlet.'"[110] But although the affair sent some Catholics
into an extended flurry of speculation regarding the habits of Jews in the
Orient, perhaps more significant was the criticism of those Jews in France
who were seen to be helping their coreligionists. For never before had
Jews been seen to act so publicly, and with such a sense of purpose and
determination. In publicly identifying with people who were depicted as
being so exotic – and possibly depraved – French Jews were confirming,
for many, that those who during the Revolution had argued that Jews in

---

[108] Balzac himself denied this association, although some historians have reported it as
fact. See, for example, Jean Tulard, ed., *Dictionnaire du second empire* (Paris, 1995), 1132.

[109] *L'Univers*, 11 March 1835.

[110] *Les Archives israélites*, March 1842, quoted in Cerfberr, 111. Some twenty years later,
in the 1863 general elections in France, the high-profile Jewish banker Isaac Pereire
stood for a seat in the Pyrenees-Orientales against the incumbent, Justin Durand, a
pillar of the Church. Those who did not wish to see Pereire win made use of antisemitic
propaganda, including references to the Damascus Affair, as one example of the terrible
things to be expected if a Jew were elected. (I am grateful to Dr Helen Davies of the
University of Melbourne for bringing this incident to my attention.) Two decades
further on again, in April 1881, the semi-official Vatican periodical *Civiltà Cattolica*
quoted from Drach's 1844 work, *De l'Harmonie entre l'église et la synagogue*, as proof
of the veracity of the 1840 charge.

France were and would remain an *imperium in imperio* had been correct in their assertion. French Jews were believed to be behaving in ways inappropriate for Frenchmen. And the most prominent among them was not even a Frenchman. Sander Gilman has described how, as he sees it, the "Christian" body became the modern body politic, always in opposition to the Jewish body. Thus the Jew, through his very body, was excluded.[111] This notion would appear to be reflected in the rhetoric surrounding the Damascus Affair.

Once again, Thiers made use of this sentiment. Thiers had come to power on 1 March, with a slim majority. He needed to strengthen his position and win over the public. He chose to take a strong stance on events in the Middle East, committing himself fully to Ali. But by October, Ali's son, Ibrahim Pasha, faced a humiliating defeat in Lebanon, at the hands of a small Anglo-Turkish force. France was forced to consider action: would they choose to go to war? Or would they allow the defeat of Egypt and their own humiliation? Thiers found himself without great backing. By mid-October, a clearly livid Thiers inspired the following attack against James de Rothschild in his mouthpiece, the *Constitutionnel*, in which the Baron's pacifism was blamed for the ultimate capitulation to England.[112] The editorial referred to a rumour that had been reported in the *Times*, that Rothschild and "other rich bankers" were attempting to use their influence to dissuade the minister from preparing for war, as he was proposing to do. "In effect," the editorial continued;

for several days now there has been a great deal of talk about Mr Rothschild and his manoeuvres. Mr Rothschild is a man of finance, and he has no wish for war. Nothing is simpler than that: Mr Rothschild is an Austrian citizen and Austrian consul-general in Paris, and as such, he has little concern for the demands of honour and of French interests; even that is understandable. But what has that to do, if you please Mr Rothschild, man of the stock exchange, Mr Rothschild, Metternich's agent, with our Chambers and their majority? By what right and on what grounds does this king of finance meddle in our

---

[111] Sander Gilman, *The Jew's Body*, 38.

[112] Lucas-Dubreton, 142. Frankel suggests that the editorial was "clearly inspired and possibly written by Thiers" (Frankel, 369, 440). Lucas-Dubreton is more certain about the source of the editorial, stating that Thiers, who was in debt to Rothschild and who therefore could not attack him directly, "attacked him through the *Constitutionnel*." Lucas-Dubreton, 142. See also David Pinkney, *Decisive Years in France, 1840–1847* (Princeton, NJ, 1986), 134.

affairs? Are the resolutions that France makes any of his business? Is he the judge of our honour? Should the interests of his bank balance prevail over our national interests? We speak of the interests of his bank balance, but here is a surprising fact! If we are to believe highly accredited rumour, it is not only financial grievances that the Israelite banker holds against the March 1 cabinet. Apparently, he also is holding a grudge for a wounded ego. Mr de Rothschild promised his coreligionists that he would have the consul-general in Damascus dismissed for the part he played in the trial of the Jews of this town. The President of the Council firmly resisted the demands of the powerful banker, and Mr Ratti-Menton retained his post. Whence the irritation of Mr de Rothschild and the ardour with which he is throwing himself into intrigues that are none of his business.[113]

This editorial, clearly pitting the nation against the Jews, and strengthening the understanding of Jewishness as implying greed and disloyalty, was widely quoted in the French press, particularly in pro-government and left wing papers.

A half century after emancipation, French society was following new paths, and French Jews were apparently becoming ever more confident at finding their own way in it. Orientalist depictions created a stereotyped and reified Jew. They arguably led to freer – and more aggressive – criticism of Jews in French society. In the wake of the Damascus Affair, reports on displays of Jewish wealth and power became commonplace. The affair served as the focal, and arguably the starting point, for such criticism, and French responses to it can be best understood against the backdrop of this dialogue of representations. The early 1840s was a period of intense Catholic proselytism among Jews in France, particularly in Paris. Kselman links this activity with the Damascus Affair, claiming that the Affair "generated increased attention to Jewish communities and their religious practices."[114] In Catholic teaching, the Jew could still represent all that lay beyond the bounds of safe and acceptable Christianity. But the new Jew also represented all that was wrong and evil in secular, capitalist society, and not only to Balzac, but also, as we shall see, to writers such as Sue, Toussenel, Fourier, and Leroux. And if capitalist society at its worst was a soulless and heartless creation that crushed the innocent and discarded tradition, Rothschild was its Prince of Darkness.

---

[113] "Editorial," *Le Constitutionnel*, 12 October 1840.
[114] Kselman, *Historical Reflections*, 94.

In the Rothschild-Jew, old criticisms were combined and developed, and the Jew as metaphor truly came of age. Frankel argued that it was "sensationalism" rather than "obsessive paranoia" that provoked the scale of the reaction to the Affair.[115] Nonetheless, the effect of the reaction was enduring, particularly in its creation of a Rothschild-Jew, who made shameless use of the wealth that gave him power. But worse than the Rothschild-Jew's power was his desire to dissemble: he worked behind the scenes; he conspired. He was, as ever, foreign and untrustworthy, but now he was also dangerous. The *Constitutionnel* may have provided a clear picture of this Rothschild-Jew, but it was the *Univers*, the voice of conservative Catholicism, which combined old and new anti-Jewish mythology to vividly depict this new evil for its readers. The quote is long, but the skill with which the author has melded together hatred of Christianity, lust for the golden calf, and newfound power, makes it worthy of full inclusion:

[W]e will say, in conclusion, a final word on this memorable event in Damascus, where Judaism, reappearing as a force, as a nationality, justifying the prophecies that make it imperishable and refuting the philanthropic theories that for some years have sought to wipe it out in the uniformity of modern civilisation, has held all of Christianity in check. It has been allowed to experience once again the power of two things that it always has at its service, intrigue and gold. Who can say now where its expectations will stop? [. . .] On the throne of David, raised up once again, would be seated that financial dynasty known and endured by all of Europe, and whose inauguration would surely be the most worthy work and most faithful expression of the venal century in which we live. [. . .] How can we be surprised, then, if the same spirit stirs around us, if grudges that do not forgive, and interests that hesitate before nothing, rouse against the ministry protecting the Christian cause in the Orient, the coreligionists of unpunished murderers? How can we be surprised and how can we even be annoyed at the more sinister possibilities that the past allows us to fear for the future? For, after all, the Jews of France, no more than those of Poland, only ever accepted the naturalisation that our laws granted them without liability to debts beyond their assets: they never knew the duties of a citizen, or the worship of the fatherland. Let us make no mistake: Judaism is less a religion than a nationality, less a community of theological opinions, than a fraternity of blood, morals and interests. Beliefs can diverge, discipline can loosen or tighten the ties, its hereditary

[115] Frankel, 437.

character remains. There will be Karaïtes in the synagogues of Hungary and Turkey, Talmudists in the consistories of Germany and England, rationalists at the Paris stock exchange, everywhere there will be foreigners, enemies of the Christians. The permanent seal of deicide will not disappear from their foreheads, whether they lean it over the tablets of the law, or in the dust at the feet of the golden calf.[116]

[116] *L'Univers*, 8 October 1840.

5

"Rothschildian Greed: This New Variety of Despotism"

O<small>N 8 JULY 1846, AT 3:05 IN THE AFTERNOON, A TRAIN TRAVEL-</small>ling from Paris to Lille was nearing the village of Fampoux, between Arras and Douai. Without warning, the locomotive and its tender skipped the rails, and five or six carriages ran down a bank and into a marsh. Newspapers recounted the horror of families awaiting their loved ones in the station at Lille, as news of the accident spread through that city, although full details of the accident were not published until the following day. Available information put the number of dead at eleven: two conductors, two soldiers, a doctor, a countryman, three women, and two young boys aged between six and eight. This number was later revised up to seventeen. The number of wounded was said to be between five and fifteen. Newspapers told graphic tales of the accident with descriptions of the heroic efforts of survivors and details of the dead and wounded. Thus, for example, General Oudinot escaped injury, but his aide-de-camp was not so lucky. He had four broken ribs, and his chances of survival, it was feared, were slim. M. Lagrenée, a former French ambassador to China, was thought to be among the dead, although the *Impartial du nord* allowed itself to hope that this news would be proved incorrect. The Princess de Ligne and her retinue, numbering seventeen, were, happily, among the survivors.[1] A journalist from the *Echo du nord*, by the name of Lestiboudois, was in the second submerged carriage as the dying passengers desperately grabbed on to one another, and he described in detail how he broke the glass of a window and was pulled from the water, his

---

[1] From *L'Impartial du Nord*, reproduced in *La Réforme*, 11 July 1846.

hands covered in blood, at the very moment when his strength was about to give way.[2]

This was not the first train accident to occur. One historian of such incidents has listed 513 accidents between 1835 and 1854 that came about as a result of human or technical error.[3] One of the worst occurred in Meudon, southwest of Paris, on 8 May 1842. Fifty-seven people died when two trains collided; most of them were burned alive. More than a hundred were seriously injured. But the accident in Meudon could be put down to an isolated driver or operator, and a one-off fault. Fampoux was different: the accident was caused by a derailment, rather than a collision, so that blame was laid on the company as a whole and its poor safety standards. This may explain the public response. For if reactions in the press are to be believed, the accident unleashed a wave of outrage. All newspapers were damning of the way the relatively new line had been constructed. The *Quotidienne* used emotive language in its coverage of the accident, seeking to ignite the "rightful indignation of honest men."[4] Even the *Charivari* departed from its usual satirical tone, noting with great seriousness that "justice" would surely discover those responsible for the "fatal imprudence" that caused the accident.[5] Indeed, "those responsible" were soon identified. The main culprit was found to be none other than the owner of the Northern line: Baron James de Rothschild. It was on his shoulders that responsibility for the deaths of innocent French men and women could be squarely laid, and a torrent of righteous fury was vented against him. The *Réforme* was quick to ensure that its readers would not forget his role in the accident, naming it "The Rothschild Disaster,"[6] or "The Rothschild drowning accident."[7] The *Univers* had by this time become the vehicle for the ultramontane propaganda of the militant Catholic journalist, Louis Veuillot.[8] His newspaper held back

---

[2] From *L'Echo du Nord*, reproduced in ibid.
[3] François Caron, "Le Rôle des accidents de voyageurs dans la gestion des chemins de fer en France," *Entreprises et Histoire* 17 (1997), 85, 87.
[4] *La Quotidienne*, 12 July 1846.
[5] *Le Charivari*, 11 July 1846.
[6] *La Réforme*, 12 July 1846.
[7] *La Réforme*, 14 July 1846.
[8] Veuillot was born into poverty in 1813 and received a limited education, although he was able to become a journalist. He worked with Lamennais on the latter's newspaper the *Avenir*. As a result of a visit to Rome in 1839, he became a devout Catholic and devoted the rest of his journalistic career to the advancement of his beliefs. Isser has

until it could announce with certainty that, on the basis of its own investigation, it had found that the accident was the result of poor and rushed workmanship, and a disregard for safety on the part of "M. de Rothschild's employees." These facts, the journal went on to note, were stated "whatever the *Journal des débats*, the *Siècle* and the *Patrie*, who have more than once and very recently shown their tender solicitude for the cherished interests of the great capitalist who is the president of the Northern Company, may think."[9] Indeed, the *Journal des débats* took a careful line, stating that, while the railway's obligations to the public must be fulfilled, that newspaper would not engage in "criticising for no reason, accusing without proof, showering with disgust and overwhelming with insults the honourable men who accepted the hard and noble task of installing a railway service for us."[10]

It is characteristic of the July Monarchy that newspapers on both the left and right of the political spectrum attacked Rothschild as owner of the Northern line. Indeed, newspapers whose political ethos was as disparate as the *Quotidienne* and the *Réforme* were united in their pursuit of Rothschild. The *Quotidienne* proudly – if somewhat self-consciously – "greatly embarrassed" Rothschild, expressing outrage at the alleged "indifference" of his train company.[11] (Although Rothschild's name was not mentioned until over a week after the accident was first reported.) Much was made in the *Quotidienne* of the fact that the company supposedly ignored all safety warnings before the accident and then denied all responsibility after it. This was interpreted as an unabashed disregard for the safety and, indeed, the lives of French citizens, in the pursuit of profit. Rothschild was apparently happy to put his income before the public interest.[12] "The greed of speculators prevailed over the most sacred interests of humanity,"[13] and in the name of speculation and profit, an unfinished railway line was opened, causing deaths. For the *Univers* also, it was a matter of "the insatiable cupidity of

discussed the extent to which Veuillot was supported by Catholics in the stance he took during the Mortara affair. Natalie Isser, *Antisemitism during the French Second Empire* (New York, 1991), 44–6.

9 *L'Univers*, 19 July 1846.
10 *Le Journal des débats*, 11 July 1846.
11 *La Quotidienne*, 19 July 1846.
12 *La Réforme*, 14 July 1846.
13 *La Quotidienne*, 12 July 1846.

a few bankers," versus "the respect due to the lives of citizens."[14] Similarly, the *Réforme* railed against Rothschild's heartless greed: in concert with government and administration, "a veil was thrown over the dead and wounded," as Rothschild "tranquilly" speculated, making money from the accident.[15] Or in the image that pamphleteer Georges Mathieu-Dairnvaell created, "Cadavers attract vultures. Great catastrophes give life to speculators." Mathieu-Dairnvaell smelled a "conspiracy of silence" about both the Northern line and the accident on the part of "Rothschild I" and his fellow stockholders. "The country's interest, the opinions of the engineers, the life of men, all have been sacrificed to H.M. Rothschild."[16]

Rothschild's detractors did not focus on stockholders and thus the stock exchange by chance. It was during the 1840s, in many ways a time of rapid evolution in France, that the nation began its entry into what we now see as the modern era of stock movement. In its newness, speculation was characterised by a flabbergasted Pierre Leroux as "the right to make a profit [. . .] from the sole fact of accumulated wealth, *without participating in any way in the useful employment of this wealth*,"[17] and for the *Réforme*, this was an era when "everything, even public misfortune, [was] exploited by the Stock Exchange."[18] Yet while so many were accusing Rothschild with great passion, the *Journal des débats*, the careful counterpart to the emotive reporting of the above, defended Rothschild with arguably as much emotion as others attacked him. Apparently, it was not possible, even for this mouthpiece of bourgeois conservatism, to discuss Rothschild dispassionately. Why not? Because Rothschild, as these newspapers drew him, was a representation of the era, and this was either to be attacked or defended, to the death.[19]

---

[14] *L'Univers*, 19 July 1846.

[15] *La Réforme*, 11 July 1846. See also Georges Mathieu-Dairnvaell, *Rothschild Ier, ses valets, et son peuple, par G. Dairnvaell. Réplique à de prétendues réponses et nouveaux faits, contre S.M. Rothschild, MM. Fould, Ch. Laffitte*, 5th ed. (Paris, 1846).

[16] Georges Mathieu-Dairnvaell, *Histoire édifiante et curieuse de Rotschild Ier, roi des juifs, par Satan*, 15th ed. (Paris, 1846), 11, 24, 35.

[17] Pierre Leroux, *Malthus et les économistes ou Y aura-t-il toujours des pauvres?* (Paris, 1897), 3: 36. Original emphasis.

[18] *La Réforme*, 10 July 1846.

[19] There were also pamphlets written in response to Mathieu-Dairnvaell and in Rothschild's defence, such as A. Deprez, *Guerre aux Juifs! Ou la vérité sur MM. De Rothschild, par A.D.***, Avocat, ancien directeur de la bibliothèque ecclésiastique (Paris: 1846); and J. B. Mesnard, *Dix jours de règne de Rothschild Ier, roi des juifs, ou notes pour servir à l'histoire de la fondation de la monarchie de ce souverain* (Paris, 1846).

What was it about this era that that led to such depth of passion? Many had seen in the July Monarchy with great hope. But those who were brought to power in the 1830 Revolution were not necessarily revolutionaries. Indeed, Casimir Périer, president of the Council from 1831 until his death from cholera the following year, declared that "there was no revolution; there was simply a change of Head of State."[20] Such were the bourgeois who, in the words of Mathieu-Dairnvaell, "triumphed" in the July Revolution and who were quick to dash any hope for an ideal nation.[21] By the 1840s, both Catholics and socialists felt under siege and alienated from the very administration which to a great extent was responsible for France's modernisation.[22] Their ideals had been compromised by Louis-Philippe and a succession of prime ministers in the name of what was seen by both left and right as individualistic opportunity. The subjects of this chapter were disillusioned by the outcome of the July Revolution; they were anxious about the future of the nation and the survival of the things they held dear. The Jew was the perfect candidate to symbolise the disempowerment of the good citizens whose champions these writers became. It was through the Jew that commentators such as Pierre Leroux, Charles Fourier, and his disciple Alphonse Toussenel expressed their anxieties about their times, and it is to their writings that I now turn. Numerous researchers have explored and commented on Leroux, Fourier, and Toussenel, and their writings and their lives, their attitude towards Jews, as well as the extent of their influence on the socialist movement in France are well known.[23] Only the pamphleteer Georges Mathieu-Dairnvaell, who used the accident in Fampoux as the background to his attacks on Rothschild, remains elusive. Even in 1846,

---

[20] Quoted in Amson, 87.

[21] Georges Mathieu-Dairnvaell, *Guerre aux fripons. Chronique secrète de la bourse et des chemins de fer*, 3d ed. (Paris, 1846), 3.

[22] See Christopher Johnson, "The Revolution of 1830 in French Economic History," in *1830 in France*, ed. John Merriman (New York, 1975), 172 and passim.

[23] See, for example, Robert Byrnes, *Antisemitism in Modern France* (New Brunswick, NJ, 1950), 118–25; Katz, *From Prejudice to Destruction*, chap. 9; George Lichtheim, "Socialism and the Jews," *Dissent* 15 (1968), 314–22; Edmund Silberner, "The Attitude of the Fourierist School towards the Jews," *Jewish Social Studies* 9 (1947), 339–48; idem, "Charles Fourier on the Jewish Question," *Jewish Social Studies* 8 (1946), 245–66; Zosa Szajkowski, "The Jewish Saint-Simonians and Socialist Anti-Semites in France," *Jewish Social Studies* 9 (1947), 46–55; Graetz, 79–84; Poliakov III: 367–79; Pierre Birnbaum, *Le peuple et les gros. Histoire d'un mythe* (Paris, 1979), 23–4.

Friedrich Engels described him as "a man nobody knows:" "a work-ing man," "the whole of whose property consists of the suit of clothes he wears."[24] Mathieu-Dairnvaell described himself as "a writer without name, position, title or rank, not even a chevalier de la Légion d'honneur or a member of the French Academy, an *obscure scribbler*."[25] Certainly, Mathieu-Dairnvaell's words seem to have resonated with readers of the day because all of the four pamphlets he wrote went through more than one edition, and his pamphlet *Histoire édifiante et curieuse de Rothschild Ier, roi des juifs* sold more than sixty thousand copies, was widely trans-lated, and went through twenty editions in 1846 alone – a feat all the more impressive given that the capital was flooded with similar works. According to Engels, "some thirty pamphlets," both for and against Rothschild, had been published. Engels noted that the public had fol-lowed the exchanges between Mathieu-Dairnvaell and Rothschild "with the greatest interest."[26] Cerfberr de Medelsheim also noted that "Lately, numerous different brochures and works that are against the Jewish monopoly have attracted the attention of the public, which showed proof of the interest it had in this discussion through the multitude of copies which were quickly sold."[27] What was it about their message that was so resonant and stirred such passionate, public debate? The success of their writings suggests that the ideas that some of the early socialists called on to frame their opposition to the July Monarchy found a sympathetic audience. For this reason, they merit another visit.

All of these men wrote about their world in a tone of outraged morality, and they had much to say about the involvement of Jews. This was the age of cold, hard pragmatism that offended the sensibilities of many, as tradi-tional relationships and spheres of influence were eroded or changed. For example, doctors appointed to hospitals by the state made inroads into the power base of the Church.[28] Relationships between landlords and

---

[24] Friedrich Engels, "Government and Opposition in France," *The Northern Star*, 5 September 1846.

[25] Georges Mathieu-Dairnvaell, *Jugement rendu contre J. Rothschild, et contre Georges Dairnvaell, auteur de l'histoire de Rothschild Ier, par le tribunal de la saine raison, accompagné d'un jugement sur l'accident de Fampoux* (Paris, 1846), 7.

[26] Engels.

[27] Cerfberr de Medelsheim, *Les Juifs, leur histoire, leurs moeurs* (Paris, 1847), preface. Medelsheim's work is discussed in detail in the next chapter.

[28] Peter McPhee, *A Social History of France, 1780–1880* (London, 1992), 124.

tenant farmers became based on money alone – a cash rent in exchange for land, animals, and tools. Indeed, perhaps one of the greatest conceptual changes of this time was to do with land. All throughout the July Monarchy, those who thought national pitted their interests against those who were historically inclined to think local. On the one hand, there were "technocrats" whose principal interest was the nation, who believed that state policy could and should make the nation prosperous, and whose interests to a large extent matched those of capitalists. They challenged the ascendancy of those whom Tudesq has labelled "notables," "whose wealth essentially was derived from land and whose social pre-eminence rested on this, their family name, and their local networks of influence."[29] This new view of land was particularly evident in the development of a rail network, a key issue on which notables – concerned primarily about the use of land in their respective regions – diverged from bureaucrats and capitalists. The 1833 law on compensation for land appropriated by the state for railways defined land as "a commodity whose value was simply its market price," as opposed to the historic understanding of land as an object of sentimental value, a thing to which one could be attached by virtue of generations of use.[30] By the mid-1840s, a rail network was being constructed throughout France, powering through lands which were now a commodity but to which some peasant or noble family perhaps still felt a sense of attachment. The Northern line, on which the accident occurred, had been a highly attractive prospect because of the probability that it would yield high profits: it was to run from Paris to Belgium and link into vital trade between France and England, as well as the Netherlands and northern Germany. The Rothschilds had been keen to acquire the concession to build the line since 1843. As the author recounting an incident, "unbelievable, and consequently, true" in the *Charivari* showed, for those who were inclined to see evil in the ideology of the era, this was epitomised precisely by railway lines such as this one:

> Last Thursday, in the general junior high school competition, the following topic was given as the subject in the Latin *prix d'honneur*, leaving teachers and students equally dumbfounded:

---

[29] Ibid., 147. See also Tudesq, 2: chap. 2, II: "Les Notables et les chemins de fer," 627.
[30] McPhee, 121. See also Johnson, 174–5.

"Charlemagne, wishing to build a canal that would link the Rhine and the Danube via the Raab and the Main, assembles his valiant knights.

"He tells them: that *peace* is a glorious thing, stability an excellent guarantee, and that *conservatives* are good people . . .

"That the best way to guarantee peace is to *create routes of communication*;

"That, for this reason, he has built roads, and wishes to build a canal . . .

"That, if he does not finish it, *one day it will be finished.*

"That he believes that one day, with the advances in *knowledge and industry, more rapid means* will be invented, and that, through the *union of fire and water* [. . .] some way to cleave open space and join *people and continents in a universal alliance* will be discovered . . . ,"

What do you have to say about this scholarly *puff*? What a Mathieu Laensberg is this Charlemagne, and moreover, what a doctrinarian, and what magnificent short-sightedness! To foresee the railways and exalt the Pritchardists ten centuries before the fact!

Is it by chance that this subject was given by M. de Rothschild, shared fifty-fifty with M. Cavillier-Fleury?

Is it not a delightful thing to see the system of endless subservience and the trickery of the Stock Exchange of 1846 prophesied by Charlemagne? And all of this to be put into Latin by rhetorical schoolchildren!

Charlemagne speaking to his valiant knights of *industry*, and the *union of peoples*, of *routes of communication* and of *vapour*! Charlemagne, head engineer! Charlemagne transformed into St Marc Girardin grafted onto Emile Pereire![31]

Yet the *Charivari* was not alone in its horror, for so many saw the world of the July Monarchy as disastrous that such a tone was common by the later

---

[31] *Le Charivari*, 23 July 1846. At the time this article was written, "Saint-Marc" Girardin, who served as a deputy during the July Monarchy, was a member of the royal council for public instruction and a senior member of the Council of State. He was also a journalist and writer, and member of the Académie française. Emile Pereire – a Jew – was a dedicated Saint-Simonian who went on to become an economic journalist and one of the leading railway financiers. He and his brother Isaac opened France's first passenger railway, the Paris-St.-Germain line, in 1837, and it was an immediate success.

years of the regime in both newspapers and pamphlets. Echoes of this criticism can be found, for example, in Marx's *Class Struggles in France*, where he described the July Monarchy as being ruled by a "finance aristocracy," which "made the laws, was at the head of the administration of the State, had command of all the organised public powers, dominated public opinion through facts and through the press," and exploited the construction of the railway. Bankers such as Rothschild ruined financial reforms that were not in their interest. This was the nation of the "Stock exchange Jews."[32] The accident in Fampoux aroused such depth of sentiment precisely because it seemed to characterise Marx's uneven struggle between honest working French citizens, and the capitalist juggernaut that was a feature of the era. Indeed, the themes explored in this chapter were rehearsed over and over in newspapers and pamphlets: French society had become decadent and was in crisis; society and the family were losing their cohesiveness.[33] "Social disorganisation" reigned.[34] The new era was one of "selfish and brutal" individualism and godlessness. Gold was king, and man was abandoning God and making himself his own deity, embracing a pagan selfishness.[35]

The Revolution of 1789 had unleashed individualism, and whether writers were for the Revolution, such as Pierre Leroux and Alphonse Toussenel, or against it, like Charles Fourier, they felt that this individualism had gone awry.[36] From the complex web of competing ideologies that characterised the years following 1789, one vital notion that emerged was that all Frenchmen were equal individuals, that no Frenchman could claim privilege or difference on the basis of membership of a specific corporation (or religion), and that all Frenchmen were expected to feel overwhelming loyalty to the great corporation that was the nation. In

---

[32] Karl Marx, *Class Struggles in France 1848–1850* (New York, 1969), 33–7. Alexis de Tocqueville also spoke about "moral decay" (*Chambre des députés; Annales du parlement français* 27 January 1848 [1849], 108–9, quoted in Pilbeam, *Republicanism*, 152).

[33] Toussenel, 233.

[34] Mathieu-Dairnvaell, *Jugement*, 23. See also Fourier, *Théorie des quatre mouvements* 252–3, quoted in Silberner, "Charles Fourier," 254.

[35] Mathieu-Dairnvaell, *Guerre*, 37.

[36] During the Revolution, Fourier, the son of a wealthy cloth merchant, joined the 1793 uprising against the Convention in Lyons. When the ensuing siege was broken and Lyons fell, Fourier was imprisoned and only just avoided being included in a group of insurgents that was later executed.

other words, citizens were to live out a sort of cooperative individual-ism. If the Revolution of 1830 had completed that of 1789, it was perhaps in that it promoted a world where man had sovereignty over his own conscience, having no moral responsibility to other men other than that prescribed by the law or that upon which they themselves decided. This was competitive individualism, and it was anathema to early socialists who believed that the ideal citizen should be an individual who cooper-ated with his fellows, rather than competing with them. It is particularly telling that, as Pam Pilbeam has discussed, men such as Fourier envisaged utopian societies based on cooperation.[37] We have seen that anxiety over the consequences of competition was shared by many across the political spectrum in the 1830s. Clearly, this sentiment carried over into the 1840s, as utopians continued to consider what might bind men together in a spirit of responsibility and solidarity. Thus many republicans during this period were, in the words of Pam Pilbeam, "far from hostile to religion as such," believing that society needed a spiritual foundation.[38] Had socialists such as Buchez and Cabet had their way, France would have experienced a reinvigorated primitive Christianity, which would surely have brought with it all the exclusivity of the Restoration. In fact, the consequences of the Revolution led conservatives and liberals alike to fear that with the breakdown of institutional Christianity, society faced nothing less than literal atomisation. In the Restoration, the Church hierarchy overwhelmingly saw the antidote to this in the resurrection of the pre-Revolutionary era. Others, like the Count Henri de Saint-Simon, proposed a new religion; a replacement for Christianity. His followers, the Saint-Simonians, sought to promote a new religion for France that would teach all humanity social values, as Christianity had attempted to do in the past.[39]

And for the writers examined here, this issue remained a pressing one into the 1840s: what could counter a competitive and individualistic society? This, in many ways, was the underlying fear that drove their work. They were fearful because, in what they saw as the materialistic atmosphere of the July Monarchy, competitive individualism could easily translate to capitalism, or, as Toussenel and others were to describe it,

[37] Pilbeam, *Republicanism*, 182–3.
[38] Ibid., 17.
[39] Leff, 76.

"financial feudalism." Indeed, for these men, medieval feudalism had never truly come to an end but had merely metamorphosed into a new form. Variously described as industrial, financial, or mercantile, this was a system where, as with its forebear, the powerful few cemented their position at the expense of the powerless majority. But this feudalism was financial: in Mathieu-Dairnvaell's words, "born in stock exchange scandals and dominating everything through usury, speculation and the vilest of dealings."[40] The feudal lord had been replaced by the banker, who waged war on his fellow men by means of lucre. Gain and profit had taken the place of "the sword and the cannon,"[41] and where men were once killed by the sword, now they succumbed to hunger.

But most of all, this was the era of cold, hard Capital. To Leroux, Capital had replaced religion, becoming "God on Earth."[42] Yet "anti-human"[43] Capital was without heart or soul, a reflection of the men who subscribed to it. The banker's heart, in Toussenel's eyes, was "lined with bronze, locked up and padlocked like his coffer."[44] Capital "spoiled and dirtied everything it touched,"[45] including the nation itself. The bankers who now ruled the nation had themselves no fixed nationality, and they cared nothing for France's fate. They were bleeding the nation white, draining it of public funds, and destroying it slowly, both physically and morally, so that it was now on the brink of disaster. Nonetheless, although the nation may have been its victim, those suffering the most were the poor innocent – and misguided – workers. Leroux and his fellow writers saw themselves as lone battlers. Mathieu-Dairnvaell depicted himself as David to Rothschild's Goliath. As a "noble-hearted man," Mathieu-Dairnvaell saw it as his "duty" to alert his fellow citizens to the evil around him. What did it matter, he asked, if his voice was weak? "A grain of sand can sometimes play a role in the fate of empires."[46] And he took care to announce his successes: he had, he noted gleefully, managed to separate "the polyp from its golden shell" and make Rothschild "leave his piles of ingots, banknotes and share coupons and [. . .] go out into the street

[40] Mathieu-Dairnvaell, *Rothschild Ier*, 7.
[41] Leroux, 1: 31.
[42] Ibid., 3: 36.
[43] Ibid., 2: 143.
[44] Toussenel, 194.
[45] Ibid., 200.
[46] Mathieu-Dairnvaell, *Guerre*, 54. See also Mathieu-Dairnvaell, *Rothschild Ier*, 6.

where public criers call out the people, the riffraff, his mortal enemies, to enjoy the spectacle of seeing Rothschild, the emperor of all Jews – Christian and non-Christian – the king of all parvenus, accused and condemned."[47] Thus, Mathieu-Dairnvaell and his fellows made themselves the champions of the little man and his cause. For having "*so gloriously snapped his irons twice* in half a century!" under the regime of financial feudalism the worker could look forward only to excessive work, low wages, "all physical and moral tortures in mature age," and an end in a hospital.[48] Yet the worker continued to arm himself mistakenly against the government, while the true culprits looked on and grew stronger on these divisions. These latter, the "barons of finance,"[49] were the workingman's true enemies.

Perhaps it would not have been so difficult for men like these writers to believe that in their world, workers indeed lived on in servitude and grinding poverty, with merely a change of master. Around them, they perceived the working classes at the mercy of capitalists' needs for a cheap labour force and for stability, unions and mutual-aid societies disbanded, the master given word over his worker, the spread of practices such as *marchandage*, concentrations, mergers and collusion, and growing competition from both an influx of cheaper labour and more efficient methods of production. And who *were* the new masters? The Jews! The spirit of "avarice and cupidity" that reigned in France was none other than the "Jewish spirit."[50] For commentators such as Toussenel and Leroux, it was the Jews, above all, who seemed to have reaped a disproportionate benefit from the Revolution, and the granting of citizenship was to them "the most shameful" of all society's recent vices.[51] For not only had they been emancipated by the Revolution, they were now thriving on the immoral individualism it had unleashed. In this time, when individualism and egotism reigned "over the ruins of all true social organisations," the Jews, egotists par excellence, had been predestined to triumph. And triumph they did. For the Jewish spirit, Leroux claimed, had risen like a wisp of smoke, "from the lowliest levels of society to

---

[47] Mathieu-Dairnvaell, *Jugement*, 7.
[48] Toussenel, 242.
[49] Mathieu-Dairnvaell, *Rothschild Ier*, 7.
[50] Leroux, 1: 31.
[51] Fourier, *Le Nouveau monde*, 421, quoted in Silberner, "Charles Fourier," 250.

its summit; it had infiltrated everywhere, it had penetrated all levels, or rather, all individuals, and today, it reigned supreme."[52] Wherever they prospered, stated an angry Fourier, neatly separating Jews from the body of the nation, it was "at the expense of the citizenry."[53]

But the Jew did not only wage war on the worker. He also dragged the nation into his clutches, making it weak, perverted, and degraded. It was the "cunning and despoiling"[54] Jews, who, as Leroux, Toussenel, and Mathieu-Dairnvaell all put it, were the kings of the era.[55] That France was in the sway of these masters was the fault of the nation's politicians. The image of the government and even royalty as ignorant and weak, the "humble vassals" of powerful Jewish bankers, was presented again and again.[56] The Jews were "omnipotent" and the government was "prostrate"; the "secret and indissoluble league" of Jews, who exerted a "preponderant" influence on the nation,[57] were "the masters our fatherland obeys."[58] The Jews were in possession of all monopolies;[59] the Jews' "cosmopolitan bank" dominated everything from all the mail-coach services to the railways and the canals.[60] Fourier produced a vivid image of the Jew, who, having no ties to the nation, allowed himself to pillage it like a pirate. For not only was the competitive and individualistic Jew the

[52] Leroux, 1: 78–9.

[53] Fourier, *Publication des manuscrits*, 3:36, quoted in Silberner, "Charles Fourier," 249.

[54] Leroux, 1: 31.

[55] Ibid., 2: 148; Toussenel. It is unclear who of the three coined this phrase. Leroux published a lengthy essay which bore this title in the *Revue sociale* in January 1846. Toussenel's pamphlet was published in 1847, and Mathieu-Dairnvaell used the epithet to describe Rothschild. See, for example, Mathieu-Dairnvaell, *Jugement*, 11. In fact, the regularity with which Mathieu-Dairnvaell's work was updated makes it difficult to know who produced their manuscript first. Mathieu-Dairnvaell quoted the "excellent writer" Alphonse Toussenel. Both noted in their discussion of the Jews – word for word – that no other race had been "more fecund in brilliant individuals," but that they had been fanatical in developing the art of "fleecing mankind." Mathieu-Dairnvaell, *Rothschild Ier*, 35–6; Toussenel, 4n. A clue to this question is perhaps offered in a note from the diary of Charles Didier: "Visit to Lamennais. He recognised all of Leroux's book, *Humanité*, as coming from Restif de la Bretonne's *Nuits parisiennes*. He showed me some passages that are identical and is writing an article on the subject that will be biting." 21 February 1841, quoted in Sellards, 91.

[56] Toussenel, 15, 65, 23.

[57] Fourier, *Théorie des quatre mouvements*, 252–3, quoted in Silberner, "Charles Fourier," 250.

[58] Toussenel, 21. See also Mathieu-Dairnvaell, *Rothschild Ier*, 7.

[59] Toussenel, 226.

[60] Ibid., 22, 90.

antithesis of everything these men envisaged as characterising the nation, the Jew himself subscribed to this notion, treating the sacred *patrie* with the utmost contempt:

The words *fatherland, religion* and *faith* have no meaning for these men who have an ecu where their heart should be. A fatherland – merchants do not have one: *ubi aurum, ibi patria* [wherever there is gold, there is the fatherland]. The cosmopolitan Jew personifies industrial feudalism.[61]

It was no wonder that the Jew did not work the land, for why would a man who had no sense of attachment to the nation choose a career that involved hard manual labour and financial uncertainty? Such work was better left to "poets and simpletons."[62] Thus the Jews shunned agriculture, devoting themselves to what for Fourier were "mercantile depravities."[63] For not only did Jews not work the land, they also owned the railways that took the land from honest French citizens, and at no more than its market price.

While in one sense the object of these men's writings is clear, in another, it remains somewhat nebulous. Who precisely were the Jews against whom they were directing their outrage? Anger could be stirred up much more effectively if a specific target could be found to be responsible for the nation's woes. Jo Burr Margadant has suggested that the depiction of an era as evil would be given all the more power if political messages also related a "moral tale" that was "rooted in intimate relations and, ultimately, focused on specific individuals."[64] Margadant was referring to King Louis-Philippe, yet this notion could be applied equally well to James de Rothschild. Rothschild had been a prominent figure in the financing of railroads, and the Northern line on which the accident occurred belonged to none other than "James the Great,"[65] "the rich son of Israel,"[66] "the divine Rothschild," "this divine golden calf," and

[61] Toussenel, 74.
[62] Ibid., 75.
[63] Fourier, *Le Nouveau monde*, 421, quoted in Silberner, "Charles Fourier," 249.
[64] Jo Burr Margadant, "Gender, Vice and the Political Imaginary in Postrevolutionary France: Reinterpreting the Failure of the July Monarchy, 1830–1848," *The American Historical Review* 104, no. 5 (1999): 1495.
[65] Mathieu-Dairnvaell, *Histoire*, 10.
[66] Mathieu-Dairnvaell, *Guerre*, 31.

"the noble Jew."[67] Rothschild "made railway lines, and exploited every-thing that could be exploited."[68] And like the newspapers with which this chapter opened, in their outrage following the accident, it was on Rothschild, the cosmopolitan Jew personified, that pamphleteers called. For Toussenel, too, James de Rothschild's power was best illustrated by the railway:

And Mr Rothschild, of the tribe of Judah, noticing that the gardens of Versailles and the forest of Saint-Germain were the principal rendezvous of the people of Paris, said to the minister: "Deliver up to me the pleasures of the Paris populace; and from now on any Parisian who goes to Saint-Germain or Versailles will be obliged to pay a tribute to me." The minister hastened to seize this opportunity to be agreeable to the king of the Jews, and conceded to him to the two lines of Versailles and Saint-Germain, the villas of Paris.[69]

But it was Mathieu-Dairnvaell who was particularly prolific in his attacks. And even as he painted Rothschild as a human super-power (James Rothschild I, "*king of Europe, Asia, Africa, America, Oceania and other places*, and especially *king of the Jews!*"),[70] Mathieu-Dairnvaell also gave Rothschild a series of nicknames, and addressed him with the familiar *tu*. In this way, Mathieu-Dairnvaell effectively recalled the contempt with which the Jew was traditionally viewed. This was reinforced in his attacks on the Rothschild family. For example, he described the founder of the dynasty, Mayer Amschel, thus: "Orphaned at the age of eleven, [...] he first wished to devote himself to teaching, but the instincts of his race having triumphed, he studied the different branches of commerce with great success."[71] Mathieu-Dairnvaell suggested that Mayer Amschel's rise to riches that began as a result of his acquaintance with the margrave of Hesse was slowed considerably in 1806 with the arrival of the French – "Mr Rothschild could no longer find someone to loan to at 4 and bor-row at 5, which momentarily prevented him from earning 200% on his little deals," and that the Rothschilds had always resented the French

---

[67] Mathieu-Dairnvaell, *Rothschild Ier*, 18. In fact, Rothschild was not the sole owner, but rather, the head of a coalition of bankers, including the Hottinguer bank, and the d'Eichtals.

[68] Mathieu-Dairnvaell, *Jugement*, 14.

[69] Toussenel, 201.

[70] Mathieu-Dairnvaell, *Histoire*, 16.

[71] Mathieu-Dairnvaell, *Histoire*, 8.

for it. Mayer Amschel died, we are told, "leaving ten million and as many children."[72] This, then, was the clan that bled France dry, remaining in France "like a leech stays on a man's vein."[73] "Dry-eyed," moved only by the passion for profit, the king of the Jews and his family were known for their hatred of France. None of the enterprises of the heartless Rothschilds were "conceived or executed for the good of humanity" but rather for "personal interest and as objects for exploitation."[74] (Nathan Rothschild's coup following Napoleon's defeat at Waterloo, where he was able to get back to England ahead of the news and thus make a fortune on the stock exchange, was for Mathieu-Dairnvaell the strongest indication of the perfidy of the Rothschild family.) And the family representative in France, James de Rothschild, was nothing if not calculating. In the eyes of Toussenel, the regime, Rothschild style, was characterised by egotism that sought "in vain to hide itself under a mask of hypocritical philanthropy. Its motto is: each man for himself."[75] In the summer of 1846, wheat crops failed across Western Europe. France was particularly badly hit, and supplies of grain became expensive, uncertain, and sparse. Rothschild imported corn and organised the distribution of free bread. Yet according to Mathieu-Dairnvaell, these acts were "a well placed *advertisement*."[76] The *Réforme* agreed. This newspaper, which complained about the "ignoble exploitation of France" by bankers from Frankfurt, read Rothschild's act as calculated to make a profit.[77] The *Réforme* exposed Rothschild as a false philanthropist who may on the surface have been seen to donate grain to the city of Paris, but who in fact sent grain to England so as to make a larger profit from it. For the *Réforme*, Rothschild's world was one of *affaires*, or business transactions. Between Rothschild the "*industrialist*" and "the merit of a philanthropist," in the eyes of the censorious *Réforme*, there was "all the distance of his cashbox."[78]

---

[72] Ibid., 9. It is worth noting that both Isaac Pereire and the Fould family also come under his scrutiny.

[73] Mathieu-Dairnvaell, *Rothschild Ier*, 25; idem, *Histoire*, 12.

[74] Mathieu-Dairnvaell, *Jugement*, 20.

[75] Toussenel, 74.

[76] Mathieu-Dairnvaell, *Histoire*, 17.

[77] *La Réforme*, 16 July 1846. Szajkowski claims that Rothschild's act of philanthropy in fact backfired: "People started whispering that Rothschild had stored up huge reserves of corn for speculation and that his bread was poisoned." Szajkowski, "Socialist Anti-Semites," 51.

[78] *La Réforme*, 19 July 1846.

But Rothschild could represent much more. Pierre Birnbaum has discussed how, at the end of the nineteenth century, Rothschild represented "the power of the foreigner, which the Other wields over all French people."[79] Already by the 1840s, however, Rothschild was clearly fixed in the popular consciousness as a synonym for wealth. On 10 July 1846, the *Charivari* announced that one Van Gend – apparently the owner of a mail-coach service – had put up a placard challenging Rothschild to a race from Paris to Brussels, promising to get there in eighteen hours, and for less than the railway charges. "When Mr de Rothschild sees the placard," the author tells us, "he won't be able to avoid squinting. I pray to God that I will not be on the boulevard des Italiens at that moment! The sight of a man squinting is always disagreeable to me, even when he is a multi-millionaire." On 27 July, the *Charivari* made reference to an advertisement that "appeals to the public's cupidity, and it is perfectly right to do so. Every notice beginning with the words *one hundred thousand francs to be won* is read by all the paper's subscribers, even by Mr de Rothschild." Thus, if the Jews were the kings of the era, it was Rothschild who was king of the Jews, for Rothschild, banker *and* Jew, personified the Jewish spirit, and thus the July Monarchy itself. He was a calculating, competitive, heartless power, with no sense of national loyalty; he was most certainly not a cooperative citizen. Indeed, Rothschild, the enemy of the nation, was conveniently Prussian, and he was known to speak with a heavy Germanic accent. (In fact, Rothschild never became a French citizen.) Mathieu-Dairnvaell made much of his origins, writing Rothschild's speech thus: "Ma chournée de chasse gommence pien." (*Ma journée de chasse commence bien*).[80] Yet what was important about Rothschild, the anti-citizen, was not his membership of another nation. It was his adherence to a nation that spread itself everywhere, but which planted roots nowhere. Before all else, Rothschild was Jewish and cosmopolitan. He was the Rothschild-Jew. Mathieu-Dairnvaell described Rothschild's heart "beating for joy" at the memory of 1830 "when the victorious people abdicated and handed over power to the millionaires."[81] For Leroux, who saw Rothschild at the head of "all the usurers of Europe,"[82] the

[79] Pierre Birnbaum, *Le peuple et les gros*, 22.
[80] Mathieu-Dairnvaell, *Rothschild Ier*, 27.
[81] Mathieu-Dairnvaell, *Jugement*, 6.
[82] Leroux, 2: 94.

face of James's brother Nathan, as depicted by the sculptor Dantan (Figure 5.1), was "the incarnation of the spirit of the time, of the dominating passions that had chosen them" as masters:

The world today is a little old man with a big fat head and a big fat belly.

Like a vulture he clasps bags of gold and wallets full of *bank notes* in his arms. These are his idols, and he squeezes them against his heart with inexpressible and exquisite pleasure. [. . .] the little old man of whom I speak is just as hideously ugly as Diana was beautiful [. . .] given up entirely to his passion, he is bizarrely twisted and you might think him epileptic: it is because all of his movements are geared towards catching and holding as much gold as possible. To this end, he is wide-eyed and distended; his legs are spread so as to seize his prey, his neck is stretched and his head is thrown back, all in the same goal. He arches his back so that his pectoral capacity forms a sort of bag or receptacle that is as wide as possible; only his belly, which is too protuberant, hampers him a little, and impedes his desires. But however much he spreads, swells and twists his avid and greedy body, there is always some gold that escapes him. It looks as though he wants to run after it, and that his despair stems from his inability to engulf the Pactolus. Wallets full of notes are partly leaking from his arms; bags are coming out of his overfilled pockets; gold coins drip like water from his fobs, all down his thighs, and from his pockets on the skirts of his clothing. He is streaming with gold; he absorbs gold, and gold seeps out from his skin like sweat. It even appears that he will metamorphose into gold; for look! There is a wart on his forehead, and this wart is a golden coin. Indeed, even more expressive than his gestures, and his body, is his face. I would like to convey the expression on this face, but I despair of succeeding. [. . .] The little old man's face has a sort of power that makes him look like Satan. A sardonic smile and joy combined with anxiety hover on his lips. [. . .] I am unable to characterise this joy. If you want to see faces that look like those I am imagining, go to the Stock Exchange and approach the handrail, you will not fail to see a speculator who will present the world's current grimace to you in nature.[83]

In mid-nineteenth century France, where so many still competed to impose their understanding of terms such as nation and citizen, the terrain was fertile for the creation of a *bouc-émissaire*. From the political

---

[83] Ibid., 1: 21–2. It is interesting to note that the above caricature differs from the imagery of the Jew that was to become so engraved in the popular consciousness by the end of the nineteenth century, suggesting perhaps that this was still in flux at this time.

5.1. Jean-Pierre Dantan (dit le Jeune), *Nathan-Meyer Rothschild*, (1777–1836). Paris, Musée Carnavalet.

writers examined in this chapter to novelists such as Eugène Sue,[84] seeking to document their times, they fashioned a Rothschild-Jew, on whose back were laden all of society's ills. Freed from the moorings of common humanity, he became a superbly efficient receptacle for all that lay beyond the bounds of the ideal world of those who created him, whatever their political beliefs. And indeed, those who released his bounds did so consciously and deliberately. In their eyes, this was the era of the "Jewish spirit."[85] Thus, just like the *Dictionnaire*, they argued that when they wrote about Jews, they were using the term Jew as it was understood in its "popular" usage; that is: "*Jew, banker, trader,*" or "*salesmen* or *second hand dealers in silver.*"[86] Leroux argued that although there might have been some link between the *bank* and the people who invented it, "since time immemorial," the term Jew had had "a generic meaning" in French. The "Jewish spirit" was one of "*gain*, of *lucre*, of *profit*, of the spirit of *business* and of *speculation*; in a word, of the *banker's spirit* (esprit),"[87] so that "Jew" was a title reserved for those who deserved it: shrewd speculators, characterised by their "insatiable cupidity," who were selfishly preoccupied with material things and who had "no soul and no heart."[88] Thus Leroux could argue that although he might have a healthy dislike for what he called the "Jewish spirit," this had nothing to do with the Jews themselves, not even, as he put it, with certain "cosmopolitan bankers," "so rich that it is said that they possess, through hypothecary enfeoffment, several of our departments." ("Such sentiment," he observed, was "no longer acceptable in France.")[89]

---

[84] While I would hesitate to label Sue's portrayal of Jews in his highly popular serialised novel of 1844 as overwhelmingly negative, there is nonetheless no escaping the connotations of the title, *Le Juif errant*, and the imagery that this would have recalled for readers. Sue himself explained to his readers that "The subject of the legend of the "Wandering Jew" is that of a poor shoemaker of Jerusalem. When Christ, bearing his cross, passed before his house, and asked his leave to repose for a moment on the stone bench at his door, the Jew replied harshly, "Onwards! Onwards!" and refused him. "It is thou who shalt go onwards – onwards – till the end of time!" was Christ's reply, in a sad but severe tone." Eugène Sue, *Le Juif errant* (Paris, 1876), 216 n. 1. Sue's wandering Jew was a solitary, unhappy character, who roamed the world, leaving death and misery in his wake.

[85] Leroux, 1: 24.

[86] Mathieu-Dairnvaell, *Rothschild Ier*, 35–6.

[87] Leroux, 1: 24. Béatrice Philippe has shown how, in Alsace in the late-eighteenth century, "Judaism" was used as a synonym for "usury." Philippe, 103–4.

[88] Mathieu-Dairnvaell, *Rothschild Ier*, 8; Toussenel, 73.

[89] Leroux, 1: 24.

But was it central to the identity of this scapegoat that he be Jewish? Or was Rothschild's Jewishness incidental to his other qualities that so perfectly characterised the era's evils? After all, in Toussenel's world, Jew and Protestant were *"one and the same thing."* According to Toussenel, a stock exchange proverb held that one Genevan was *"worth six Jews."*[90] Yet Toussenel's work was not entitled *Les Protestants, rois de l'époque*, and in the end all authors returned to the Jews. For although Protestants could be found in France, Protestantism and the competitive individualism with which this religion was associated had its home in Switzerland and England. Geneva, for Toussenel, was the true fatherland of financiers and the root of the notion of Capital.[91] Thus Protestantism could be identified with the evils of a type of society, as exemplified by these two nations, and Protestant, for writers like Toussenel and Leroux, was interchangeable with Geneva, Switzerland, or England.

But the Jews had no true home; they had planted roots nowhere. They were everywhere, and they could be everything to the writers who saw this group at the root of their anxieties. Indeed, the fact that the identification of the Jew as representative of the evils of the era was not incidental is demonstrated by the difficulty all three had in maintaining a clean separation between the Jew as metaphor and the Jew as human being. Schechter has argued that the Jew cannot be viewed as part of a pool of alterity that also includes, among others, blacks and women; but rather, that they should be understood as uniquely other.[92] I would put it, rather, that in the catalogue of alterity, Jews, like other others, occupy their very own page. And among the things that gave the Jew as other his uniqueness were his geographical situation, and his place in the story told by Catholicism. The writings of Toussenel, Leroux, and Mathieu-Dairnvaell provide evidence to support this. All of these men were insistent in their view of the Jews as a great people. Toussenel wrote about "the superior character of the Jewish nation."[93] Leroux would have awarded the Jews the "prize for humanity" had such a thing existed.[94] In a passage addressed "to the Israelites," Mathieu-Dairnvaell

[90] Toussenel, 177–8.
[91] Ibid., 84.
[92] Schechter, 236–48.
[93] Toussenel, 4n.
[94] Leroux, 1: 31.

protested that he saw the *Jews* as his brothers and venerated them for their antiquity.[95] Sartre would have told these authors that their praise cost them little in their creation of an evil Jew. For Sartre argued that figures such as Toussenel, Leroux, and Mathieu-Dairnvaell envisaged the Jew as an "indivisible totality," where the whole was greater than the sum of its parts, and where all the Jew's characteristics were governed by his innate evil. Thus such authors could willingly acknowledge the Jew's good qualities, believing all the while that in fact, the more virtues the Jew had, the more dangerous he could be, because his virtuous façade could effectively mask his true nature.[96] Moreover, an evil nature would use even the most positive of attributes in a negative way, and so it was, predictably, that the Jews were also damned by the very history that highlighted their greatness. This is where the Jew as human being and Jew as metaphor tended to become one. For example, from the medieval image of the Jew as usurer, the depiction of the Jew as banker could follow, as though it were a natural progression,[97] or, as Jacob Katz put it, hatred of the Jews was transferred from "the marketplace of the Alsatian town to the scene of the economic transactions in Paris."[98] Thus Leroux, who in fact promised to "show" what a Jew was, linked the stigmatised Jew of Catholic teaching with the Jew of his time, who still maintained a "vendetta" against humankind.[99] Mathieu-Dairnvaell, who had "too much love for equality to incite hatred of Jews," nonetheless used the name *Jew* deliberately as a punishment, because one part of the Jewish population, which had "remained Jews of the Middle Ages, instead of showing themselves to be worthy of the public rights that have been granted them" and which still inspired "an instinctive repulsion," con-tinued to deserve the name.[100] Toussenel "understood" why the Romans, Christians, and "Mohammedans" had all persecuted the Jewish people. "The universal repulsion that the Jew inspired for such a long time was merely the rightful punishment for his implacable arrogance," and, he continued, with a sudden leap in time, "our disdain" was a legitimate

[95] Mathieu-Dairnvaell, *Rothschild Ier*, 35–6.
[96] Sartre, 40.
[97] See Graetz, 84.
[98] Katz, *From Prejudice to Destruction*, 127.
[99] 1: 33. See also Leroux, 1: 55, chap. 6: "I will show you what a Jew is."
[100] Mathieu-Dairnvaell, *Rothschild Ier*, 35.

retaliation for the Jews' hatred of the rest of humankind.[101] Leroux made a similar connection, criticising the Jews of his world for their continued crucifixion of Christ, through "speculation and capital."[102]

This legacy of Catholicism, or perhaps the sense of its absence, that is evident in the discussions of all these men, best underscores the importance of the Jewishness of the Rothschild-Jew. French men and women had lived through forty years of revolutionary upheaval and were now faced with the challenge of making sense of capitalism. Those who sought comfort in angry criticism of the system could draw on a Catholic worldview that had only been superficially uprooted by the Revolution. For such people, the Catholic overtones evident in the censure of the kings of the era would have made it all the more resonant. The supposedly anti-Christian philosophers of the eighteenth century did not shy away from "hurling ancient Christian insults at the Jews," as Schechter has put it.[103] How much more straightforward then, for Mathieu-Dairnvaell, Toussenel, Fourier, and Leroux, who all clearly understood their world through their adherence to Catholicism? For Leroux, whose ideas were informed by a strong adherence to the Catholic faith, the present world was one where Economic Science had entered into battle with the Gospel. Chapters in his work were entitled "The law of nature of economists is against the law of God";[104] "Political economy removes our salvation, and at the same time destroys faith, hope and charity";[105] or "Political economy orders for poor children to be killed, the Gospel orders for them to be saved."[106] Toussenel had worked on the staff of the ultra-conservative paper, *La Paix*, during the thirties, and there he had met Veuillot. He, too, was a religious man and faith informed his understanding of his world. Thus his greatest wish was to see the people emancipated from financial feudalism, for this would allow them to find their faith again. In the eyes of Mathieu-Dairnvaell, who set up Rothschild and his fellows against "carpenters,"[107] the Jew was still clearly the other, the one who did not belong, in a Catholic nation. He suggested that if Rothschild had

---

[101] Toussenel, 4n.
[102] Leroux, 1: 22.
[103] Schechter, 65.
[104] Leroux, 2: 166.
[105] Ibid., 2: 171.
[106] Ibid., 2: 156.
[107] Mathieu-Dairnvaell, *Guerre*, 9.

been a Christian, he would have been less hated. But Christians could not forgive the fact that the Jewish principle had "infiltrated into the Christian bourgeoisie and become its soul."[108] Even Fourier, who disliked the Church, based his "whole system" "on a set of unquestioned assumptions concerning God and the nature of Divine Providence."[109] For Fourier, as for Mathieu-Dairnvaell, Jews were clearly a discrete group within society. This was how, for example, they could continue to hate Christians.[110]

In an article on socialism and the Jews, George Lichtheim argued that it was "irrelevant" that, alongside his criticisms of Jews as representative of modern society, Fourier "also dragged up some standard abuse."[111] Yet for all these men, and particularly for Fourier, who read very little, such "standard abuse" is as strong as possible an indication of the continuing pervasiveness of this aspect of Catholic ideology in France. These men, among them the founders of socialist thought in France, were – consciously or not – clearly able to comfortably combine their modern criticism of Jews with "standard" Catholic teachings about the place of the Jew. Both Mathieu-Dairnvaell and Leroux looked to the writings of a Catholic who saw no contradiction between his religiosity and the socialist doctrine: Félicité de Lamennais. Lamennais saw no alternative other than Catholicism, but he also understood that the Church must move forward. To this end, he sought to rejuvenate it, working towards a union of Christianity and liberalism. Rather than "trembling" at the prospect of liberalism, he set out to "Catholicise" it, and he enjoyed a great success with the works in which he linked Christianity with social issues.[112] Mathieu-Dairnvaell quoted his work and saw him as a "great writer."[113] In Leroux's eyes, Lamennais was "a famous man of our time, a great and venerable genius," and the "emancipating spirit of the Evangelist" breathed through his *Paroles d'un croyant*.[114] Indeed, Leroux's work read like that of Lamennais in the intensity of its

---

[108] Mathieu-Dairnvaell, *Jugement*, 16.
[109] Jonathan Beecher, *Charles Fourier: The Visionary and His World* (Berkeley, 1987), 196.
[110] Silberner, "Charles Fourier," 247.
[111] Lichtheim, 317.
[112] Félicité de Lamennais, *Le Prêtre et l'ami: Lettres inédites à la Baronne Cottu*, ed. Comte d'Haussonville (Paris, 1910), 219; quoted in Peter Stearns, *Priest and Revolutionary: Lamennais and the Dilemma of French Catholicism* (New York, 1967), 63.
[113] Mathieu-Dairnvaell, *Guerre*, 53.
[114] Leroux, 1: 63.

spirituality. Even Toussenel must have felt his influence, for he worked with Veuillot, who, as a student of Lamennais' influential Mennaisien movement, collaborated with him on his newspaper the *Avenir* before going on to found his journalistic career. Thus, although most liberals were opposed to Lamennais' brand of liberal Catholicism, some chose to embrace it. Leroux, for example, opposed capitalism, in part, on the basis that it did not offer a solution to the religious crisis.[115] As a young man in the Restoration, Leroux was a founder of the *Globe* newspaper, as well as flirting briefly with Saint-Simonianism. The band of young liberals that formed around the newspaper believed that the Church and the Revolution could be reconciled. Leroux, concerned, as Lamennais was, with the atomisation of modern society, wrote of solidarity, and infused this term with an unmistakeable Christian religiosity. In fact, in rhetoric that is strikingly redolent of the writings of early socialists, conservative Catholics had been the first to express their horror in the face of the egotism unleashed, first by the Enlightenment, and then, in what they perceived to be the liberalism of the Restoration.[116] Lamennais had sought to bridge the gap between Catholicism and liberalism by infusing the latter with the former, because Catholic faith was the necessary glue, in his eyes, for any society. Leroux and his fellow socialists may have remained anticlerical. Nonetheless, they clearly also felt it necessary that society retain some element of religiosity. In this sense, they were able to find common ground with the groundbreaking liberalist Christian. And the Jew, who knew neither "faith" nor "religion," was clearly representative of the cult of the individual, and thus he presented a threat to French society itself. These socialist thinkers created a Rothschild-Jew rooted in traditional Catholic imagery. It is little wonder that works such as those of Mathieu-Dairnvaell were so resonant with the population. But although the Rothschild-Jew sprang from Catholic teaching, these men loosened his chains and allowed him to go far beyond his modest origins.

It is important to place these writings in perspective. If we can group critics of the July Monarchy such as Leroux, Fourier, and Toussenel in terms of the role assigned to Jews in their writings, we must also make

---

[115] Bakunin, 222.
[116] See McMahon, for example, 47–53.

mention of major figures such as Louis Blanc or Etienne Cabet, also socialists and critics of the regime, but not critics of Jews, or members of the Fourierist movement, such as Victor Hennequin, or Jean Czynski, who took it upon themselves to defend Jews against criticism.[117] It is certainly the case, also, that beyond their focus on Jews, it is only possible to group these men in the loosest sense. As Pam Pilbeam has pointed out, at this time there were as many brands of socialism as there were socialists,[118] and not all those who wrote to expose the evils of the regime and to propose a replacement for it incorporated Jews into this scheme. Moreover, although negative attitudes to Jews most certainly feature in the works of Leroux, Toussenel, Mathieu-Dairnvaell, and Fourier, and they were even innovative, at the same time, these attitudes are not the principal aspect of their works. Anti-Jewish sentiment was not the natural corollary of anti-capitalism for all socialist writers in July Monarchy France. Nonetheless, more than a few of them saw it thus, and it is important to acknowledge this, and to seek to understand why they chose the Rothschild-Jew to play the role of evildoer in their tales of woe.

Old and new myths regarding Jews were ever-present in July Monarchy society. The intense speculation generated by the Damascus Affair provides just one illustration. Members of the public were fed with reminders of such myths: even just the title of Halévy and Scribe's opera or of Eugène Sue's highly successful novel meant that throughout the July Monarchy, notions of the *belle juive* or of the "wandering Jew" presented themselves to the nation's consciousness. And the most visible of Jews in France was clearly a highly accessible target, even if not all those who attacked him made his religious affiliation clear. But did they need to? When the *Réforme* made Rothschild a major object in its criticism of capitalism, it did not expressly refer to his Judaism. Perhaps Rothschild in his "opulence" was truly no more to this newspaper than the most visible of the bourgeois bankers who represented the capitalism it so abhorred. Nonetheless, the *Réforme* duly noted the appearance of advertisements for Mathieu-Dairnvaell's *Histoire édifiante et curieuse de*

---

[117] See Poliakov, III: 373. I would, however, disagree with Poliakov's contention that figures such as Blanc, Blanqui, and Cabet refrained from criticising Jews, "probably because their understanding had not been clouded by the historical legacy of Christianity." I would, rather, offer the suggestion that such men simply chose not to use the Jew to express their own ambivalence towards the boundaries of their world.

[118] Pilbeam, *Republicanism*, 156.

Rothschild Ier, roi des Juifs.[119] Moreover, oblique references to Rothschild's "coreligionists"[120] or the "Sanhedrin of the Ponts et Chaussées"[121] would suggest that Rothschild's religious affiliation was indeed featured in the background of the image that this newspaper painted of him. Perhaps it was even easily accessible for those who wished to find it. After all, the pamphlets of Mathieu-Dairnvaell, to which the *Réforme* made reference, of Leroux and Toussenel, and even of Lamennais, were busy making this connection explicit in their works that sold so well. From their writings, sternly moral, comes a strong message of horror at competitive individualism unleashed. Those who sought someone on whom to lay the blame for the current situation could easily choose to see Rothschild looming large on their horizon. For them, it would seem, none symbolised this new regime better than those who were seen to have derived the most benefit from it. This was the epoch of the "Jewish spirit," and "avidity and greed,"[122] deceptiveness and dishonour, cold-heartedness, all characteristics of the competitive individual, were all familiar Jewish qualities. However, if once they had been rooted in the bodies of men such as Simon Deutz and his coreligionists in the Orient, now they no longer needed to be contained within the Jew. Rothschild's attackers made him into a symbol, a "new variety of despot,"[123] and this was a role that he could play to perfection, for Rothschild was the anti-citizen personified. He was visibly (and audibly) foreign. He was fabulously wealthy and powerful. He cared nothing for his fellow citizens. He stood firm against the tide of the national will. And most important, perhaps, he was Jewish.

[119] *La Réforme*, 18 July 1846.
[120] *La Réforme*, 13 July 1846.
[121] *La Réforme*, 15 July 1846.
[122] Leroux, 1: 30.
[123] *L'Univers*, 19 July 1846.

6

∾

Evolutions in the Jewish Question

WHAT HISTORIANS HAVE COME TO LABEL THE JEWISH question has been posed by different groups and in varying guises over a long period. But what, exactly, is it? Perhaps we could characterise the Jewish question as a direct expression of ambivalence: if Jews raise a question, it is precisely because they challenge the dimensions of the "orderly world" of their describer.[1] It follows, then, that over time, this so-called question has changed with a changing world, and more; at a given point in time, the question has existed in different forms, depending on the one who posed it and on their specific utopia. In eighteenth-century France, as the Enlightenment brought challenges to the existing order, the Jewish question came to relate specifically to new ways in which France and the French were being envisaged: as citizens, and as a nation. Ronald Schechter has shown how, by the 1770s, Jews were increasingly becoming "good to think," as he puts it, about questions of citizenship and nationhood.[2] In 1787, in the context of Hell's forged receipts and the ongoing debate regarding how Jews in Alsace should be viewed and treated, the Société royale des sciences et des arts de Metz chose to pose their own Jewish question: was there a way "to make the Jews more useful and happier in France?"[3] Jews in eighteenth-century France maintained their community structures, and in the eyes of those who used Jews as the prism through which to understand their world, they lived among the French, but not with them. They formed a separate community under the one French roof. Was it possible to remake them as fellow citizens?

---

[1] Bauman, "Allosemitism: Premodern, Modern, Postmodern," 144.
[2] Schechter, 67.
[3] "Est-il des moyens de rendre les Juifs plus utiles et plus heureux en France?"

Sepinwall describes three positions taken by those who considered this question in the late 1780s: alongside the conditionalism of those such as Grégoire, there was what she has called unconditionalism – or those who argued that Jews should simply be allowed to be citizens with no specific conditions imposed. We might say that unconditionalists were driven by a great optimism in the ability of their ideological system to incorporate a Jewish population. Sepinwall has named the third position imposs-bilism. This position stated that Jews were unredeemable and therefore inadmissible, under any conditions, into society;[4] that the world was unimaginable without Jews forever situated on its margin. Perhaps the most powerful of the discourses that was to emerge in the Revolutionary discussions of the matter was the conditionalist approach. According to this schema, the unimproved Jew represented the counter-image of each of the ideal citizen's qualities, but he was nonetheless perfectible, or at the least improvable, if certain specific conditions were met.

Schechter makes an important point when he underscores the dispro-portionate amount of energy that the National Assembly devoted to dis-cussions of Jews. There are different ideas as to why this might have been the case.[5] For our purposes, it is important to note that Jews were called on repeatedly just as questions of citizenship were at their most concrete and acute. As deputies debated the possibility of making Jews citizens, they were considering broader questions of central importance to their endeavour: what constituted a citizen? What was the nation? In calling on the Jew to think through these concepts, revolutionary culture was self-consciously parading its modernity, while drawing on a centuries-old tradition to make sense of this.[6] But then, even the anti-revolutionary movement was using Jews to think of the world of the Revolution. Ouzi Elyada has shown that as the Revolution intensified, and up until the fall of the monarchy in August 1792, through the medium of journals, anti-revolutionaries used Jews to explain the evils that were occurring, be they the civil constitution of the clergy, the patriotic clubs, and of course, the emancipation of the Jews. Thus, for example, when in March 1790

---

[4] Sepinwall, 62.
[5] Ibid., 156–65; Gary Kates, "Jews into Frenchmen: Nationality and Representation in Revolutionary France," in *The French Revolution and the Birth of Modernity*, ed. Ferenc Fehér (Berkeley, 1990), 103–16.
[6] Schechter, 163.

the National Assembly sought to nationalise the Church's property, anti-revolutionary journals such as the *Gazette de Paris* understood events as a Judeo-Protestant conspiracy. As Elyada puts it, those who saw events as evil were not interested in Jews per se; rather, Jews served to under-score the wrongs of the Revolutionary project.[7] Another of the evils of the era, in the eyes of such critics, was the voice of moderation that was Count Stanislas de Clermont-Tonnerre. Discussions, of which this was a part, on Jewish separateness, could be said to betray an anxiety regarding the means of binding newly forged citizens, of all faiths, to the state. Would the Jewish sense of community be a barrier to their performance of citizenship? Could a citizen maintain a secondary or dual loyalty? This question, of whether Judaism could be compatible with French citizen-ship, began with the Revolution, but the process of responding was to stretch across the nineteenth century. Perhaps the most explicit posing of a Jewish question – to Jews themselves – was Napoleon's convocation of Jewish leaders known as the Assembly of Notables in 1806, and the ensuing Sanhedrin in the following year. In this final chapter, I would like to trace the *parcours* followed by this question beyond Napoleon, across the period I have examined in this book, and thus explore another aspect of the evolutions that I have described.

By the 1820s, where this chapter begins, Napoleon had been in distant exile for some years and France was restoring itself to the fold of Catholi-cism as the eldest daughter of the Church. One feature of Napoleon's rule had been the employment of the methodology of description and classification that was a strong legacy of the Enlightenment and of ancien régime bureaucracy. In his fascination with facts, Napoleon was in fact continuing the work begun by doctors and naturalists in the seven-teenth and eighteenth centuries of "classing" and thus understanding the world.[8] (The Société royale des sciences et des arts of Metz that set the 1787 essay question on the Jews to which the Abbé Grégoire wrote his celebrated response had in the two previous years set questions on "the most useful and least cumbersome type of wine press," and how

[7] Ouzi Elyada, "La rhétorique antijuive dans la presse contre-révolutionnaire 1789–1792," in Ilana Y. Zinguer and Sam W. Bloom, ed., *L'Antisémitisme éclairé. Inclusion et exclusion depuis l'Epoque des Lumières jusqu'à l'affaire Dreyfus* (Leiden, 2003): 141–50.
[8] Marie-Noëlle Bourguet, "Race et Folklore: l'image officielle de la France en 1800," *Annales ESC* 31 (1976): 805.

"to ensure the livelihood of bastards and make them more useful to the state.") Under Napoleon, the gathering of information became a way to administer, a manner of putting into practice his ideas about how the state should be organised, and the best way to undertake this.[9] An optimistic faith in the power of administration led to the expectation that the possession of detailed knowledge of society's different facets would make the latter well ordered.[10] For example, Napoleon's organisation of French Jewry into Consistories (along the model of the Protestant church) was expected to facilitate their supervision and regeneration.[11] Thus, it was necessary to gather statistical information on the population, including descriptions of cultural practices and physical appearance. Not surprisingly, such pursuits led to generalisations and a dehumanisation, or anonymisation of the subjects. Stuart Woolf argues that Napoleon's prefects would take their cue from the *philosophes* and economists of the enlightenment, as well as from more recent writings on the science of man and progress of civilisation, and allocate "social groups and entire peoples [. . .] to an appropriately labelled and preformulated box, as 'idle' or 'industrious,' 'superstitious' or 'enlightened,' 'feudal' or 'civilised,' and so forth."[12] Or as one well-known member of the generation of 1820 put it: "To organise is a word of the Empire."[13] In the 1820s, the emperor's system of administration lived on, now run by this generation of men whose maturity had coincided with the collapse of the Empire. To them, the world, now at peace, was "in process of definition,"[14] and the possibilities that this presented were infinite. Theirs was the challenge to take their place in the great task of defining the world. They took Napoleon's legacy as their inspiration. Yet a particular test presented itself to them. For as far as they were concerned, in the midst of French society there still existed a Jewish population with a way of life that had remained seemingly unchanged since the Revolution. Jews were now French citizens. Nonetheless, although freed from external restrictions, many had chosen to maintain their observance of Jewish law. If Jews defied categorisation within the new system, the so-called Jewish question was essentially

---

[9] Stuart Woolf, *Napoleon's Integration of Europe* (London, 1991), 125.
[10] Ibid., 85.
[11] See, for example, Albert, *Modernization*, 50, 143–6.
[12] Woolf, 84.
[13] Honoré de Balzac, quoted in ibid., 83.
[14] Spitzer, 269.

a reflection of the ambivalence that this untidiness engendered: if the world had been re-made in perfect form, what was to be done with this population that continued to maintain a double allegiance, challenging this perfection? Was it possible to reform the Jews – a culturally inferior population living in the superior French family – so that they might fit into the "new grid of classification" that had stemmed from the Revolution?[15] Thus, in the post-Revolutionary world, the nature of the Jewish question had changed, for with the non-renewal of Napoleon's Infamous Decree in 1818, it was clearer than ever that the question of whether the Jews should be granted citizenship was no longer open for debate. Now the Jewish question involved finding a way for these citizens to fit into the greater French family.

In the 1820s, two learned societies in France set essay questions that sought to come up with an answer to the apparent unchanged existence of the Jews. It was a long-standing tradition at this time already to use history as a means of explaining the present and planning the future. During monarchical reign in France, it was not uncommon for statistical enquiries to implicitly assume that 'today' could be understood through a study of 'yesterday', as though time and evolution were in themselves explanatory.[16] In 1823, the Académie des inscriptions et belles-lettres of Rouen held a competition inviting its participants to take just this approach. The topic called on competitors to "Examine the state of the Jews in France, Spain and Italy, from the beginning of the fifth century of the common era to the end of the sixteenth century, under the headings of civil rights, trade and literature." If the Jew was to be civilised, that is, if his external condition was to be regenerated, it was necessary to begin by examining and perfecting his internal nature: his religious beliefs, his philosophy, and his contributions to the fields of science, letters, and the arts.[17] Two responses were published.[18] One year later, an essay

---

[15] Marie-Noëlle Bourguet, *Déchiffrer la France: la statistique départementale à l'époque napoléonienne* (Paris, 1989), 212.

[16] Jean-Claude Perrot, *L'Age d'or de la statistique régionale française (An IV – 1804)* (Paris, 1977), 5.

[17] Berkovitz, *Shaping*, 47.

[18] These were Arthur-Auguste Beugnot, *Les Juifs d'Occident, ou "Recherches sur l'état-civil, le commerce et la littérature des Juifs en France, en Espagne et en Italie pendant la durée du Moyen âge"* (Paris, 1824), and Charles Joseph Bail, *Etat des Juifs en France, en Espagne et en Italie, depuis le commencement du cinquième siècle de l'ère vulgaire jusqu'à la fin du seizième, sous les divers rapports du droit civil, du commerce et de la littérature; ouvrage*

contest was proposed by the Société des sciences, agriculture et arts du département du Bas-Rhin. The – somewhat rhetorical – essay question, detailed in an issue of the society's newsletter, was:

1. To determine the most appropriate means to enable the Israelite population of Alsace to enjoy the benefits of civilization. 2. To investigate whether the causes that estrange the members that compose this population from society are at all the product of superstitious practices and of the obstinacy to persevere in the ancient customs that the times and changes in the political situation should have modified.[19]

The Société pointed the entrants to the consideration of a few issues in particular: whether the Sanhedrin decisions could be used to achieve the desired results; whether changes to Jewish ritual that had been introduced elsewhere in France and Europe might be applicable to the Jewish population of Alsace; whether Jewish (Mosaic) law would enable the bringing into line of Jewish holidays and state holidays; and finally, whether it would be useful to establish an école normale israélite in Alsace, where "educated and enlightened men" – as opposed to rabbis – would act as teachers. Four essays were submitted.[20]

Regeneration or the French *régénération* was a central notion to this type of thinking and discourse. In its post-Revolutionary form, the concept found its roots in the Enlightenment, and specifically in Diderot's *Encyclopédie*. This movement had affirmed the power of knowledge and reason and the relationship of these to progress and the ascent towards civilisation. The optimism of the Revolution that took as its catchcry the word *régénération* developed these notions, and made *régénération* an intrinsic part of the purifying process that led from a degraded ancien régime to a nation characterised by its enlightenment and civilisation.

qui a concouru au prix décerné par l'Académie des inscriptions et belles-lettres de l'Institut de France, dans le mois de juillet 1823 (Paris, 1823).

[19] "Variétés: Programme," *Journal de la société des sciences, agriculture et arts, du département du Bas-Rhin*, 1 (1824): 114–16. Marie-Noëlle Bourguet has noted that terms like "superstitious" were used in a general – as opposed to a religious – sense by some Napoleonic prefects to describe the inhabitants of their region (e.g., "la superstition forme le caractère général".) Bourguet, "Race," 815.

[20] "Rapport de la Commission chargée d'examiner les mémoires qui ont concouru pour le prix proposé en 1824, par la Société des sciences, agriculture et arts du département du Bas-Rhin," *Journal de la société* 2 (1825), 299. The content of these works has been examined in detail elsewhere. See Berkovitz, *Shaping*, chap. 2.

Régénération was vital in the creation of citizens who could contribute to the nation, and thus form part of the national will. Thus, for example, Lepelletier de Saint-Fargeau (a noble-born Jacobin), spoke thus of his project to establish a school designed to train Revolutionary male elites: "I dared to conceive of an inspiration more vast than that of mere instruction. Having considered the extent to which the human species has been corrupted by the vice of our former social system, I became convinced of the need to operate a complete regeneration, and, if I dare to speak in this manner, of the need to create a new people."[21] The notion of *régénération* had already been used in consideration of the Jewish question during the ancien régime.[22] But where at that time *régénération* may have retained its original, religious connotation of baptism and thus rebirth, the idea of *régénération* had been secularised, first by the encyclopedists and then by the Revolution. Sepinwall has detailed how in the introduction to the *Encyclopédie*, d'Alembert self-consciously used the word in a distinctly new way, linking it to the development of new ideas. Where *régénération* had previously signified rebirth through God, the new use of the word was a reflection of the new belief that human beings could determine the order of things.[23] Where Jews were concerned, then, the requirement that they regenerate was an onus placed upon them. And in post-Revolutionary France, it was perceived that the need for Jews to regenerate was overwhelming. This was perhaps tied up with the imperative for each French citizen to do the same so that the Revolutionary *nation* could exist. Thus, *régénération* offered the Jewish population a means of inclusion, but at the same time it demanded of them that they change themselves so as to fit; in this sense the notion gave, but it also took away. To someone like Grégoire, therefore, the Jewish idea that it was possible to be a true Frenchman and still maintain distinct Jewish practices was absurd.[24]

The power of the notion that Jews must somehow regenerate is indicated by the fact that it was also taken on by a section of the Jewish elite. In fact, the prize for the question set by the Strasbourg Société was

[21] Quoted in Patrice Higonnet, "Cultural Upheaval and Class Formation during the French Revolution," 102n, in Fehér, 69–102.

[22] The Abbé Grégoire's prize-winning essay of 1785 was entitled *Essai sur la régénération physique, morale et politique des Juifs.*

[23] Sepinwall, 57.

[24] Ibid., 94.

sponsored by an Alsatian Jew named Worms de Romilly (originally Olry-Hayem Worms), a banker, who was to serve as president of the Central Consistory in the 1840s. He offered 300 francs in prize money. After 1830, members of the French Jewish community – mostly young men who had not experienced the process of emancipation – formed a *Mouvement régénérateur*. For inspiration, these Jewish intellectuals drew on the similar movement in Germany, known as Haskalah – or Jewish Enlightenment. For them, regeneration signified as much a religious as a civic rebirth. In this sense, they did not advocate assimilation. They sought to modernise French Jewry, but not at the expense of Judaism. Rather, Jewish education was to be reorganised so as to produce Jews who would be good French citizens but also good Jews. In fact, one member of the *Mouvement régénérateur*, Michel Berr, a prominent lawyer, criticised the Strasbourg Société for the phrasing of the second question.[25] It is telling that most of the movement's members were actively involved in either the adaptation of Jewish studies to fit into a greater secular academe or the bringing of secular studies to Judaism. Thus, for example, Gerson-Lévy taught French at the École centrale rabbinique in Metz, while Adolphe Franck was professor of Greek and Latin philosophy at the Collège de France, and also published works on Jewish mysticism. In a sense, the *Mouvement* worked to bring Jews back to Judaism, and from there, into French society.[26]

The Strasbourg Société set its essay question in terms of regeneration, although this did differ from the *Mouvement régénérateur*. Rather, as the preamble to the question explained, the Société was motivated by a desire to assist the Jewish people first by either reawakening the latter's dormant seeds of perfection or making them aware of methods used by other populations, and then by publicising the various means of assistance that could be provided by the general population. The preface argued that the Jewish people was "foreign to other nations," even though it made up part of their populations, and that only a small number of its members were included in the great European family. This phenomenon was explained by the perseverance with which Jews maintained their

[25]   Michel Berr, *Lettre au rédacteur de l'Argus*, Paris, 1824, 4–5; quoted in Berkovitz, *Shaping*, 258n.
[26]   For a wider discussion on the *Mouvement régénérateur*, see Berkovitz, *Shaping*, chap. 6, 128–49.

rituals, as well as by the persecution and isolation that were a result of this very perseverance and, for the Society, it seemed time to hold out a helping hand to the Jews. In this chapter, I examine four works that present a variety of approaches to the Jewish question – the winning entry to the Strasbourg competition, an entry in the Rouen competition, and two other works on the same subject – to shed light on the evolution of the question in the context of the world in which it was posed.

Who were the authors of these works? These men had neither age nor politics in common. A member of the nobility, a long-time member of Napoleon's military and administrative corps, a career public servant in the Restoration, and the secretary to the Strasbourg Société – what united them was their consensus on the existence of a Jewish question. For although their approach to minutiae differed in places, they all agreed that the Jewish population in France presented a problem, and they were equally in agreement as to how it should be approached. The Jews were to be regarded impassively and with impartiality, so that even though, in the eyes of the devoutly Catholic Count Arthur-Auguste Beugnot, they had killed Christ, it was necessary to tell their story without prejudice. Second, the question was to be solved by means of reason, in which all of the authors had such faith that they were optimistic regarding the possibility of a positive solution to the question under review.

Beugnot was a lawyer and historian, and a member of the Rouen Académie that had set the 1823 essay, but his greatest love was study, and he took time out from the law to devote himself to it at several stages in his life. Beugnot also spent time as editor of the *Ami de la religion*. He was so confident of his ability to find an answer to this question that he entered both the competition set by the Strasbourg Société and the one held in Rouen the year before.[27] (He received an honourable mention in Rouen, and was declared the winner in Strasbourg.) Another entrant to the Rouen competition had less success than Beugnot, although he had already published a work on the same subject. Charles-Joseph Bail, who had achieved some notoriety in 1816 with his *Des Juifs au dix-neuvième*

---

[27] Beugnot's winning entry was not published, although a number of passages from it and a summary of his arguments were included in the *Journal de la société* 2 (1825): 312. Because his arguments are essentially the same in both works, I focus on the 1823 work that was published in full and which thus provides greater opportunity for interpretation.

siècle, was perhaps spurred on by this success to revisit the theme in response to the 1823 Rouen competition. Although his work was not awarded the prize by the Rouen Academy, he chose to publish it himself, in the interest – as he explained it – "of science, history and truth."[28]

Also published at this time was Michel Betting de Lancastel's *Considérations sur l'état des Juifs dans la société chrétienne et particulièrement en Alsace.*[29] Lancastel was a career public servant originally from Alsace who was serving as sub-Prefect of the district of Colmar. Thus he was part of the network of men who administered the nation. Amédée Tourette, the secretary of the Strasbourg Société, makes up this quartet. Although it is not explicitly stated that the work of Amedée Tourette was written in response to the question set by the Société, his position and the title of his work – *Discours sur les Juifs d'Alsace* – would suggest that this was the case.[30] Little is known about his circumstances, but it can be stated with certainty that Tourette was clearly a great believer in the powers of strong government, and Revolutionary ideals. Tourette distanced himself from Christianity, interpreting a passage from the Bible but excusing himself, hoping that he had "properly understood the spirit of the holy book that Jesus Christ's disciples left us."[31]

These men had in common their awareness of one another. Beugnot, Bail, Tourette, and Lancastel took inspiration from each other's work in their attempts to solve the Jewish question. Betting de Lancastel borrowed from Beugnot and, in particular, from Bail, and quoted both of them with admiration. Tourette referred his readers to Beugnot's work, of which he was a great admirer, calling *Les Juifs d'Occident* "the best piece of work that has yet appeared on this topic; in it, one finds a thorough knowledge of Jewish history; a mass of insights that are both noble and just, and a very engaging style."[32]

All four authors set great store by the value of impartiality, and they were confident of their ability to undertake their work in this spirit. Bail prided himself on the fact that his 1816 work had not been "without use

---

[28]   Bail, *Etat des Juifs*, vi.
[29]   Michel Betting de Lancastel, *Considérations sur l'état des Juifs dans la société chrétienne et particulièrement en Alsace* (Strasbourg, 1824).
[30]   Amédée Tourette, *Discours sur les Juifs d'Alsace* (Strasbourg, 1825).
[31]   Tourette, 4.
[32]   Ibid., 30n.

to the Jewish cause,"[33] and he called himself an impartial friend of the Jews: "severe, rather than a flatterer or a panegyrist."[34] Bail undertook research into the work of contemporary men of science to support his own ideas, and inserted a clause on the nobility of his motives and the objectiveness of his approach. Lancastel promised opinions "based on indisputable evidence,"[35] and impartiality in his research and his views. He was certain that a civilising influence on what he called the Jewish nation would see "exalted sentiments" take root.[36] Lancastel's faith in the authority of Napoleon's initiative was absolute and this led him to be absolute regarding those who had failed it. In one chapter, entitled "That those foreign Jews who have settled in Alsace can be expelled from there," Lancastel stated that "Nothing would be both more natural and legal than [. . .] to expel from the kingdom those foreign [Jews] who are of no use to society."[37] In the interest of impartiality, Beugnot carefully examined claims that there was something "antisocial" in the Jewish character, although he himself was confident that the effect of poor treatment of the Jews could stand alone as justification for their actions.[38]

The fact that they set great store by the need to maintain a scientific distance from their subjects ultimately led these authors to depict the former as a passive class. Their faith in the inheritance of Enlightenment thought and the Revolutionary construction of the nation was such that they believed that nothing – not even what they saw as the continued refusal of a proportion of the Jewish community to take on the duties of citizenship – could stand before reason, science, and knowledge. As such, their approach to the Jewish question involved seeking to categorise and thus define Jews: much as they might have done were they classing butterflies. Tourette spelled out his view of the Jews as a "passive class" early on in his essay, making himself their puppeteer:

The regeneration of a people can only be carried out if there is exact agreement between the intentions of the regenerator and the duties of the class of men who are passive in the reforming action. I draw two consequences from

[33] Bail, *Etat des Juifs*, x.
[34] Ibid., xi.
[35] Lancastel, vii.
[36] Ibid., 8.
[37] Ibid., 118.
[38] Beugnot, *Les Juifs*, 280.

this principle: firstly, the necessity of granting the passive class all possible means of rising to the same social condition and intellectual dignity as that where the regenerator is placed; secondly, not to allow, in the very heart of the latter, elements that are contrary to the efficient application of the agreed means to subsist.[39]

Beugnot also cast his subjects as a passive mass: throughout his work he referred to "the Jews," making no exceptions and barely singling out individuals (with the exception, for example, of a figure such as Maimonides). The actions of these men were also echoing an integral part of Napoleonic administration. Marie-Noëlle Bourguet has shown that under Napoleon, prefects all over France were already describing that nation's inhabitants and their physiognomy as a function of their habitat, approaching the varieties of the human species as they would the fauna and flora, looking for influences in the surrounding environment.[40] As administrator of Napoleon's provinces in Westphalia, Charles-Joseph Bail had produced a *Statistique générale* of the region for which he was responsible,[41] and his studies of the Jewish population were undertaken in the same spirit.

   If it was a tradition of the Napoleonic style of description to imagine different groups as passive, it was equally so to see them as a problem. One prefect under the Empire, observing the Gypsy population in his department, wrote that they

secretly practised a religion particular to them [. . .] They fed on bad poultry, contaminated fish, dogs, and rotting cats [. . .] they [had] their own language that was unintelligible to the native inhabitants, and they carefully concealed any knowledge of it from them. [. . .] Their features were irregular and announced their membership of a transplanted race.

They were "a miserable, isolated caste, foreign to society which tolerates them only with excessive disdain."[42] And just as this prefect suggested

---

[39]   Tourette, 6.
[40]   "A la pointe Saint-Mathieu, sauvage et aride," "les hommes sont de couleur olitre," mais dans la presqu'île de Plougastel, toute proche," "les femmes sont plus jolies, plus grandes," épanouies comme les fleurs et les primeurs qui poussent dans ce climat de rêve." Bourguet, *Déchiffrer la France*, 240, 241.
[41]   Charles-Joseph Bail, *Statistique générale des provinces composant le royaume de Westphalie, dans l'ordre où elles subsistaient au 1er octobre 1807, avec l'indication de la nouvelle division départementale* (Göttingen, 1809).
[42]   From Delon, *Annales de Statistique*, vol. 2, pp. 31–6, cited in Bourguet, "Race et Folklore," 812.

that the degraded character of the Gypsy could be read in his appearance
and his situation, Bail also went looking for the influence of the internal
environment on the Jew, seeking evidence of the Jewish character in the
Jew's physical appearance. To do this, he borrowed from the work of the
Swiss priest Johann Caspar Lavater with whom, like many of his time,
he was familiar. Lavater, a Protestant pastor, was born in Zurich in 1741.
He was known for his *Essai sur la physiognomie, destiné à faire connoître
l'homme et à le faire aimer* (1781–1803). In this work, he, with the help of
other contributors, set out his theory of physiognomy – with examples –
and argued for its recognition as a science.[43] The Abbé Grégoire also
called on the theories of Lavater when he wrote about Jews. Bail noted
that, according to Lavater, the average Jew generally had

a pallid face, a hooked nose, deep-set eyes, a prominent chin, the constrictor
muscles around the mouth were highly pronounced, their hair was frizzy
and coloured red or brown, and they had a light beard, the standard sign of
an effeminate temperament.[44]

Bail also drew on another theorist of mankind whose work appears
to have been in the popular canon; this was Anthony Ashley Cooper,
Third Earl of Shaftesbury, and his *Characteristicks of Men, Manners,
Opinions, Times.*[45] Shaftesbury described Jews as naturally "gloomy" and
melancholy – characteristics of men surrounded for a long time by terrors
and fears – for "the property of slavery was to condemn the soul."[46] Bail
produced his own specific description of the Alsatian Jew to show how
interior degeneration was reflected in the Jew's exterior. For if physical
degradation followed moral degradation, the Alsatian Jew provided a
good example of this notion. He was:

generally reproached for being cunning, fertile in expedients, obstinate in
his plans, perseverant in overcoming obstacles so as to satisfy his greed,
and barely scrupulous in his choice of means. In his obsequious subtlety, in
his degraded exterior, his shifty look reminds one of a Greek oppressed by

---

[43]   Christopher Rivers, *Face Value: Physiognomical Thought and the Legible Body in Mari-
      vaux, Lavater, Balzac, Gautier, and Zola* (Madison, 1994), 66.
[44]   Lavater, quoted in Bail, *Etat des Juifs*, 30.
[45]   Anthony Ashley Cooper, Third Earl of Shaftesbury, *Characteristics of Men, Manners,
      Opinions, Times*, ed. Lawrence Klein (Cambridge, 1999). Klein claims that Shaftesbury's
      work found an audience right throughout the eighteenth century – and, seemingly,
      into the nineteenth.
[46]   Shaftesbury, quoted in Bail, *Etat des Juifs*, 29.

the crescent on the ruins of Athens. When he accosts you, he is round-about; he makes a deep bow and speaks in a soft voice; one is always tempted to say to him: "*Speak up, and stand straight.*" His language is a sort of slang, a Germanic jargon mixed with corrupted Hebrew, unknown to those around him, and very useful for perpetuating ignorance or masking deceit.[47]

We have seen the power of Catholic narration in making this degradation part of the punishment for the crime of Jesus' death. However, in stories such as the one told by Bail, it was linked to power and its loss, as though Jews and Judaism could not keep up with modernity. Indeed, not only Bail but also Beugnot and Lancastel told the story of a nation that was once powerful, maintaining a monopoly in trade. But by the end of the sixteenth century, overtaken by the opulence and activities of Christian merchants, of industry, and of the progress of science, this same nation was left standing still "like a tree, which, in the middle of a delightful garden, can only produce dead man's fruit."[48] Such descriptions echo Enlightenment depictions of Jews as eternal, static, and unable to change with a changing world.[49] By the nineteenth century, the Jews existed as an obstinate and barely tolerated *imperium in imperio*; "plunged in ignorance, degraded by misery, deadened by a long exile."[50] In their bid to enrich themselves, they used "fraudulent measures" to cheat Christians,[51] and they refused in the face of moral reprobation to mix with surrounding populations, be it in terms of ritual, custom, morality, and language, or most important, blood. Whence such stubbornness? Part of the blame had to be placed on the Talmud, for over centuries it had "restrained, shrunken and stifled" the Jews, making them "superstitious, timid, extravagant, [and] short-sighted."[52] All four writers agreed on the evil nature of the Talmud and its influence on Jewish behaviour, although not one of them appears to have gone to the source itself: none

---

[47] Bail, *Etat des Juifs*, 160.
[48] Ibid., 134.
[49] Schechter, 38, 55.
[50] Arthur-Auguste Beugnot, "Notice sur un projet formé à Varsovie de publier une TRADUCTION FRANÇAISE DU TALMUD, précédée d'un Essai intitulé: THÉORIE DU JUDAISME APPLIQUÉE A LA RÉFORME DES JUIFS," *Revue encyclopédique ou Analyse raisonnée des productions les plus Remarquables dans la littérature, les sciences et les arts* 38 (1828): 24.
[51] Lancastel, 87.
[52] Bail, *Etat des Juifs*, 134.

of them offered quotes from it or specific references to it. Indeed, Bail, Beugnot, Tourette, and Lancastel argued in general terms, using similar categories to Drach in his condemnation of this work. Thus, the Talmud was blasphemous, nonsensical, and dangerous: it was an outrage to good sense, "a monument to the misdemeanours of the human mind"[53] and a work of absurdly extravagant superstition. Most important, perhaps, it was "antisocial," producing "evil,"[54] dangerous for its nonsense and imprecations against Christians,[55] and for its influence over "Jews of little learning."[56] For Beugnot, the Talmud was a "poison" that should not be made available to the general public, a useful tool for a people "dedicated to misery and animated by the most hostile of sentiments towards those nations foreign to its religion."[57] And just as the Jew dissembled, the Talmud was inaccessible: not for the Jews the transparency of the good citizen.[58]

In fact, as we have seen, all those who attacked Judaism, attacked the Talmud. The criticism laid out here is, of course, resonant of these men's Catholic contemporaries – one need only think back to Drach. But at the same time, these essayists could equally draw on Enlightenment rhetoric, such as that of Voltaire, or the encyclopaedists, where the Talmud was depicted as fantastical and ridiculous. Even Jewish scholarship echoed this mainstream view of the Talmud as thoroughly discredited and attempted to recast Jewish religiosity in terms of biblical Judaism, criticizing Talmudic practices as "superstitious," "overly stringent," or "contradictory to the findings of modern-day science."[59] If Judaism was a medium through which one could make sense of the world, it would seem that the Talmud – the source of Jewish law, and thus of Judaism as it was practised – was the means through which to make sense of Judaism. For figures such as Voltaire, it highlighted the superstitious nature of religion. According to Catholic criticism, it proved that Judaism had no basis in credible theological reasoning.

---

[53] Beugnot, *Notice*, 29. Tourette focused less on the Talmud than on the role of the rabbi in the community.
[54] Lancastel, 19.
[55] Bail, *Etat des Juifs*, 28.
[56] Lancastel, 13.
[57] Beugnot, *Notice*, 20.
[58] For Rousseau's discussion of this notion, see Schechter, 62.
[59] Berkovitz, "Jewish Scholarship and Identity," 20.

As we saw in the first chapter, the French image of the stubborn, separate, and degraded Jew was also shared across the ideological spectrum.
The nature of the Jewish question had perhaps evolved since the days
when the French knew no other role than that of subjects of a most
Catholic king, but – in terms of the way in which Jews were viewed –
the new world clearly retained traces of the old. The self-conscious
even-handedness with which Beugnot approached his subjects was not
evident in a later article, in which he reviewed a project to translate the
Talmud into French.[60] In 1828, the Abbé Luigi Chiarini (professor of
ancient oriental languages at Warsaw Royal University) made known his
intention to translate the Talmud into French, in the hope that if Christians were familiar with its content, they would "acquire the means to
confound the rabbis' bad faith and make all Jews aware of the enormity
of their errors, and consequently crush talmudism."[61] Beugnot, a devout
Catholic, wrote to respond to this proposal, and he was categorical in his
objections to the project. Beugnot could not see how the translation of
this work would change the opinions of the Jews, who, in Beugnot's eyes,
were "obstinate," motivated by hatred for non-Jews[62] and characterised
by "hateful habits, hereditary vices and degrading cupidity."[63] Beugnot
made another borrowing in his criticism of Jewish cosmopolitanism. For
him, this could especially be seen in the behaviour of rabbis, whose theology took nothing from the nations in which they dwelt, but rather was
self-sufficient, passing with ease from one nation to another, planting
no roots, and "taking no regrets."[64] Such criticism was not new. In his
Philosophical Dictionary, Voltaire sought to make the point that everything in Jewish culture had been borrowed from others. Indeed, as he
saw it, the only thing that the Jews could claim true ownership of was
"their stubbornness, their new superstitions, and their hallowed usury."[65]
Bail made a similar criticism, although he couched it in terms of Jewish
creativity – or the lack thereof. Thus, for example, Jewish literature, written in sterile "*Rabbinic Hebrew*"[66] had produced few books worthy of

---

[60] Beugnot, "Notice".
[61] Quoted in ibid., 25.
[62] Ibid., 24.
[63] Ibid., 26.
[64] Beugnot, *Les Juifs*, 246.
[65] Voltaire, *Philosophical Dictionary*, 499, quoted in Hertzberg, 303.
[66] Bail, *Etat des Juifs*, 120.

being read. Bail also traced the history of bills of exchange – a Jewish invention – and found that their influence was to make "the treasures of the Jews [become] invisible; they were everywhere, but left no trace."[67] In the eyes of Beugnot and Bail, cosmopolitan Jews may have managed to find some type of belonging everywhere they lived, but this also meant that they truly belonged nowhere.

These were the men, degenerate, cosmopolitan, and secretly powerful, who were the subjects of the Jewish question. Although it may have been possible to an extent to make sense of their sorry state as the result of a sad history, the Jews had used up their quota of tolerance. Those who had taken charge of the world wanted the Jew now to adapt to fit within it. It was time for action, and it is hardly surprising that, having depicted the Jews as they did, Beugnot, Bail, Tourette, and Lancastel all found that the Jews' place in the nation needed to change. For Bail, the serious issue of Jewish national allegiance remained to be resolved: were Jews capable of finding a balance between the duties and obligations imposed by citizenship and their national prejudices and superstitions? Did the Jews themselves even wish to be emancipated? Bail did not believe so. Some, he argued, merely wished to take advantage of the benefits of citizenship without shouldering its responsibilities. Others believed that emancipation would mean the weakening of Jewish law and ultimately the end of Judaism. Lancastel agreed. Napoleon had convened the Sanhedrin because he could not accept that Jews could maintain a dual allegiance; yet they, awaiting the announcement of the return of their fatherland, could not renounce it.

In harking back to the Sanhedrin, Lancastel was recalling an important distinction. For the days of the meetings of the Assembly of Notables and the Sanhedrin were marked by ongoing disagreements between secular and orthodox Jews or, along broad brush lines, the Sephardic Jews of the southwest and the Ashkenazic Jews of the east of France.[68] It was generally believed that the Sephardic Jews of Bordeaux had lived up to the trust placed in them by the Revolutionary government, *fusing* into the French nation. In contrast, the greater part of France's Jewish population,

---

[67] Ibid., 101.
[68] On the Assembly of Notables and the Sanhedrin, see, for example, Paula Hyman, *The Jews of Modern France* (Berkeley, 1998), chap. 3, "The Napoleonic Synthesis," 37–52.

living in Alsace, remained "unworthy of admission to common law."[69] It was these latter on whom these authors turned their gaze. For although they generally referred to Jews as a whole, what they depicted was the perceived image of the Jew of Alsace specifically, and not just for those who were writing in response to the essay question set by the Strasbourg Society.

Through all these writings, the Jews of Alsace were a constant presence. It was clear to Lancastel that the problem was that "almost all Alsatian Jews" refused to recognise the decisions of the Sanhedrin he so admired.[70] Bail believed that thirty years after emancipation, despite the best efforts of legislators (and of some Jews), "legislation that was beneficial, gentle and equitable had produced no noticeable improvement" in the Jews of Alsace.[71] Paula Hyman has shown that well into the nineteenth century, Jews in Alsace continued largely to live in poverty throughout the many villages that still dot the Alsatian landscape. Moreover, they were still clustering in the professions linked to the commercial middleman,[72] into which they had been pushed centuries before, through limitations placed on the occupations they could practice, by rulers, the Church, and organisations such as guilds that required that their members be Christian. In the eyes of their critics, members of the Alsatian Jewish community were perceived to be practising the worst type of middleman's work – that of the moneylender or usurer – in overwhelming proportions. For such critics, this was the strongest example of the way in which members of this community were bad citizens, because usury – long condemned by the Church – was "exploitation," a plague on society, threatening to "plunge" Alsatian farmers "into misery"[73] and making Alsace the "victim" of Jewish immorality.[74] In Beugnot's eyes, the practice of usury was the strongest criticism that could be levelled at the Jews, and Lancastel saw it as the primary evil in their story, although he did argue that Christians who practiced usury should be punished and watched just like their

[69] Lancastel, 4.
[70] Ibid., 21.
[71] Bail, *Etat des Juifs*, 88.
[72] Hyman, *Emancipation*. See also David Cohen, "L'Image du juif dans la société française en 1843, d'après les rapports des préfets," *Revue d'histoire économique et sociale* 55, no. 1–2 (1977): 70–91.
[73] Lancastel, 130.
[74] Tourette, 20.

Jewish fellow citizens.[75] The continued practice of usury was perceived as being the clearest indication that a significant group still resisted the ascent towards civilisation. It was another of the unacceptable qualities that all critics chose to see in the Jews. Moreover, while persecution may have contributed to the Jews' usurious practices, in general it was the Jews themselves who, by dint of their own weakness and greed, were primarily responsible for their situation.

The Alsatian Jew was not only a scourge on French society, however; he was also a bad Jew. Commentators who distinguished between good (Mosaic) Judaism and bad (Rabbinic) Judaism generally associated these with good Sephardic Jews and bad Alsatian Jews. The Judaism practised in Alsace was that ruled by the Talmud in all its most negative connotations. For example, the Talmud encouraged usury, because the hatred it engendered enabled the Jew to demand criminally high rates of interest from his neighbour. Thus, if a Jew followed the teachings of the Talmud, this cast doubt on his ability to regenerate.[76] The Alsatian Jew threatened the nation in that he challenged the most fundamental requirements of citizenship. What was to be done about him? Just like their forebears in the Constituent Assembly, these men believed that the Jews could not be trusted to take control of their own fate. Nonetheless, "arbitrary power" was not the answer, but rather, strong and reliable laws that would instil in the Jews "those notions of order, wisdom and patience" that they lacked.[77] Similarly, the prefect of the Pyrénées-Orientales, so discomfited by the local Gypsy population, was nonetheless confident that "rigorous policing, laws that are gentle but vigilant, and paternal care would give back this degenerate race the dignity of the morals it had lost in the oblivion and misery that follow it."[78]

Like a good social scientist, Tourette believed that prejudice – on the part of Christians – and "superstitious practices" – such as the continued use of the "Hebrew language and its characters"[79] – still stood in the way of what he called "social fusion."[80] In the early part of the nineteenth

[75] Lancastel, 122.
[76] Berkovitz, *Shaping*, 34. On the Talmud as damaging to the Jewish character, see also Jacob Katz, *From Prejudice to Destruction*, 41–2, and Hertzberg, chap. 9.
[77] Beugnot, *Les Juifs*, 47.
[78] Bourguet, "Race et Folklore," 812.
[79] Tourette, 37, 27.
[80] Tourette, 9.

century, there was a growing use by both non-Jewish commentators and Jewish community leaders of the term *fusion sociale* to define the goal of Jewish modernisation. The term, introduced during the Restoration to discuss the question of the success of Jewish emancipation, assumed the rejection by Jews of those practices that distinguished them.[81] Just as Jewish advocates of *régénération* sought to take ownership of the term, so the chief rabbi of France, Abraham de Cologna, sought to dissociate political from religious assimilation (or fusion).[82] Tourette saw a challenge in the notion of fusion: to ensure that the "way" was not merely shown to the Jews but also opened up and made passable.[83] He was optimistic about the prospect of success. He believed the Jewish question could be solved much like a mathematical equation, with "calculations."[84] The "sought-after reforms" could be achieved through the combination of the following:

1. the propagation of knowledge among the Jews [. . .] 2. the reward that will be offered to them so that they enter into agricultural habits and interests; 3. the application of Israelite youth to the industrial arts, and its calling to honourable professions.[85]

Bail, something of an impossibilist, stood firm against this tide of optimism. As far as he was concerned, the Jews represented a danger, waiting patiently in their oppression for a time when a "universal revolution" would enable them "to dominate all nations."[86] Thus, the benefits of Jewish emancipation had to be weighed against the inconvenience it could cause to the people among whom the Jews lived.[87] Bail died not

---

[81]   Berkovitz, *Shaping*, 128–9. See also idem, "The French Revolution and the Jews: Assessing the Cultural Impact," *AJS Review* 20, no. 1 (1995): 74. Stuart Woolf notes that 'fusion' was an "operational word in the search for stability" after Brumaire, implying reconciliation of former political opponents from the Revolution and an end to social distinctions. Woolf, 109.

[82]   This was a letter written in response to Silvestre de Sacy's letter that formed the basis of the discussion in Chapter 1. De Cologna, *Réflexions addressées à M. S. de S.* (Paris, 1817), quoted in Posener, "The Immediate Economic and Social Effects of the Emancipation of the Jews in France," *Jewish Social Studies* 1 (1939), 325.

[83]   Tourette, 9.

[84]   Ibid., 4.

[85]   Ibid.

[86]   Bail, *Etat des Juifs*, 6.

[87]   Ibid., 80.

long after the publication of his second work, in 1827. Had he lived to read considerations of the Jewish question that were published some two decades later, he may well have felt that his caution was vindicated. For twenty years after the essay writers of the 1820s had turned their attention to the Jews in their midst, Alsatian Jews were still seen to be resisting any changes to their lives, even if these were designed to make them into good citizens. The question apparently remained the same: how were the Jews to be made into citizens? Among those who set out to examine the situation of Alsatian Jewry in the world of 1840s France were Cerfberr de Medelsheim, a journalist, and Théophile Hallez, a lawyer to the royal court and a republican. Although twenty years and a revolution separate these works from one another, and although there are vital differences in the way these men approached the Jewish question, there are also striking similarities in the ways they dealt with their subjects, providing a fascinating insight into both the constancy and the changing nature of the Jewish question.

Who were these two authors? Hallez's words are a resounding echo of those of his fellow citizens a generation before.[88] Indeed, Hallez let his readers know that he took inspiration from Beugnot's "excellent" work of 1824, *Les Juifs Occident*. Hallez claimed to have been motivated to set pen to paper by the publication of a document written for the High Court for an anonymous appeal regarding the Jews in Alsace. In fact, he may have been the author of this work, probably written in 1844 (reference is made to the Jews of Alsace in 1844), which discussed the validity and relevance of the *more judaïco* oath in Alsace.[89] (In early-nineteenth-century France, use of *more judaïco* was widespread and intentionally humiliating to Jews, especially in the East of the nation, although the practice was not limited to this region.) Oaths such as *more judaïco* were understood to be a religious act. Throughout the nineteenth century, those who chose to see Jews as separate by virtue of their religion could choose to understand logically that they must have an oath that was

---

[88] Théophile Hallez, *Des Juifs en France. De leur état moral et politique depuis les premiers temps de la monarchie jusqu'à nos jours* (Paris, 1845).

[89] "Observations sur le serment *more judaïco*." F¹⁹ 11031: Plaintes et réclamations contre faits d'intolérance, 1820–1902.

unique to them.[90] This was the crux of Hallez' argument: as an advocate *for* the *more judaïco*, Hallez was driven by his obsession with the need to maintain the "beautiful unity" of his nation, for he loved it truly. This is typical of the one posing the Jewish question. Whoever the Jew might be, his critic was the nation; he defined it, he sat at its very heart, and thus he knew and loved it best. For example, François Hell, the source of the false receipts for Jewish loans in Alsace in 1778, cast himself as the patriot and protector of an innocent and moral Alsatian peasantry.[91] Hallez, for his part, wished to see only "Frenchmen in France" and the disappearance of divisions and hatreds based on religion. What was a Frenchman? He was a patriot, fully aware of the "holy and inviolable duties"[92] that citizens owed to their nation, and who, to enjoy the advantages that society had to offer, was prepared to give up the exclusiveness of his own individuality. The Jews were a problem, in Hallez's eyes, precisely because they had maintained their "national individuality unchanging and intact" in the midst of French society,[93] and the continued resistance of what he called

[90] Phyllis Albert has argued that the perpetuation of the *more judaïco* suggests the persistence of hostility towards Jews in official quarters, and particularly in the Ministry of Justice. She notes that as early as 1826, a supreme court decision ruled that Jews could take regular oaths, but that the practice was not brought to an end until the middle of the century. Jewish communities worked hard to change this practice, and Albert defines three distinct periods in this campaign: first, between 1809 and 1815, demands in the courts that Jews swear *more judaïco*, for example, on a Torah scroll, were increasing, while Jewish communities sought to limit oath-taking to swearing on a Bible. Despite support from the Ministère des Cultes, this campaign was unsuccessful. From 1816, Jewish representatives changed their tack and rejected the validity of the special oath – and with it, any distinction between Jew and non-Jew – entirely. Over this period, they were bolstered in their cause through a number of court rulings in their favour; in particular, the high courts ruled that Jews might not be coerced into swearing *more judaïco*. Although these rulings did not bring about the abolition of the *more judaïco*, its usage did decline. Crémieux was instrumental in this campaign. Around 1830, he was in Paris, becoming involved in the Central Consistory as a delegate from Marseilles. He was to serve for fifteen years, including being vice-president, then president. Among his causes was the abolition of the *more judaïco*. Albert details the campaigns of what she calls "antisemitic polemicists" who from around 1847, began to call for the re-introduction of the *more judaïco* oath. Ultimately, even though the Ministère de Justice could have ended the practice with a directive to the courts, the oath was abolished because of court-generated independent rulings, and not due to any official act. Indeed, the Ministère continued to pursue rabbis who refused to administer the oath, until all legal avenues were closed. Albert, "Jewish Oath".
[91] See Schechter's discussion of François Hell's rhetoric in Schechter, 69–70.
[92] Hallez, i–ii.
[93] Ibid., xii.

the "Jewish race" to the nation's assimilatory force formed the main focus of Hallez's work. From the opening pages of *Des Juifs en France*, Hallez set up a strong and resonant image of Jewish isolation with the words of the Jew Shylock in Shakespeare's *The Merchant of Venice*: "I will buy with you, sell with you, talk with you, walk with you, and so on; but I will not eat with you, drink with you, nor pray with you."[94] In fact, Hallez's criticisms are echoes of the reports submitted in 1843 by prefects in regions where there were Jewish populations (they had been asked to provide observations on the Jews in their respective departments). The prefect of Bordeaux, for example, observed that while the lack of mixed marriages resulted in a "pure" Jewish race, "this race, which has not interbred with the people, is physically polluted."[95] The responses of these prefects also show a fascinating continuity with their forebears, in that they were still using vocabulary such as "crafty, lazy, indolent" (but also "sober, tolerant" and "polite") to describe the Jewish populations in their departments. Hallez also looked to the past. He was critical of the generosity shown by his forebears in 1789. "Seduced by the principles of philanthropy that are sacred to all," they had not been sufficiently severe with the Jewish population. Where they had seen "oppressed individuals, and an exiled religion,"[96] they should have recognised that it was the Jews "alone," who stubbornly persisted in their isolation and their hatred of the French, making it "a point of honour" to remain a nation within a nation.[97] The Jewish desire for separateness, he argued, had not been sufficiently taken into account, and yet this desire was so overwhelming that it shaped all of Jewish life in France.[98] Now, fifty years after the Jews had been granted citizenship, the decisions of the Sanhedrin that Hallez, like his forebear Lancastel, found so worthy of admiration, had not become practice, and "obstinate" Jews had "maintained their aversion for property ownership and useful industry, their predilection for monetary transactions, and their fraudulent and usurious customs towards their

---

[94] Hallez, x.
[95] Quoted in Cohen, 83.
[96] Hallez, 162.
[97] Ibid., iii. This perception of religion remaining a barrier to assimilation was echoed in the 1843 reports. See Cohen, 91.
[98] Hallez, 160.

non-Israelite compatriots."[99] For Hallez's Jew was a usurer, and he was Alsatian.

In the eyes of Cerfberr de Medelsheim, too, "the type and prototype of the Jew as he is described and as we know him in general," was the Jew of Alsace.[100] But so was Cerfberr himself. Indeed, Cerfberr's family pedigree reached back into one of Alsace's most prominent Jewish families. Cerfberr was the cousin of Louis Ratisbonne, a Jewish poet, and a member of the Alsatian Jewish family that included the apostates Théodore and Alphonse. Cerfberr's father had converted to Christianity before Cerfberr was born, but there is no doubt that he was very aware of his origins. "Even though the German Jew normally dies without having made his final penitence," he wrote, perhaps with his own family in mind:

sometimes he mends his ways, especially when he has made his fortune. These Jews are then truly good and generous; they are charitable without being ostentatious, and they live neither in splendour nor in pride; they give their children a solid and liberal education; they are useful citizens, and the fatherland can count on them in times of danger; they are honest and loyal, they recognise the errors of their nation, and since they are not obliged by any interest to hide their feelings, they confess the truth and are almost all converts to Christianity."[101]

Cerfberr was a writer by profession, and at the time of writing *Juifs de France*, he was working for the Ministry of the Interior, implementing the program of a government that saw public order and moral rehabilitation as the two-pronged solution to social ills, by creating schools in prisons. Perhaps it was Cerfberr's links to the Jewish community in Alsace that inspired him to apply this thinking to this other social ill, and he would certainly appear to have struck a chord. His work sold 20,000 copies and, as Cerfberr himself announced to the readers of its second edition, was "loudly lauded in the daily newspapers."[102]

In the eyes of these two men, the Jews of Alsace had not changed. Not only their customs, but also their character and even their physiognomy had remained the same.[103] They were still "ignorant, fanatical, usurious,"

[99] Ibid., 264.
[100] Cerfberr, *Juifs de France*, 46.
[101] Ibid., 63.
[102] Ibid., preface.
[103] Hallez, iv.

and superstitious,[104] as well as wily cheaters of Christians. Moreover, the Alsatian Jew remained a bad Jew so that, although he would never come to the table "without covering his head, reciting a few prayers and performing an ablution," this latter only reached "as far as the fingertips."[105] Worst of all, however, was their continued practice of usury. Using "shameful and perfidious methods," the Jews had variously "amassed half of Alsace's property," or were "ruining the country."[106] This was the way Jews served the *patrie*, in return for the granting of "the dignity and all the rights of citizenship."[107] Yet, although for Cerfberr usury was "the great plague of our time,"[108] he nonetheless found it perfectly understandable that Jews should have stooped to using trickery and fraud. After all, were they not merely "satisfying the sordid demands of their persecutors?" Cerfberr painted the Jews as perpetual victims: the "scape-goats of the centuries." To any Jew born into the world, he noted, could be said the "terrible" words of Dante: *Abandon hope, all ye who enter here.*[109] Perhaps seeing his own ancestors only too clearly in this tale, Cerfberr found that in the midst of "all types of debasement," the Jews had nonetheless shown "admirable patience and deep self-denial" and that, if the Jews seemed worthy of punishment because their morality emerged a little the weaker from this sad tale, they should not be blamed.[110] Rather, with the memory of long persecutions in mind, they should be pitied, and "perhaps even forgiven."[111]

Nonetheless, fifty years had shown that forgiveness and pity alone were not sufficient to make citizens out of degenerate Alsatian Jews. What was to be done? Cerfberr and Hallez drew on the ideology of their regime, itself preoccupied with the improvement of those on the margins of society. Governments during the July Monarchy took a paternalistic view of groups like the poor, prisoners, or prostitutes, combining concern with a stern morality. Yet where the regime saw a Christian morality, but not necessarily Christianity itself, as the means to rehabilitation, for Cerfberr

[104] Ibid., 194.
[105] Cerfberr, 60.
[106] Ibid., 48.
[107] Hallez, ix, 91.
[108] Cerfberr, 48.
[109] Ibid., 6.
[110] Ibid., 135.
[111] Ibid., 5.

the Catholic, the Jews had only two choices: to renounce Judaism (or undertake its complete reform) or to give up their French citizenship. In Judaism's present state, the two were incompatible.[112] In contrast with Cerfberr, Hallez believed that Jews could become Frenchmen without becoming Christians. This would not be a straightforward task, however, for Hallez himself was "gathering proof that shows that the Jews have never wanted and still do not want to merge with the rest of the nation."[113] Nonetheless, like Beugnot on whose work he drew, Hallez was nothing if not an optimist. Like the government he served, he believed in the reforming power of education.[114] "By free will or by force," Hallez sought, "with all [his] heart," to bring about the fusion of the Jews into the French nation.[115] After all, the "Jewish race" was in possession of "admirable faculties, which would be of great use to the country, if they decided to orient them in the direction of the general interest."[116] Apparently, in the eyes of Hallez, even "fused," the "Jewish race" would remain just that, retaining its distinctive qualities – and thus its separateness.

The experience of Simon Deutz had shown that for Catholics who found an echo of their views in newspapers such as the *Quotidienne* and the *Gazette du Languedoc*, the Jew was inseparable from his Judaism. Was Hallez's attitude a legacy of Church ideology that he carried with him, despite the scorn with which he treated religion? There is a striking constancy in these writings, a generation apart, and that is the presence of traditional Catholic anti-Judaism. It would appear that, where the Jew was concerned, Catholic mythology held a particular power and resonance for many Frenchmen. The devoutly and proudly Catholic Cerfberr saw Jews as powerful and vindictive yet, at the same time, forever marked with the brand of deicide. But even Hallez, the fervent republican, noted with disdain that there was nothing to stop his headstrong subjects from persisting "in their superstitious practices" and continuing "to wait for the messiah who they crucified eighteen centuries ago,"[117] if they wished to do so (although this would be at the expense of citizenship). And it was Hallez who, once again underscoring the apparent inability of Jews

[112] Ibid., introduction.
[113] Hallez, xxx.
[114] Ibid., 265.
[115] Ibid., 272, 276.
[116] Ibid., 279.
[117] Ibid., v.

to change their ways, stated that the Jews of Alsace "were in 1844 what they had been in 1789."[118]

But were they? For the nation itself had changed significantly, and as society and the things it held dear changed, so did its evils – and with them the nature of the Jew. Yet if anything remained constant, it was that Jews continued to represent what was beyond the bounds of safety and acceptability. What had become unacceptable in French society? Beugnot, Bail, and their contemporaries lived in a world where it was possible to feel in control of the nation's future, and thus to be optimistic about it. Catholics could could find proof that the Church had been restored to its hallowed position in France, and liberals that the Revolution had left an important legacy in Louis XVIII's charter. Moreover, this world was being efficiently managed by a strong administrative corps that had its roots in the ancien régime and the Napoleonic era.

But the Revolution of 1830 had brought with it great changes, and by the 1840s, both Catholics like Cerfberr and republicans like Hallez felt under siege and alienated from the very administration in which Lancastel had placed so much faith and which to a great extent was responsible for France's modernisation.[119] Their ideals had been compromised by Louis-Philippe and a succession of prime ministers in the name of what was seen by both left and right as individualistic opportunity. Men like Cerfberr and Hallez were disillusioned by the outcome of the July Revolution; they were anxious about the future of the nation and the survival of the things they held dear. Hallez, harking back to the greatness of Napoleon and his Sanhedrin, found it necessary to write because he felt so strongly regarding the dangers of disunity in a society that had "so often been shaken to its very foundations."[120] In the midst of Catholic struggles for the freedom to establish Church-run schools, and tirades by men such as Louis Veuillot against the irreligion of the age from the helm of the Catholic newspaper, the *Univers*, the Catholic Cerfberr saw religion being attacked "from all sides: in its ritual, its traditions, its ministers and its

---

[118] Ibid., 240.
[119] See Christopher Johnson, "The Revolution of 1830 in French Economic History," in *1830 in France*, ed. John Merriman (New York, 1975), 172 and passim.
[120] Hallez, xii.

works." "Cold materialism and disappointing selfishness" had left their imprint on his world.[121]

Who better to symbolise the disempowerment of good citizens like Cerfberr and Hallez than the bad citizen who was personified in the figure of the dissembling, greedy, untrustworthy Jew? The idea of the powerful Jew was not new. François Hell – of the forged receipts – cast the Jews of Alsace as malevolent and powerful. In 1806, Bonald wrote of the same population that they were the region's "high and powerful lords."[122] This rhetoric continued into the 1820s. In 1824, the *Ami de la religion* noted how authorities in Frankfurt and in Russia had placed restrictions on the Jewish communities in their jurisdiction, because they were becoming concerned "about the Jews' progress, about their growing wealth, and the means of which many of them make use to increase it even more."[123] The perception of the Jews as powerful and dissimulating clearly continued through the 1830s. In 1835, a reviewer of Halévy's opera *La Juive* described fifteenth-century Jews as hoarding "vast treasures that they removed from circulation and enjoyed mysteriously."[124] In the same year, one author was promising several volumes unveiling a Jewish conspiracy:

There is a class of men unfortunately too little known, whose principles of invasion and expansion would become disastrous, if the progressive pace of its proliferation and ambitious plans were not stopped: *this is the class of the Jews.*

Since the emancipation of the Jews in France, their number has increased so much, that in the provincial towns where barely a few hundred could be counted, they currently number in the thousands. What has not been taken over by their usurious designs? In what business have they not, through their hidden and skilfully devised ruses, ruined a mass of respectable businessmen? Where is the brilliant fortune that is not theirs? [...] Thus this singular people, apart from all others although living among them, has disastrous and destructive principles, plans for power and invasion that must be revealed, made known, and the Sovereigns must be alerted or rather begged to stop them!!! [125]

---

[121] Cerfberr, xviii.
[122] Bonald, "Sur les Juifs," 365.
[123] *L'Ami de la religion*, 15 September 1824.
[124] *La Quotidienne*, 27 February 1835.
[125] This extract is from a publisher's prospectus, which appeared under the same title as that below. The promised volumes appear not to have been published. The work is

And in the Legitimist *Gazette du Languedoc* the headline of an article on the activities of the Rothschild family announced, in a rare use of capitals: "THE JEWS HAVE THE UPPER HAND EVERYWHERE."[126]

This alarmist tone set the scene for the years to come. Authors who decried the usurious practices of the Jews of Alsace might be concerned or even outraged by the prospect of this usury, yet not fearful of it. But the notion of Jewish plans for domination of France, and perhaps the world, evoked tones that did not fall far short of hysteria. Hallez, who saw vindictiveness in the Jews' separateness, believed the latter potentially to "forever remain a danger to society."[127] Cerfberr saw powerful Jews everywhere; they were "hungry wolves,"[128] or alternately birds of prey, tangling honest men in their "deadly network."[129] They made use of their sorry history to claim "at the slightest provocation" and "in the name of ancient persecutions, the broadest immunities and tolerances." With "all the favours and especially all the advantages," their hand was in every transaction, and more:

There is no post that they do not desire, no position that they do not exploit, and they, who number barely one hundred thousand in France, fill, thanks to their insistence, proportionately more posts than the Catholic and Protestant religions. Their disastrous influence makes itself felt especially in those affairs that weigh the heaviest on the country's fortune; there is no enterprise of which the Jews do not have a large part, no public loan that they do not monopolise, no disaster that they have not prepared and from which they do not profit.[130]

The lowly Jew who in the 1820s could still be cast as a passive subject had by the 1840s become powerful and active, aggressively pursuing those who challenged him. Revealing of this new Jew was the attitude of Hallez and Cerfberr towards their subjects. Where men like Bail and Beugnot had been at pains to point out their impartiality in their treatment of passive subjects, Hallez and Cerfberr saw themselves standing up against their

---

Renault Bécourt, *Conspiration universelle du judaïsme, entièrement dévoilée, dédiée à tous les souverains de l'Europe, à leurs ministres, aux hommes d'état et généralement à toutes les classes de la société, menacées de ses perfides projets* (Nancy, 1835).

[126] *La Gazette du Languedoc*, 25 September 1835.

[127] Hallez, 162.

[128] Cerfberr, xxxiii.

[129] Ibid., 172.

[130] Ibid., xviii.

powerful protagonists. They made much of the nobility of their actions and the courage that their task necessitated. As Hallez wrote, he was aware that, in seeking to make Jews adopt the burdens of citizenship along with its rights, he would be inviting hostility and accusations and that attempts would be made to throw an unfavourable light on his work. Certain of the necessity of the task, Hallez allowed himself to believe that the book would "speak for itself."[131] Despite his most sincere protestations, Cerfberr clearly saw himself in opposition to the Jews, describing them as his "adversaries," who themselves furnished him "with arms with which to fight them."[132] Indeed, Cerfberr cited "a veritable conspiracy," funded by "the denarii of a famous foreign banker," allegedly working against him.[133]

Yet while the prospect of the powerful Jew might have been alarming, men like Hallez and Cerfberr, and those who followed, were to take this image even further. The Jew to those who wrote on the topic in the 1820s was in a sense like his forebear who, according to medieval Catholic teaching, could possess horns and a tail and still be a concrete human entity. By the 1840s, the Jew was becoming utterly inhuman. Hallez complained that the Jews distinguished between their "brothers" – or co-religionists – and Frenchmen, demanding no interest from the former, but practising "sordid and merciless usury" towards the latter. They took sons from mothers and the last penny from a poor family, all the while asking to be treated like brothers. But "why?" asked an exasperated Hallez of his subjects, "why do you want us to treat you like Frenchmen, when you don't want to stop being Jews?"[134]

What did Hallez understand by "stopping" being a Jew? Was it the renunciation of usury? The "greedy" and "hostile"[135] Jews who were the focus of Hallez's lament were Jew-usurers, one term implying the other. Under "Juif" in the *Dictionnaire de l'Académie française* could be found the following definition:

JEW: We do not put this word here to represent the name of a Nation, but rather, because it is used figuratively in certain sentences in the Language.

[131] Hallez, xxx.
[132] Cerfberr, 167.
[133] Ibid., introduction.
[134] Hallez, ix.
[135] Ibid., 150.

Thus a man who practises usury and who sells goods at exorbitant prices is called a *Jew: He is a Jew, he makes loans at fifteen percent; That merchant is a real Jew*. It is used, in the familiar style, to describe all those who demonstrate a great greed for money and ardour in making it. It is said proverbially that *A man is as rich as a Jew*, to mean that he is very rich, etc., etc.[136]

For Cerfberr, too, the word Jew held greater meaning. In his own posing of the Jewish question, he asked whether the Jews had "ceased to be Jews in the negative sense given to the word, so as to become French."[137] Cerfberr and Hallez were presaging the break between the meaning imparted to the word Jew, and the Jew himself. And while in the eyes of Hallez, a Jew could be any usurious member of that religion from Alsace, ultimately none was to epitomise this negative understanding of Jew better than the Jew par excellence: the Baron James de Rothschild. It was Cerfberr who captured the metamorphosis of the Rothschild-Jew, from lowly Alsatian Jew of "degraded exterior," and "shifty look," to powerful, dissembling German baron:

In effect, take the most disgusting Jew, the most ignorant and crass, in the most tattered getup, with the most mutilated language, have him washed, his hair combed and face shaved, fit his feet in boots that are not yet worn at the heel, dress him in nearly-new clothing; to his white shirt fix imitation buttons for 39 sols each, put his mushroom head to the service of a fixed-up hat [...] slip a few crowns in his pocket, and suddenly you will see this Quasimodo stand up straight and laugh: he will have a haughty air, a self-confident expression, lively gestures, arrogant and staccato speech, he will stroll like a dandy along Ghent Boulevard; and, with his Alsatian gibberish and his foreign accent, he will pass for a German Baron, and will dine out on his dupe that very evening at the Paris Café.[138]

Those who chose to pose the Jewish question in the nineteenth century were faced with the challenge to articulate radically new concepts, such as citizen, and nation, and to incorporate Jews into these. Catholics and republicans pooled resources as they formulated their understanding of the Jew and his place in society. Overwhelmingly, the Jew – and specifically, the Alsatian Jew – was cast as the anticitizen. In this sense, as Schechter argues, it was more straightforward to establish what the

[136] Quoted in Leroux, 1: 24.
[137] Cerfberr, 136.
[138] Ibid., 49.

ideal citizen was *not*: the Jew provided the prototype for this.[139] For the idea of citizenship itself was as open to competing definitions as the idea of nation has been shown to be. Thus, although the essayists speculated on whether it was possible to remake recalcitrant Jews as citizens, they were never to go beyond this speculation, because the Jewish question involved the invocation of a utopia. And this was to guarantee, not only that the question would be "repeatedly rehearsed,"[140] but also that it would remain unanswered – in a word, the most rhetorical of questions.

[139] Schechter, 77.
[140] Ibid., 109.

Conclusion

*T*HE INFLUENTIAL THINKER FÉLICITÉ DE LAMENNAIS HAD BURST
onto the Catholic scene in 1817 with his *Essai sur l'indifférence en
matière de religion*. But within eight years, he was to shift his focus
significantly, turning away from the spiritual world and directing his
gaze towards the material world and its woes. Ultimately, Lamennais was
to catholicise liberalism[1] and to be inscribed in the historiography as "the
father of Christian progressivism and sociology."[2] Such was his concern
for the dispossessed that in his own time, he attracted homage from
writers such as Georges Mathieu-Dairnvaell and Pierre Leroux. But in
fact, as early as 1825, Lamennais was stealing a march on his great admirers
who saw the Jews as the incarnation of the era. They, too, would link the
Jew solidly to the evils of the age, but not until the 1840s. Lamennais was
already laying the world's troubles at their door in 1825, associating them
with the world of heartless finance:

Meanwhile, politics, reduced to internal intrigues, and having become nothing more than a dispute over positions, the nation will rapidly lose all respect
and influence outside the country: it will be delivered up to men of money,
and as soon as they dream of making some profit from it, sold; perhaps to
a Jew.[3]

Lamennais's life encapsulates much of the story of ambivalence towards
Jews in early-nineteenth-century France that has been traced out here. In

---

[1] "Au lieu de trembler devant le libéralisme il fallait le catholiciser." Lamennais, *Correspondance*, II, 166. Letter of December 24, 1829. Quoted in Stearns, 63.
[2] Cholvy, 91.
[3] Lamennais, "De la Religion, considérée dans ses rapports avec l'ordre civil et politique,"
in *Oeuvres complètes*, 4: 28.

his writings may be found the mix of evolution and tradition that charac-
terises this sentiment. A committed Catholic in 1817, he could assign Jews
the lowly place that Catholicism had always reserved for them. But his
confidence that the restored Bourbon monarchy would deliver the world
that he hoped for was to be short-lived. In 1825, the recently crowned
Charles X held an elaborate coronation ceremony at the cathedral of
Reims. This overt and ostentatious display of Charles X's intention to
reinstate a national Church in France must have angered the committed
ultramontane Lamennais. At the same time, he was faced with constant
reminders of the legacy of the Revolution from which Jews had benefited so inordinately. The inclusion of Judaism and Protestantism in
the sacrilege law of 1825 incited Lamennais to express his outrage at the
notion that it could be legally recognised, "without the least opposition,"
that "to steal a table, a seat, or a tablecloth from a Calvinist church, or
a Bible from a synagogue, constituted a veritable sacrilege; and consequently, that the objects used in these different rituals are no more or
less sacred than those used in Catholic ritual."[4] Disillusioned with the
nation, threatened by a charter that maintained the religious freedom of
heretics and deicides, it would not have been difficult for this Catholic
priest, taught to see Jews as representative of all evil, to blame the latter
for troubles in his own world.

Lamennais, twice condemned by Rome, may ultimately have been lost
to the Church.[5] He may have become more concerned with the temporal
than the spiritual world. Nonetheless, in a reflection of the enduring
strength of Catholic ideology with regard to Jews, his faith remained
a keenly felt presence throughout all his work. The journal he established after 1830, entitled the *Avenir*, took as its motto *Dieu et la liberté*.
But as he was drawing on Catholic teaching in his depictions of Jews,
Lamennais was also adapting the Jew's role to a changing world. Where
once his writings on Jews, much like the speeches of Labouderie, were
overwhelmingly concerned with their historical place, Lamennais's anti-
Jewish writings came to be situated firmly in the present. For Lamennais,
this was a world in which brotherhood was discarded in favour of the
enslavement of many to a handful of men, who used their power to

---

[4] Ibid., 37.
[5] These were the two papal encyclicals, *Mirari vos*, in 1832, and *Singulari vos*, in 1834.

dominate. Indeed, his own writing would not have looked out of place in the works of Leroux, Hallez, or Toussenel. The Jews were "a people devoured by a thirst for gold,"[6] driven by their "abject avidity."[7] In his *Gospels*, supposedly set in ancient times, Lamennais managed in 1846 to present a very contemporary view of the Jew:

These were Christ's great adversaries, his most ardent enemies, those who believed that in killing him, they also killed the future, those to whom Jesus declared that the blood of all the prophets, spilled since the beginning of the world, would be asked for once more, for they were of the race of murderers, and the spirit of this race was still well and truly alive in them. Immortal here below, as evil will never be entirely destroyed here, it has survived here and will continue to survive here until the end. There will always be hypocritical Scribes and Pharisees, sepulchres on whom men walk without knowing it, doctors of the Law, who hold the key to knowledge and who do not enter there at all, and repel those who endeavour to enter. For that is another of their characteristics: they love the dark, they delight in it; the light would be an annoying disturbance for them, but most importantly, it would ruin their authority over the people.[8]

In this extract can be discerned a fundamental shift in his rhetoric; once again, a clear echo of the way in which the place of the Jew was evolving. For if in his early work, the Jews were a downtrodden, lowly people, thirty years later, he depicted a nebulous, powerful, Jewish world. Jews could no longer be described in terms of their guilt and lowly status. They were now symbols, or metaphors, for a greater evil.

Catholic thinking had taught its adherents to see the Jew as representative of all that was unacceptable. Those Catholics who felt vulnerable during the Restoration could choose to find a convenient scapegoat in the Jews. For the Jews had benefited from the very Revolution that had spelled the end of the Church's absolute legitimacy. As we have seen, Catholics such as Lamennais and Bonald understood the role of Catholicism in the post-Revolutionary world differently. Nonetheless, in this world, where God's presence could no longer be keenly felt, all Catholics had to come to terms with the fact that they were now no different from the Jew in the eyes of the law. The tone with which apostates addressed their former

---

6 Lamennais, *Esquisse d'une philosophie*, in *Oeuvres complètes*, 9: 455.
7 Idem., *Pensées diverses*, in ibid., 8: 466.
8 Idem., *Les Evangiles*, in ibid., 10: 270–1.

co-religionists is as clear as possible an indicator of the anxiety with which some Catholics viewed these new citizens and the difficulty they faced in acknowledging Jews as equals. And almost fifty years after Jews had been emancipated in France, some Catholics were still clinging to the notion that Jewish hatred for Christianity ran so deep that at least foreign Jews remained capable of committing brutal ritual killings.

Negative depictions may have been used by some to legitimate and explain their claims to represent the nation. But not by all. For some, the presence of Jews in French society was not an evil; on the contrary, Jews could serve as the ultimate example of the virtues of the new era. Jews were "good to think," in myriad ways.[9] Many liberals, and groups such as the Saint-Simonians, saw the Jew as a *good* example of the success of the republican integrative project. The depth of their belief is illustrated by the fact that one such as Adolphe Crémieux, who lived his Jewishness very publicly, was able to enjoy such success. But to return to ambivalence in a negative key: even Crémieux was attacked by the very press that normally showed him so much respect when he publicly came to the aid of his imprisoned coreligionists in Damascus. For those who identified with the Catholic tradition were not the only ones to project anxiety onto the Jewish population. Discussions of Jews in the context of the notion of citizenship endured beyond the Revolutionary debates. The Jewish question continued to be posed. As we have seen, in the eyes of adherents to the Revolutionary legacy, so concerned with creating a nation of ideal citizens, the Jew, still practising usury, still adhering to the precepts of the Talmud, still refusing to renounce his sense of belonging to Judaism, came to represent the anti-citizen par excellence. Yet over the course of the nineteenth century, the concepts of citizenship and nationhood were subject to competing ideologies and a changing world. We should not be surprised, then, to find that those who turned their attention to this question found that it was not possible to make citizens out of this recalcitrant and degenerated group of Alsatian Jews. Men such as Charles-Joseph Bail and Théophile Hallez most certainly did not believe so. Fourier argued that were they to be given freedom, the Jews, "far from becoming reformed, would corrupt the morals of the French."[10] And if this Jew

---

[9] Schechter, 7.
[10] Quoted in Silberner, "Charles Fourier," 251.

did not become a citizen, then what would he become? The answer to this question – and this was one question that could be answered for men such as these – lay in the Rothschild-Jew. Indeed, in Rothschild, all the anxiety regarding the Jewish question came to a head. In imagining the place of this emancipated Jew, the most determinedly secular of revolutionaries drew on a Catholic tradition, that of seeing the Jew as representative of all that lay beyond the bounds of the acceptable world. Instead of cooperating, contributing, and participating in the nation, the Rothschild-Jew competed, exploited, and dissembled. These were the qualities that the Rothschild-Jew's creators were to designate as specifically Jewish. Indeed, this unassimilated Jew, the one who had not fulfilled the promise of emancipation and who had instead become the Rothschild-Jew, was easily identified by his Jewishness. The notion was powerful: during the 1880s and 1890s, there was an explosion of works excoriating Rothschild in exactly the same terms as had done Leroux, Toussenel, and their contemporaries.[11]

Jewishness, then, was representative of all that went against the nation. In this time, characterised by competing ways of remembering the Revolution and the ensuing years, and of imagining the nation, Jewishness was a wonderfully fluid notion that could lend itself equally – albeit in different terms – to secular left wing and to conservative Catholic rhetoric. No event illustrates this more clearly than the Damascus Affair and Rothschild's involvement in it. Universal to those who sought to cast the Jew in a negative role was that Jewishness was placed permanently beyond the bounds of the nation and its citizens. Those sensitive to the connotations behind Jewishness created the Israelite; shorthand for Jews who had fulfilled the expectations of emancipation. Adolphe Crémieux was – for the most part – one such Jew. For Mathieu-Dairnvaell, there were "noble Israelites," who merited the generosity of the nation, and there was the "Jewish mass," which misused the freedom the nation had granted them.[12] Yet although it could be argued that as individuals, Jews, or more correctly, Israelites, could be citizens of France, the characteristics of Jewishness would never be far behind them. The most "noble

---

[11] See Stephen Wilson, *Ideology and experience: Antisemitism in France at the Time of the Dreyfus Affair* (East Brunswick, NJ, 1982), 256–8.

[12] Mathieu-Dairnvaell, *Rothschild Ier*, 35–6; Mathieu-Dairnvaell, *Histoire*, 35.

Israelite" of this era, Adolphe Crémieux, was open for attack if he was seen to be too overt in his expression of loyalty to Judaism.

In the medieval era, Catholics taught that Jews had horns and a tail. However damaging this might have been to the Jewish population, this Jew-devil was a concrete figure, in that his Jewishness was anchored in his body. By the middle of the nineteenth century, the Jew had been set loose from the fetters that linked Judaism with humanity and allowed to soar high into the stratospheric regions of the metaphor. What had changed? Society had changed. Through historical circumstance, the Jew had practised professions linked to the movement of money. For many centuries, to deal in and amass money had been seen as somehow dirty, and this dirtied the Jew by association. His usury was a scourge on the population but not necessarily a danger. Rather it served as a proof of his antisocial nature. At best, his skills with money might be useful, if distasteful. But when the desire to accumulate wealth was legitimised, first by the wealthy members of the Third Estate who came to power through the Revolution and then, definitively, by a materialist government after 1830, the Jew as moneymaker supreme surged to a position of power. The Jew might once have represented an evil power, but it could be disdained and controlled because the Jew himself could be ostracised – expelled, or burned at the stake, as had happened on occasion in France. But his emancipation meant that now he was at the very heart of the nation and could no longer be separated out from it. The Jewish evil now posed a direct threat to the sanctity of French life, however this might be idealised.

Nonetheless, the nature of the Jew as he was imagined might have changed with the changing world, but the Catholic inheritance of "religious Jew-hatred"was not discarded, even by the most secular of republicans. In a study of a much earlier period, David Nirenberg has shown how fourteenth-century accusations against Jews drew on "an ancient hoard of stereotypes," which were then used in new ways to express opposition to changing rule.[13] Herein lies the link between the period covered here and those which both preceded and followed it, including the Enlightenment and the "antisemitic moment" of 1898.[14] At all times, those who

---

[13] Nirenberg, 93.

[14] Birnbaum, "Introduction," in Ilana Zinguer and Sam W. Bloom, eds, *L'Antisémitisme éclairé. Inclusion et exclusion depuis l'Epoque des Lumières jusqu'à l'affaire Dreyfus* (Leiden, 2003). 10.

chose to use the Jew to think drew on what they knew, what was around them, and what was important to them as a vehicle for their thinking. Adam Sutcliffe has detailed how Judaism troubled the new boundaries that Enlightenment writers such as Voltaire sought to establish: as Sutcliffe put it, Judaism encapsulated "the residuum of myth and tradition" that held fast against Enlightenment logic; it provided a messy challenge to Enlightenment efforts to discredit the Bible.[15] Birnbaum has argued of the end of the nineteenth century that if there is such a thing as a peculiarly French antisemitism, it is linked to ownership of the state, or what I would call the imagining of the nation.[16] Just as the possibility for the Terror was at the heart of the Revolution, so the possibility for hatred lay at the heart of the Revolutionary understanding of Frenchness. The question revolved around how this Frenchness should be conceptualized; or in other words, what France was one for? And what place might there be for Jews in this France? If in 1898 the wrangling over what the state should be reached an apogee with the Dreyfus Affair, discussions on the same topic went on nonetheless right across the century.

The continuity is striking: at all times, the Jew was used to explain away frustration at a world that would not conform to an ideal. (Or indeed, in the case of a group such as the Saint Simonians, the Jew's inclusion could be seen as an example of what the idealised world could achieve.) Writers would either draw on tools at hand or develop new ways to understand this Jew that fitted in with new boundaries. In the interplay of traditions and changing events over the course of the early nineteenth century, imaginings of the Jew most certainly evolved, but in this respect they also remained static. This is, arguably, a reflection of the era. For the early nineteenth century can be characterised by intense and ongoing competition as to how the nation should be imagined. Ultras turned Legitimists, secular republicans, socialists outraged by their government – all ideologies envisaged a nation in which the Jew, such as he was, had no place. The Jew was left to choose the "sauce" with which he was to be eaten, as Sartre put it;[17] to convert or to assimilate, depending on

---

[15] Sutcliffe "Voltaire in context," 123.
[16] Birnbaum, "Introduction," 10.
[17] Sartre saw the antidemocratic antisemite, struggling to assert a true and real France over a fabricated 'Jewish' one, as the natural product of a democracy and his struggle as an underhand form of what is called the citizen's struggle against the powers that be. Yet

the voice he accorded the greater legitimacy. And the stories of David Drach, Simon Deutz, and James de Rothschild (or, more specifically, the Rothschild-Jew) tell us that to make a choice was no guarantee of acceptance. For by the mid-nineteenth century, Jewishness had become a quality independent of the Jew and yet inextricably linked to him. His Jewishness could escape him and take on whatever quality the Jew-hater desired, so that the Jew could never escape it.

This work is delineated arbitrarily – by a Revolution – and the steadfastness with which I keep to this boundary sits in contrast to the sentiments on the spectrum of ambivalence that I have explored herein. My research has left me convinced that incidents where French non-Jews expressed such ambivalence towards their Jewish fellow citizens in the nineteenth century cannot be viewed as random or parenthetical.[18] Rather, the story of these ideas of the Jew throughout this period can and must be told as a continuous one. Nor should we understand this period as a tranquil interlude before what Pierre Birnbaum has described as the "extreme rejection" of emancipation, the thundering climax of the nineteenth century that was the Dreyfus Affair.[19] On the other hand, though, as I have stressed, we should not see the stories I have described as a puzzle, which, when solved, displays an antisemitic France. Rather, what I believe the tales contained here suggest is that as conservative Catholics and secular Republicans alike made their way through the early nineteenth century, they constantly adapted, modified, and renegotiated the place of the Jew. The process of making sense of Jewish emancipation, whether this meant outright rejection or the taking of some other position on the spectrum of ambivalence, was ongoing. And it is central to the story of France at this time. In the early nineteenth century, the French were faced with

although Sartre's antisemite is antidemocratic, and indeed could "only show himself in the context of the Republic," it does not necessarily follow that the democrat is a friend of the Jew. The antisemite sees the world in terms of synthesis, but the democrat analyses: everything can be broken down into its composite parts, including the social or religious group. Thus, for the democrat, there is no such thing as a Jew, there is only a man, and his defence of the Jew "saves the Jew as a man and annihilates him as a Jew." The antisemite reproaches the Jew for *being* a Jew; the democrat would willingly reproach him for *seeing himself* as a Jew. Between his adversary and his defender, in Sartre's eyes, the Jew seems to be in a fairly sorry state. Sartre, 38, 69.

[18] On the notion of parentheses in a different historical context, see Henry Rousso, *Le Syndrome de Vichy (1944–198 . . .)* (Paris, 1987), 322.

[19] Birnbaum, "Introduction," 8.

the challenge to adapt and make sense of a changing world. To accompany them on this journey, a significant number chose the Jew – always "relevant"[20] and always evolving, eternal, inexorably, and uniquely other.

[20] On the idea of the "relevant Other," see Michael Burns, *Rural Society and French Politics: Boulangism and the Dreyfus Affair, 1886–1900* (Princeton, NJ, 1984), 124.

Appendix A

A L'HOMME QUI A LIVRE UNE FEMME
Victor Hugo
Œuvres poétiques vol. 1, Avant l'exil, 1802–1851 (Paris, 1964), 848–50.

> O honte ! ce n'est pas seulement cette femme,
> Sacrée alors pour tous, faible cœur, mais grande âme,
> Mais c'est lui, c'est son nom dans l'avenir maudit,
> Ce sont les cheveux blancs de son père interdit,
> C'est la pudeur publique en face regardée
> Tandis qu'il s'accouplait à son infâme idée,
> C'est l'honneur, c'est la foi, la pitié, le serment,
> Voilà ce que ce juif a vendu lâchement !
>
> Juif ! les impurs traitants à qui l'on vend son âme
> Attendront bien longtemps avant qu'un plus infâme
> Vienne réclamer d'eux, dans quelque jour d'effroi,
> Le fond du sac plein d'or qu'on fit vomir sur toi !
>
> Ce n'est même pas un juif ! C'est un payen immonde,
> Un renégat, l'opprobre et le rebut du monde,
> Un fétide apostat, un oblique étranger
> Qui nous donne du moins le bonheur de songer
> Qu'après tant de revers et de guerres civiles
> Il n'est pas un bandit écumé dans nos villes,
> Pas forçat hideux blanchi dans les prisons,
> Qui veuille mordre en France au pain des trahisons !
>
> Rien ne te disait donc dans l'âme, ô misérable !
> Que la proscription est toujours vénérable,
> Qu'on ne bat pas le sein qui nous donna son lait,

Qu'une fille des rois dont on fut le valet
Ne se met point en vente au fond d'un antre infâme,
Et que, n'étant plus reine, elle était encor femme !

Rentre dans l'ombre où sont tous les monstres flétris
Qui, depuis quarante ans, bavent sur nos débris !
Rentre dans ce cloaque ! et que jamais ta tête,
Dans un jour de malheur ou dans un jour de fête,
Ne songe à reparaître au soleil des vivants !
Qu'ainsi qu'une fumée abandonnée aux vents,
Infecte, et dont chacun sc détourne au passage,
Ta vie erre au hasard de rivage en rivage !

Et tais-toi ! que veux-tu balbutier encor !
Dis, n'as-tu pas vendu l'honneur, le vrai trésor ?
Garde tous les soufflets entassés sur ta joue.
Que fait l'excuse au crime et le fard sur la boue !

Sans qu'un ami t'abrite à l'ombre de son toit,
Marche, autre juif errant ! marche avec l'or qu'on voit
Luire à travers les doigts de tes mains mal fermées !
Tous les biens de ce monde en grappes parfumées
Pendent sur ton chemin, car le riche ici-bas
A tout, hormis l'honneur qui ne s'achète pas !

Hâte-toi de jouir, maudit ! et sans relâche
Marche ! et qu'en te voyant on dise : c'est ce lâche !
Marche ! et que le remords soit ton seul compagnon !
Marche ! sans rien pouvoir arracher de ton nom !
Car le mépris public, ombre de la bassesse,
Croît d'année en année et repousse sans cesse,
Et va s'épaississant sur les traîtres pervers
Comme la feuille au front des sapins toujours verts !

Et quand la tombe un jour, cette embûche profonde
Qui s'ouvre tout à coup sous les choses du monde
Te fera, d'épouvante et d'horreur agité,
Passer de cette vie à la réalité,
La réalité sombre, éternelle, immobile !
Quand, d'instant en instant plus seul et plus débile,
Tu te cramponneras en vain à ton trésor
Quand la mort, t'accostant couché sur des tas d'or,
Videra brusquement ta main crispée et pleine

Comme une main d'enfant qu'un homme ouvre sans peine,
Alors, dans cet abîme où tout traître descend,
L'un roulé dans la fange et l'autre teint de sang,
Tu tomberas, perdu sur la fatale grève
Que Dante Alighieri vit avec l'œil du rêve !
Tu tomberas damné, désespéré, banni !
Afin que ton forfait ne soit pas impuni,
Et que ton âme, errante au milieu de ces âmes,
Y soit la plus abjecte entre les plus infâmes !
Et lorsqu'ils te verront paraître au milieu d'eux,
Ces fourbes dont l'histoire inscrit les noms hideux,
Que l'or tenta jadis, mais à qui d'âge en âge
Chaque peuple en passant vient cracher au visage,
Tous ceux, les plus obscurs comme les plus fameux,
Qui portent sur leur lèvre un baiser venimeux,
Judas qui vend son Dieu, Leclerc qui vend sa ville,
Groupe au louche regard, engeance ingrate et vile,
Tous en foule accourront joyeux sur ton chemin,
Et Louvel indigné repoussera ta main !
Juillet 1835

Appendix B

LA SULTANE FAVORITE
Victor Hugo
Les Orientales (Paris, n.d.), 91–93.
   "Perfide comme l'onde." – Shakespeare.

> N'ai-je pas pour toi, belle juive,
> Assez dépeuplé mon sérail ?
> Souffre qu'enfin le reste vive.
> Faut-il qu'un coup de hache suive
> Chaque coup de ton éventail ?
>
> Repose-toi, jeune maîtresse.
> Fais grâce au troupeau qui me suit.
> Je te fais sultane et princesse,
> Laisse en paix tes compagnes, cesse
> D'implorer leur mort chaque nuit.
>
> Quand à ce penser tu t'arrêtes,
> Tu viens plus tendre à mes genoux ;
> Toujours je comprends dans les fêtes
> Que tu vas demander des têtes
> Quand ton regard devient plus doux.
>
> Ah ! jalouse entre les jalouses !
> Si belle avec ce cœur d'acier !
> Pardonne à mes autres épouses.
> Voit-on que les fleurs des pelouses
> Meurent à l'ombre du rosier ?

Ne suis-je pas à toi ? Qu'importe,
Quand sur toi mes bras sont fermés,
Que cent femmes qu'un feu transporte
Consument en vain à ma porte
Leur souffle en soupirs enflammés ?

Dans leur solitude profonde,
Laisse-les t'envier toujours ;
Vois-les passer comme fuit l'onde ;
Laisse-les vivre. A toi le monde !
A toi mon trône, à toi mes jours !

A toi tout mon peuple qui tremble !
A toi Stamboul qui, sur ce bord
Dressant mille flèches ensemble,
Se berce dans la mer, et semble
Une flotte à l'ancre qui dort !

A toi, jamais à tes rivales,
Mes spahis aux rouges turbans,
Qui, se suivant sans intervalles,
Volent courbés sur leurs cavales
Comme des rameurs sur leurs bancs !

A toi Bassora, Trébizonde,
Chypre où de vieux noms sont gravés,
Fez où la poudre d'or abonde,
Mosul où trafique le monde,
Erzeroum aux chemins pavés !

A toi Smyrne et ses maisons neuves
Où vient blanchir le flot amer !
Le Gange redouté des veuves !
Le Danube qui par cinq fleuves
Tombe échevelé dans la mer !

Dis, crains-tu les filles de Grèce ?
Les lys pâles de Damanhour ?
Ou l'œil ardent de la négresse,
Qui, comme une jeune tigresse,
Bondit rugissante d'amour ?

Que m'importe, juive adorée,
Un sein d'ébène, un front vermeil !

Tu n'es point blanche ni cuivrée,
Mais il semble qu'on t'a dorée
Avec un rayon de soleil.

N'appelle donc plus la tempête,
Princesse, sur ces humbles fleurs,
Jouis en paix de ta conquête,
Et n'exige pas qu'une tête
Tombe avec chacun de tes pleurs !

Ne songe plus qu'aux frais platanes,
Au bain mêlé d'ambre et de nard,
Au golfe où glissent les tartanes ...
Il faut au sultan des sultanes ;
Il faut des perles au poignard !

22 octobre 1828.

SARA LA BAIGNEUSE
Victor Hugo
Les Orientales (Paris, n.d.), 125–29.

Sara, belle d'indolence,
Se balance
Dans un hamac, au-dessus
Du bassin d'une fontaine
Toute pleine
D'eau puisée à l'ilyssus ;

Et la frêle escarpolette
Se reflète
Dans le transparent miroir,
Avec la baigneuse blanche
Qui se penche,
Qui se penche pour se voir.

Chaque fois que la nacelle,
Qui chancelle,
Passe à fleur d'eau dans son vol,
On voit sur l'eau qui s'agite
Sortir vite
Son beau pied et son beau col.

Elle bat d'un pied timide
L'onde humide
Où tremble un mouvant tableau
Fait rougir son pied d'albâtre,
Et, folâtre,
Rit de la fraîcheur de l'eau.

Reste ici caché, demeure ;
Dans une heure,
D'un œil ardent tu verras
Sortir du bain l'ingénue,
Toute nue,
Croisant ses mains sur ses bras.

Car c'est un astre qui brille
Qu'une fille
Qui sort d'un bain au flot clair,
Cherche s'il ne vient personne,
Et frissone,
Toute mouillée au grand air.

Elle est là, sous la feuillée,
Eveillée
Au moindre bruit de malheur ;
Et rouge pour une mouche
Qui la touche,
Comme une grenade en fleur.

On voit tout ce que dérobe
Voile ou robe ;
Dans ses yeux d'azur en feu,
Son regard que rien ne voile
Est l'étoile
Qui brille au fond d'un ciel bleu.

L'eau sur son corps qu'elle essuie
Roule en pluie,
Comme sur un peuplier ;
Comme si, gouttes à gouttes,
Tombaient toutes
Les perles de son collier.

Mais Sara la nonchalante
Est bien lente
A finir ses doux ébats ;

Toujours elle se balance
En silence,
Et va murmurant tout bas :

"Oh ! si j'étais capitane,
Ou sultane,
Je prendrais des bains ambrés,
Dans un bain de marbre jaune,
Près d'un trône,
Entre deux griffons dorés !

"J'aurais le hamac de soie
Qui se ploie
Sous le corps prêt à pâmer ;
J'aurais la molle ottomane
Dont émane
Un parfum qui fait aimer.

"Je pourrais folâtrer nue,
Sous la nue,
Dans le ruisseau du jardin,
Sans craindre de voir dans l'ombre
Du bois sombre
Deux yeux s'allumer soudain.

"Il faudrait risquer sa tête
Inquiète,
Et tout braver pour me voir,
Le sabre nu de l'heiduque,
Et l'eunuque
Aux dents blanches, au front noir !

"Puis, je pourrais, sans qu'on presse
Ma paresse,
Laisser avec mes habits
Traîner sur les larges dalles
Mes sandales
De drap brodé de rubis."

Ainsi se parle en princesse,
Et sans cesse
Se balance avec amour
La jeune fille rieuse,
Oublieuse
Des promptes ailes du jour.

L'eau, du pied de la baigneuse
Peu soigneuse,
Rejaillit sur le gazon,
Sur sa chemise plissée,
Balancée
Aux branches d'un vert buisson.

Et cependant des campagnes
Ses compagnes
Prennent toutes le chemin.
Voici leur troupe frivole
Qui s'envole
En se tenant par la main.

Chacune, en chantant comme elle,
Passe, et mêle
Ce reproche à sa chanson :
Oh ! la paresseuse fille
Qui s'habille
Si tard un jour de moisson !
Juillet 1828.

Selected Bibliography

ARCHIVAL SOURCES

Archives nationales

BB/18/1328, 1332, 1333: Duchesse de Berry, politique.
F¹ᶜIII: Bas-Rhin/15.
F⁷ 12171, 12173 (no. 19³), 12175.
  9819 dossier 63956: Israélites, agression contre eux. Délits usuraires.
  9430 dossier 14314A: la disparition de Mme Drach.
F¹⁹ 11031: Plaintes et réclamations contre faits d'intolérance. 1820–1902.

Archives départementales du Bas-Rhin

3M: Police générale et administrative. 15, 18, 19, 28, 42, 49.
V: 23, 30, 79, 179, 411.

PRINTED PRIMARY SOURCES

Almanach populaire du Languedoc pour l'année 1833. Toulouse: Senac, 1833.

Anne, Théodore. *La prisonnière de Blaye.* Paris: Charpentier, 1832.
Bail, Charles Joseph. *Etat des Juifs en France, en Espagne et en Italie, depuis le commencement du cinquième siècle de l'ère vulgaire jusqu'à la fin du seizième, sous les divers rapports du droit civil, du commerce et de la littérature; ouvrage qui a concouru au prix décerné par l'Académie des inscriptions et belles-lettres de l'institut de France, dans le mois de juillet 1823.* Paris: Eymery, 1823.
———. *Réplique et commentaire de M. Bail, . . . aux observations de M. de Cologna, . . . grand rabbin . . . de France, sur la 2e édition des Juifs au 19e siècle.* Paris: Treuttel et Wurtz, 1817.
———. *Des Juifs au dix-neuvième siècle, ou Considérations sur leur état civil et politique en Europe, suivies de la Notice biographique des Juifs anciens et modernes qui se sont illustrés dans les sciences et les arts, par M. Bail.* 2d ed. Paris: Treuttel et Wurtz, 1816.

————. *Statistique générale des provinces composant le royaume de Westphalie, dans l'ordre où elles subsistaient au 1er octobre 1807, avec l'indication de la nouvelle division départementale.* Gottingen: H. Dieterich, 1809.

Balzac, Honoré de. *Cousin Pons.* Paris: Furne et Cie, 1848.

Bautain, Louis-Eugène-Marie (Abbé). *Philosophie du christianisme, correspondance religieuse de L. Bautain, professeur de philosophie à l'Académie de Strasbourg. Publiée par l'abbé H. de Bonnechose.* 2 vols. Paris: Dérivaux, 1835.

Bécourt, Renault. *Souscription. Conspiration universelle du judaïsme, entièrement dévoilée, dédiée à tous les souverains de l'Europe, à leurs ministres, aux hommes d'état et généralement a toutes les classes de la société, menacées de ses perfides projets.* Nancy: F. A. Bachot, 1835.

————. *Questions sur divers passages de la Bible. Réponse à la première de ces questions par Abraham-Elie Caisson.* Paris: Duverger, 1828.

Berr, Michel. *Un mot de M. Michel Berr, avec des notes, en réponse à un pamphlet anonyme, intitulé: un mot à M. Michel Berr, publié par les Juifs de Paris.* Paris: Sétier, 1824.

Betting de Lancastel, Michel. *Considérations sur l'état des Juifs dans la société chrétienne et particulièrement en Alsace.* Strasbourg: F.-G. Levrault, 1824.

Beugnot, Arthur. *Les Juifs d'Occident; présentation de G. Bertier de Sauvigny.* Paris: Champion, 1979.

————. "Notice sur un projet formé à Varsovie de publier une TRADUCTION FRANÇAISE DU TALMUD, précédée d'un Essai intitulé: THÉORIE DU JUDAISME APPLIQUÉE A LA RÉFORME DES JUIFS." *Revue encyclopédique ou Analyse raisonnée des productions les plus remarquables dans la littérature, les sciences et les arts* 38 (1828): 20–31.

————. *Les Juifs d'Occident, ou "Recherches sur l'état-civil, le commerce et la littérature des Juifs en France, en Espagne et en Italie pendant la durée du Moyen âge."* Paris: F.-G. Levrault, 1824.

Bonald, Louis de. *Essai analytique sur les lois naturelles de l'ordre social. Du divorce considéré au XIXe siècle, relativement à l'état domestique et à l'état public de la société. Pensées sur divers sujets. Discours politiques.* Paris: Le Clere et Cie, 1858.

————. *Mélanges littéraires, politiques et philosophiques.* 3rd ed. Paris: Le Clere et Cie, 1852.

Cerfberr de Medelsheim, Maxmilien Charles Alphonse. *Les Juifs, leur histoire, leurs moeurs.* Paris: Albert frères, 1847.

————. *Ce que sont les Juifs de France.* Strasbourg: Dérivaux et Drach, 1843.

Chiarini, Louis-A. (Abbé). *Le Talmud de Babylone traduit en langue française, et complété par celui de Jérusalem et par d'autres monuments de l'antiquité judaïque.* 2 vols. Leipzig: Weigel, 1831.

————. *Théorie du judaisme, appliquée à la réforme des Israélites de tous les pays de l'Europe, et servant en même temps d'ouvrage préparatoire à la version du Talmud de Babylone.* 2 vols. Paris: Barbezat, 1830.

————. *Observations sur un article de la "Revue encyclopédique," dans lequel on examine le projet de traduire le Talmud de Babylone; suivies du programme de la théorie du judaïsme appliquée à la réforme des israélites de tous les pays de l'Europe.* Paris: F. Didot, 1829.

Clarétie, Jules. *La Vie à Paris, 1881.* Paris: Havard, 1883.

Cologna, Abraham de. *Quelques Observations sur la deuxième édition de l'ouvrage intitulé: "Des Juifs au XIXe siècle," de M. Bail.* Paris: Sétier, 1817.

————. *Réflexions adressées à M. le baron S. de S . . . (Silvestre de Sacy) sur sa lettre à M***, conseiller de S. M. le roi de Saxe, relativement à l'ouvrage intitulé "Des Juifs au XIXe siècle."* Paris: Sétier, 1817.

Deprez, A. *Guerre aux Juifs! ou la vérité sur MM. de Rothschild, par A. D***, avocat, ancien directeur de la bibliothèque ecclésiastique.* Paris: Martinon, 1846.

Dermoncourt, P.F.S. (Général). *Deutz ou Imposture, ingratitude et trahison par l'auteur de "La Vendée et Madame."* Paris: Dentu, 1836.

————. *Considérations sur l'existence civile et politique des israélites.* Mainz: Zabern, n.d.

Dermoncourt, P. F. S. (Général), and Alexandre Dumas (père). *La Vendée et Madame.* 2d ed. Paris: A. Guyot, 1833.

Deutz, Simon. *Arrestation de Madame.* Paris: chez les libraires associés, 1835.

Didier, Charles. "Le Maroc." *La Revue des deux mondes.* 1 November 1836: 241–69.

Drach, P. L. B. [David]. *De l'Harmonie entre l'église et la synagogue, ou perpétuité et catholicité de la religion chrétienne, par le chevalier P.-L.-B. Drach.* 2 vols. Paris: P. Mellier, 1844.

————. *Du Divorce dans la synagogue, par le chevalier Drach.* Paris: A. Le Clère, n.d.; Rome: Collège urbain, 1840.

————. *Hymne de louange en l'honneur de . . . Grégoire XVI, au 1er jour de la 8e année de son règne, par le chev. abbé P.-L.-B. Drach.* Rome: F. Bourlié, 1838.

————. *Relation de la conversion de miss L. T. H. à la sainte église catholique romaine.* Rome: n.p., 1836.

————. *Ode hébraïque sur l'hospice de saint-Michel, par le chevalier P.-L.-B. Drach.* Rome: l'Hospice apostolique, 1835.

————. *Lettre sur une question d'usure . . . par le chevalier P.-L.-B. Drach.* Rome: nel Collegio Urbano, 1834.

————. *Troisième lettre d'un rabbin converti aux Israélites, ses frères, sur les motifs de sa conversion. Première partie, prophétie d'Isaïe VII, 14, expliquée par les traditions de la synagogue.* Rome, l'auteur; Paris: Bricon, 1833.

————. *L'Inscription hébraïque du titre de la Sainte Croix restituée, et l'heure du crucifiement de N. S. J. C. déterminée. Deux dissertations en formes de lettres par M. P.-L.-B. Drach.* 2d ed. Rome: F. Bourlié, 1831.

————. *Relation de la conversion de M. Hyacinthe Deutz, baptisé à Rome le 3 février 1828, précédée de quelques considérations sur le retour d'Israël dans l'église de Dieu.* Paris: l'auteur, 1828.

————. *Deuxième lettre d'un rabbin converti aux Israélites ses frères sur les motifs de sa conversion. Les Prophéties expliquées par les traditions de la synagogue.* Paris: l'auteur, 1827.

————. *Lettre d'un Rabbin converti aux Israélites, ses frères, sur les motifs de sa conversion.* Paris: Beaucé-Rusand, 1825.

————. *Discours prononcé aux obsèques de M. Lan (Léon), célébrées à Paris le 14 janvier 1823, par D. Drach.* Paris: P. Dupont, 1823.

————. *Discours prononcé aux obsèques de Mme Claire Javal aînée, qui ont eu lieu le 10 juin 1822, par le rabbi Drach.* Paris: Sétier, 1822.

————. *Ode hébraïque sur la consécration du temple élevé par le consistoire israélite de Paris, par le Rabbi D. Drach.* Paris: Sétier, 1821.

Gauthier, Théophile. *Le voyage en Italie.* Paris, 1860.

Goslin, Abbé. *Méthode courte et facile pour se convaincre de la vérité de la religion catholique, d'après les écrits de Bossuet, Fénélon, Pascal et Bullet.* Paris: Demonville, 1822.

Guibourg, Duke de. *La Relation fidèle et détaillée de l'arrestation de S. A. R. Madame, duchesse de Berry.* Nantes: C. Merson, 1832.

Hallez, Théophile. *Des Juifs en France. De leur état moral et politique depuis les premiers temps de la monarchie jusqu'à nos jours.* Paris: G.A. Dentu, 1845.

Hamont, M. P.-N. *L'Egypte sous Méhémet-Ali.* 2 vols. Paris: Léautey et Lecointe, 1843.

Hugo, Victor. *Oeuves poétiques. Vol 1, Avant l'exil 1802–1851.* Edited by Pierre Albouy. Paris: Gallimard, 1964.

————. *Les Orientales.* Paris: Maison Quantin, n.d. [1829].

Laboudrie, Abbé. *Discours pour le baptême de Joseph-Marie-Louis-Jean Wolf, juif converti, prononcé à Saint-Eustache, le 23 mai 1818 par M. l'abbé Laboudrie.* Paris: Demonville, 1818.

————. *Discours pour le baptême d'Ange-Alexandre-Bernard-Jean Mayer, juif converti, prononcé à Saint-Nicholas-du-Chardonnet, le 23 avril 1818.* Paris, Demonville, 1818.

————. *Discours prononcés à Notre-Dame, le 7 mars 1817, à l'occasion du baptême, du mariage, de la première commission de sieur Alphonse-Jean-Sébastien-Louis Jacob, juif converti, par M. l'abbé Laboudrie.* Paris: Demonville, 1817.

————. *Discours de M. l'abbé Laboudrie, . . . pour le baptême de M.D.J.B. Lévy cadet, juif converti, à la métropole de Paris le 14 juin 1815.* Paris: A. Clo, 1815.

————. *Discours pour le baptême de Philippe-Rigobert Vahl, juif converti, dans la chapelle du Collège royal des Écossais, le 12 novembre 1818.* n.p.n.d.

————. *Discours pour le baptême de Anna et Louise Vahl, prononcé à Saint Germain-l'Auxerrois, le 24 mars 1819, par M. l'abbé Laboudrie.* n.p.n.d.

Lamennais, Félicité de. *Oeuvres complètes.* Geneva: Slatkine, 1980.

Laurent, Achille. *Relation historique des affaires de Syrie depuis 1840 jusqu'en 1842: statistique générale du Mont-Liban et procédure complète dirigée en 1840 contre des juifs de Damas à la suite de la disparition du Père Thomas.* 2 vols. Paris: Gaume Frères, 1846.

Leroux, Pierre. *Malthus et les économistes ou Y aura-t-il toujours des pauvres?* Paris: Librairie de la bibliothèque nationale, 1897.

L'évèque, Nicolas. *Erreurs des juifs en matière de religion.* Paris: J.-J Blaise, 1828.

de Maistre, Joseph. *Joseph de Maistre: Textes choisis et présentés par E.M. Cioran.* Monaco: Éditions du Rocher, 1957.

Malet, Chevalier. *Recherches politiques et historiques, qui prouvent l'existence d'une secte révolutionnaire, son antique origine, son organisation, ses moyens, ainsi que son but; et dévoilent entièrement l'unique cause de la révolution française, par le chevalier de Malet, ancien officier au corps royal de l'artillerie.* Paris: n.p., 1817.

Marx, Karl. *Class Struggles in France 1848–1850*. New York: International Publishers, 1969.

Mathieu-Dairnvaell, Georges. *Guerre aux fripons. Chronique secrète de la bourse et des chemins de fer*. 3rd ed. Paris, 1846.

———. *Histoire édifiante et curieuse de Rotschild Ier, roi des juifs, par Satan*. 15th ed. Paris, 1846.

———. *Jugement rendu contre J. Rothschild, et contre Georges Dairnvaell, Auteur de l'histoire de Rothschild Ier, par le tribunal de la saine raison, accompagné d'un jugement sur l'accident de Fampoux*. Paris, 1846.

———. *Rothschild Ier, ses valets, et son peuple, par G. Dairnvaell. Réplique à de prétendues réponses et nouveaux faits, contre S.M. Rothschild, MM. Fould, Ch. Laffitte*. 5th ed. Paris, 1846.

Mesnard, J.-B. *Dix jours de règne de Rothschild Ier, roi jes juifs, ou notes pour servir à l'histoire de la fondation de la monarchie de ce souverain*. Paris, 1846.

———. *Grand procès entre Rothschild Ier, roi des juifs, et Satan dernier, roi des imposteurs. Arrêt rendu sur le réquisitoire de Junius, rapporteur général*. Paris, 1846.

Morel, Ignace Xavier. *La vérité sur l'arrestation de MADAME Duchesse de Berry, ou les mensonges de Deutz dévoilés, suivie, de plusieurs pièces et documens pour servir à la biographie des gens de Nantes, par Ty . . . Morel, docteur-médecin; Avec portrait du traitre; augmentée de l'homme qui a livré une femme, par Victor Hugo*. Paris: Levasseur, 1836.

———. *Renseignements relatifs à la persécution dont M. Drach, rabbin converti, a été l'objet*. Paris: Gueffier, [1826].

Moureau, Agricole. *De l'incompatibilité entre le judaïsme et l'exercice des droits de cité et des moyens de rendre les Juifs citoyens dans les Gouvernements représentatifs*. Paris: Crochard, 1819.

Notice sur l'état des Israélites en France, en réponse à des questions proposées par un savant *étranger*. Paris: Pillet Ainé, 1821.

Ratisbonne, Marie-Alphonse. *Conversion de M. Marie-Alphonse Ratisbonne. Relation authentique par M. Le Baron Th. de Bussières; suivie de la lettre de M. Marie-Alphonse Ratisbonne à M. Dufriche-Desgenettes, Fondateur et Directeur de l'Archiconfrérie du Très-Saint et Immaculé Coeur de Marie, établie en l'église de Notre-Dame-des-Victoires, à Paris*. 3d ed. Paris: Sagnier et Bray, 1844.

———. *Conversion de Monsieur M.-A. Ratisbonne, racontée par lui-même*. Le Mans: Gallienne, 1842.

Ratisbonne, Marie-Joseph-Louis-Théodore. *La Question juive*. Paris: Dentu, 1868.

———. *Eclaircissement sur l'enseignement de M. Bautain, en réponse au coup d'oeil de l'Abbé D. . . . sur cet enseignement*. Paris: Dérivaux, 1835.

———. *Essai sur l'éducation morale. Discours couronné par la société des sciences, agriculture et arts du Bas-Rhin*. Strasbourg: Silbermann, 1828.

Rousseau, Auguste, Marc-Antoine-Madeleine Désaugiers, and Jean-Baptiste Mesnard. *Le Juif: Comédie anecdotique en deux actes, mêlée de vaudevilles, par MM. A. Rousseau, Désaugiers et Mesnard, représentée, pour la première fois, sur le théâtre de la porte Saint-Martin, le 14 mai 1823. In Fin du répertoire du théâtre français*. Paris, 1824.

Sacy, Silvestre de. *Lettre à M***, conseiller de S. M. le roi de Saxe, relativement à l'ouvrage intitulé: "Des Juifs au XIXe siècle." Par M. le Bon S. de S. ([Silvestre de Sacy].* 10 février 1817. Paris: De Bure frères, 1817.

Scott, Sir Walter. *Ivanhoe.* Edited by A. N. Wilson. London: Penguin Books, 1984.

Sue, Eugène. *Le Juif errant.* Paris: A. Lacroix et Cie, 1876.

de Tocqueville, Alexis. *The Old Regime and the Revolution.* Translated by Alan Kahan. Edited by François Furet and Françoise Mélonio. Chicago: University of Chicago Press, 1998.

————. *Recollections.* Translated by George Lawrence. New York: Doubleday, 1971.

Tourette, Amédée. *Discours sur les Juifs d'Alsace.* Strasbourg: F.-G. Levrault, 1825.

Toussenel, Alphonse. *Les Juifs, rois de l'époque. Histoire de la féodalité financière.* Paris: Renouard, 1847.

"Variétés: Programme." *Journal de la société des sciences, agriculture et arts, du département du Bas-Rhin, séant à Strasbourg.* 1 (1824): 114–16.

de Vigny, Alfred. *Poèmes antiques et modernes.* Paris, 1826.

Wittersheim, P. *Mémoire sur les moyens de hâter la régénération des Israélites de l'Alsace.* Metz, 1825.

JOURNALS

L'Ami de la religion et du roi, journal ecclésiastique, politique et littéraire
Le Charivari
Le Constitutionnel
La Gazette de France
La Gazette du Languedoc
Le Journal des débats
La Quotidienne
La Réforme
L'Univers

BIOGRAPHICAL REFERENCES

Archives biographiques françaises, I & II.

SECONDARY SOURCES

Adorno, T. W., et al. *The Stars Down to Earth, and Other Essays on the Irrational in Culture.* Edited by Stephen Crook. London: Routledge, 1994.

————. *The Authoritarian Personality. Studies in Prejudice.* Edited by Max Horkheimer and Samuel H. Flowerman. New York: Norton, 1969.

Ages, Arnold. "Bonald and the Jews." *Revue de l'Université d'Ottawa* 44, no. 1 (1974): 32–43.

————. "Veuillot and the Talmud." *Jewish Quarterly Review* 64 (1974): 229–60.

————. "Lamennais and the Jews." *Jewish Quarterly Review* 63 (1972): 158–70.

Agulhon, Maurice. *1848 ou l'apprentissage de la République 1848–1852*. Paris: Seuil, 1973.

Albert, Phyllis Cohen. "Ethnicity and Solidarity in Nineteenth-Century France." In *Mystics, Philosophers, and Policitians. Essays in Jewish Intellectual History in Honor of Alexander Altman*, ed. Jehuda Reinharz and Daniel Swetschinski, 249–74. Durham, NC: Duke University Press, 1982.

————."The Jewish Oath in Nineteenth-Century France." *Spiegel Lectures in European Jewish History*. Tel Aviv, 1982.

————. *The Modernization of French Jewry: Consistory and Community in the Nineteenth Century*. Hanover: Brandeis University Press, 1977.

————."Le rôle des Consistoires Israélites vers le milieu du dix-neuvième siècle." *Revue des études juives* 130 (1971): 231–54.

Allison, John M. S. *Thiers and the French Monarchy*. Boston, New York: Houghton Mifflin, 1926.

Amson, Daniel. *Adolphe Crémieux. L'oublié de la gloire*. Paris: Seuil, 1988.

Anchel, Robert. "Contribution levée en 1813–1814 sur les Juifs du Haut-Rhin." *Revue des études juives* 92 (1926): 495–501.

Artz, Frederick. *Reaction and Restoration, 1814–1832*. 3d ed. New York: Harper and Row, 1966.

————. *France under the Bourbon Restoration, 1814–1830*. New York, 1963.

Babut, Étienne, and Danielle Delmaire. "Minorités protestantes et juives dans le nord de la France." *Historiens et géographes* 81, no. 331 (1991): 245–53.

Badia-Evzline, Suzy. "Histoire d'une beauté idéale ou un certain reflet de la femme juive à travers la littérature française du XIXe siècle." *Combat pour la diaspora* 8 (1982): 49–58.

Badinter, Robert. *Libres et égaux... l'émancipation des Juifs 1789–1791*. Paris: Fayard, 1989.

Bailyn, Bernard. *The Ideological Origins of the American Revolution*. Enlarged edition. Cambridge, MA: Harvard University Press/Belknap Press, 1992.

Bakunin, Jack. *Pierre Leroux and the Birth of Democratic Socialism, 1797–1848*. New York: Revisionist Press, 1976.

————."National Socialists and Socialist Antisemites." *Patterns of Prejudice* 11, no. 2 (1977): 29–33.

Bauman, Zygmunt. "Allosemitism: Premodern, Modern, Postmodern." In *Modernity, Culture and 'the Jew'*. Edited by Brian Cheyette and Laura Marcus. Stanford, CA: Stanford University Press, 1998. 143–56.

Becker, Jean-Jacques, and Annette Wieviorka, eds. *Les Juifs de France. De la Révolution française à nos jours*. Paris: Liana Levi, 1998.

Beecher, Jonathan. *Charles Fourier: The Visionary and His World*. Berkeley: University of California Press, 1987.

Bénichou, Paul. "Sur quelques sources françaises de l'antisémitisme moderne." *Commentaire* 1 (1978): 67–79.

Berger, David, ed. *History and Hate: The Dimensions of Anti-Semitism*. Philadelphia: Jewish Publication Society, 1986.

Berkovitz, Jay R. *Rites and Passages: The Beginnings of Modern Jewish Culture in France, 1650-1860*. Philadelphia: University of Pennsylvania Press, 2004.

_____."Jewish Scholarship and Identity in Nineteenth-Century France." *Modern Judaism* 18, no. 1 (1998): 1–33.

_____."The French Revolution and the Jews: Assessing the Cultural Impact." *Association for Jewish Studies Review* 20, no. 1 (1995): 25–86.

_____. *The Shaping of Jewish Identity in Nineteenth-Century France*. Detroit, MI: Wayne State University Press, 1989.

Bertier de Sauvigny, Guillaume. "La Conspiration des légitimistes et de la duchesse de Berry contre Louis-Philippe, 1830–32." *Études d'histoire moderne et contemporaine* 3 (1951): xvii-125.

Birnbaum, Pierre. *Jewish Destinies: Citizenship, State, and Community in Modern France*. Translated by Arthur Goldhammer. New York: Hill and Wang, 2000.

_____. *Un mythe politique: La "république juive."* Paris: Gallimard, 1995.

_____. *Le peuple et les gros. Histoire d'un mythe*. Paris: Grasset, 1979.

Blumenkranz, Bernard. *Les Juifs et la révolution française*. Toulouse: Privat, 1976.

Bourgin, Georges. "Contribution à l'histoire des origines de l'antisémitisme en France." *Revue politique et parlementaire* 59, no. 665 (1957): 195–8.

Bourguet, Marie-Noëlle. *Déchiffrer la France: La statistique départementale à l'époque napoléonienne*. Paris: Éditions des archives contemporaines, 1989.

_____."Race et folklore; l'image officielle de la France en 1800." *Annales: économies, sociétés, civilisations* 31 (1976): 802–23.

Burns, Michael. *Dreyfus: A Family Affair, 1789–1945*. New York: HarperCollins, 1991.

_____. *Rural Society and French Politics: Boulangism and the Dreyfus Affair, 1886–1900*. Princeton, NJ: Princeton University Press, 1984.

Bury, J. P. T., and R. P. Tombs. *Thiers 1797–1877: A Political Life*. London: Allen and Unwin, 1986.

Byrnes, Robert. *Anti-Semitism in Modern France: The Prologue to the Dreyfus Affair*. New York: Fertig, 1969.

Caron, François. "Le rôle des accidents de voyageurs dans la gestion des chemins de fer en France." *Entreprises et histoire* 17 (1997): 85–93.

Catrice, Paul. *L'Harmonie entre l'église et le judaïsme d'après la vie de Paul Drach*. Thèse présentée pour le doctorat en théologie devant la faculté de théologie de Lille, 1978. Unpublished thesis. Lille, 1978.

Chazan, Robert. *Medieval Stereotypes and Modern Antisemitism*. Berkeley: University of California Press, 1997.

_____. *Daggers of Faith: Thirteenth-Century Christian Missionizing and Jewish Response*. Berkeley: University of California Press, 1989.

Chevalier, Louis. *Labouring Classes and Dangerous Classes in Paris During the First Half of the Nineteenth Century*. Translated by Frank Jellinek. London: Routledge and Kegan Paul, 1973.

Cholvy, Gérard, and Yves-Marie Hilaire. *Histoire religieuse de la France contemporaine*. Toulouse: Privat, 1985.

Cohen, David. "L'image du juif dans la société française en 1843 d'après les rapports des préfets." *Revue d'histoire économique et sociale* 55, no. 1–2 (1977): 70–91.

Cohen, David K. "The Vicomte de Bonald's Critique of Industrialism." *Journal of Modern History* 41 (December 1969): 475–84.

Cohen, Richard. "Conversion in Nineteenth-Century France: Usual or Common Practice?" *Jewish History* 5, no. 2 (1991): 47–54.

Collingham, H. A. C. *The July Monarchy. A Political History of France 1830–1848.* London: Longman, 1988.

Collins, Irene, ed. *Government and Society in France, 1814–1848.* London: Edward Arnold, 1970.

————. *The Government and the Newspaper Press in France 1814–1881.* Oxford: Oxford University Press, 1959.

Compagnon, Antoine. *Connaissez-vous Brunetière? Enquête sur un antidreyfusard et ses amis.* Paris: Seuil, 1997.

Cox, Marvin. "The Liberal Legitimists and the Party of Order under the Second French Republic." *French Historical Studies* 5 (1968): 446–64.

Crook, Malcolm, ed. *Revolutionary France, 1788–1880. The Short Oxford History of France.* Oxford: Oxford University Press, 2002.

Crossley, Ceri. "Anglophobia and Anti-Semitism: The Case of Alphonse Toussenel." *Modern and Contemporary France* 12, no. 4 (2004): 459–72.

Dahan, Gilbert, ed. *Les Juifs au regard de l'histoire: Mélanges en l'honneur de Bernhard Blumenkranz.* Paris: Picard, 1985.

Dansette, Adrien. *Religious History of Modern France. Vol. 1, From the Revolution to the Third Republic.* Translated by John Dingle. New York: Herder and Herder, 1961.

Delpech, François. "De 1815 à 1894." In *Histoire des juifs en France.* Edited by Bernard Blumenkranz. Collection Franco-Judaïca. Toulouse: Privat, 1972.305–46.

————."La seconde communauté juive de Lyon (1775–1870)." *Cahiers d'histoire* 13 (1968): 51–66.

Dreyfus, Robert. *Alexandre Weill, ou Le prophète du Faubourg Saint-Honoré.* Paris: Durlacher, 1907.

Dundes, Alan, ed. *The Blood Libel Legend; A Casebook in Anti-Semitic Folklore.* Madison: University of Wisconsin Press, 1991.

Dunham, Arthur. *The Industrial Revolution in France, 1815–1848.* New York: Exposition Press, 1955.

Elyada, Ouzi. "La rhétorique antijuive dans la presse contre-révolutionnaire 1789–1792." In *L'Antisémitisme éclairé. Inclusion et exclusion depuis l'Epoque des Lumières jusqu'à l'affaire Dreyfus.* Edited by Ilana Y. Zinguer and Sam W. Bloom. Leiden: Brill, 2003. 141–50.

Endelman, Todd. "Anti-Semitism and Apostasy in Nineteenth-Century France: A Response to Jonathan Helfand." *Jewish History* 5, no. 2 (1991): 55–64.

————, ed. *Jewish Apostasy in the Modern World.* New York: Holmes and Meier, 1987.

————."Comparative Perspectives on Modern Anti-Semitism in the West." In *History and Hate: The Dimensions of Anti-Semitism.* Edited by David Berger. Philadelphia: The Jewish Publication Society, 1986.

Ettinger, Shmuel. "The Origins of Modern Anti-Semitism." In *The Catastrophe of European Jewry.* Edited by Yisrael Gutman and Livia Rothkirchen. Jerusalem: Yad Vashem, 1976: 3–39.

Feuerwerker, David. *L'Émancipation des Juifs en France: de l'Ancien régime à la fin du Second Empire.* Paris: A. Michel, 1976.

Ford, Caroline. *Creating the Nation in Provincial France:Religion and Political Identity in Brittany.* Princeton, NJ: Princeton University Press, 1993.

Frankel, Jonathan. *The Damascus Affair.* London: Cambridge University Press, 1997.

Frederking, Bettina. "'Il ne faut pas être le roi de deux peuples': Strategies of National Reconciliation in Restoration France." *French History* 22, no. 4 (December 2008): 446-68.

Friedemann, Joë. *Alexandre Weill, Ecrivain contestataire et historien engagé (1811–1899)*. Strasbourg: Istra, 1980.

Gemie, Sharif. "Balzac and the Moral Crisis of the July Monarchy." *European History Quarterly* 19, no. 4 (1989): 469–94.

Gibson, Ralph. *A Social History of French Catholicism 1789–1914*. London: Routledge, 1989.

Gilman, Sander. "Salome, Syphilis, Sarah Bernhardt and the Modern Jewess." In *The Jew in the Text: Modernity and the Construction of Identity*. Edited by Linda Nochlin and Tamar Garb. London: Thames and Hudson, 1995. 97–120.

_____. *The Jew's Body*. New York: Routledge, 1991.

_____. *Jewish Self-Hatred: Anti-Semitism and the Hidden Language of the Jews*. Baltimore, London: Johns Hopkins University Press, 1986.

Girard, Patrick. *Les Juifs de France*. Paris: B. Huisman, 1983.

_____. *Les Juifs de France de 1789 à 1860: de l'émancipation à l'égalité*. Paris: Calmann-Lévy, 1976.

Glasberg, Victor. "Intent and Consequences: The "Jewish Question" in the French Socialist Movement of the Late Nineteenth Century." *Jewish Social Studies* 36, no. 1 (1974): 61–71.

Graetz, Michael. *The Jews in Nineteenth-Century France: From the French Revolution to the Alliance israélite universelle*. Translated by Jane Marie Todd. Stanford, CA: Stanford University Press, 1996.

Green, Nancy. "Assimilation et antisémitisme: deux siècles d'histoire juive en France." *Esprit* 10 (1983): 266–270.

Hallman, Diana. *Opera, Liberalism, and Antisemitism in Nineteenth-Century France; the Politics of Halévy's* La Juive. Cambridge: Cambridge University Press, 2002.

Hamache, Magy. "Les juifs dans les arts dramatiques au XIXe siècle: regards croisés sur la tragédienne Rachel (1821–1858)." *Revue historique* 293, no. 1 (1995): 119–33.

Harel, Yaron. "Le consul de France et l'affaire de Damas à la lumière de nouveaux documents." *Revue d'histoire diplomatique* 113, no. 2 (1999): 143–70.

Hartman, Mary. "The Sacrilege Law of 1825 in France: A Study of Anticlericalism and Mythmaking." *Journal of Modern History* 44, no. 1 (1972): 21–37.

Helfand, Jonathan. "Assessing Apostasy: Facts and Theories." *Jewish History* 5, no. 2 (1991): 65–71.

_____. "Passports and Piety: Apostasy in Nineteenth-Century France." *Jewish History* 3, no. 2 (1988): 59–83.

Hertz, Deborah. *How Jews Became Germans: The History of Conversion and Assimilation in Berlin*. New Haven, CT: Yale University Press, 2007.

_____. "Seductive Conversion in Berlin, 1770–1809." In *Jewish Apostasy in the Modern World*. Edited by Todd Endelman. New York: Holmes and Meier, 1987. 48–82.

Hertzberg, Arthur. *The French Enlightenment and the Jews*. New York: Columbia University Press, 1968.

Heschel, Susannah. *Abraham Geiger and the Jewish Jesus*. Chicago: Chicago University Press, 1998.

Hess, Jonathan M. *Germans, Jews, and the Claims of Modernity*. New Haven, CT: Yale University Press, 2002.

Higonnet, Patrice. "Cultural Upheaval and Class Formation During the French Revolution." In *The French Revolution and the Birth of Modernity*. Edited by Ferenc Fehér. Berkeley: University of California Press, 1990. 69–102.

Hours, J. "Un précurseur oublié de l'antisémitisme français, le Vicomte de Bonald." *Cahiers sioniens* 4 (1950): 165–70.

Hyman, Paula. *The Jews of Modern France*. Berkeley: University of California Press, 1998.

———. *The Emancipation of the Jews of Alsace: Acculturation and Tradition in the Nineteenth Century*. New Haven, CT: Yale University Press, 1991.

———. "The History of European Jewry: Recent Trends in the Literature." *Journal of Modern History* 54, no. 2 (1982): 303–19.

Isser, Natalie. *Antisemitism during the French Second Empire*. New York: Peter Lang, 1991.

Isser, Natalie, and Lita Linzer Schwartz. *The History of Conversion and Contemporary Cults*. New York: Peter Lang, 1988.

———. "Sudden Conversion: The Case of Alphonse Ratisbonne." *Jewish Social Studies* 45 (1983): 17–30.

Jardin, André, and André-Jean Tudesq. *Restoration and Reaction, 1815–1848*. Translated by Elborg Forster. Cambridge: Cambridge University Press, 1983.

Johnson, Christopher. "The Revolution of 1830 in French Economic History." In *1830 in France*. Edited by John Merriman. New York: Franklin Watts, 1975. 139–89.

Joubin, André, ed. *Journal de Eugène Delacroix. Tome Premier: 1822–1852*. Paris: Plon, 1932 (1950).

Judaken, Jonathan. *Jean-Paul Sartre and the Jewish Question: Anti-Antisemitism and the Politics of the French Intellectual*. Lincoln: Nebraska University Press, 2006.

Kalmar, Ivan Davidson, and Derek J. Penslar, eds. *Orientalism and the Jews*. Waltham, MA: Brandeis University Press, 2005.

Kates, Gary. "Jews into Frenchmen: Nationality and Representation in Revolutionary France." In *The French Revolution and the Birth of Modernity*. Edited by Ferenc Fehér. Berkeley: University of California Press, 1990. 103–16.

Katz, Jacob. *From Prejudice to Destruction: Anti-Semitism, 1700–1933*. Cambridge, MA: Harvard University Press, 1980.

———. *Out of the Ghetto: The Social Background of Jewish Emancipation, 1770–1870*. Cambridge, MA: Harvard University Press, 1973.

———. *Emancipation and Assimilation: Studies in Modern Jewish History*. Westmead, England: Gregg International Publishers, 1972.

———. *Tradition and Crisis*. New York: Glencoe, 1961.

———, ed. *The Role of Religion in Modern Jewish History: Proceedings of Regional Conferences of the Association for Jewish Studies Held at the University of Pennsylvania and the University of Toronto in March–April 1974*. Cambridge, MA: Association for Jewish Studies, 1975.

Kertzer, David. "The Montel Affair: Vatican Jewish Policy and French Diplomacy under the July Monarchy." *French Historical Studies* 25, no. 2 (2002): 265–93.

———. *The Popes against the Jews: The Vatican's Role in the Rise of Modern Antisemitism*. New York: Knopf, 2001.

Klein, Charlotte. "Jews, Christians, Muslims under Turkish Rule." *Patterns of Prejudice* 12, no. 4 (1978): 25–29.

Klein, Luce. *Portrait de la juive dans la littérature française.* Paris: Nizet, 1970.

Klein, Paul. "Mauvais juif, mauvais chrétien." *Revue de la pensée juive* 7 (1950): 87–103.

Klinck, David. *The French Counterrevolutionary Theorist, Louis de Bonald (1754–1840).* New York: Peter Lang, 1996.

Kroen, Sheryl. *Politics and Theater: The Crisis of Legitimacy in Restoration France, 1815–1830.* Berkeley: University of California Press, 2000.

Kselman, Thomas. "Turbulent Souls in Modern France: Jewish Conversion and the Terquem Affair." *Historical Reflections/Réflexions historiques* 32, no. 1 (2006): 83–104.

———. "The Bautain Circle and Catholic-Jewish Relations in Modern France." *The Catholic Historical Review* 92, no. 3 (July, 2006): 177–96.

———. "Social Reform and Religious Conversion in French Judaism: Alphonse Ratisbonne and the 'Société d'encouragement pour le travail parmi les israélites' of Strasbourg." *Proceedings of the Western Society for French History: Selected Papers of the Annual Meeting.* Vol. 28. Boulder: University of Colorado Press, 2001.

Kudlick, Catherine. *Cholera in Post-Revolutionary Paris.* Berkeley: University of California Press, 1996.

Langmuir, Gavin. *History, Religion and Antisemitism.* Berkeley: University of California Press, 1990.

———. *Toward a Definition of Antisemitism.* Berkeley: University of California Press, 1990.

Lathers, Marie. "Posing the "Belle Juive" – Jewish Models in 19th-Century Paris." *Womans Art Journal* 21, no. 1 (2000): 27–32.

Lecanuet, R. P. *Montalembert.* 3 vols. Paris: J. De Gigord, 1920.

Leff, Lisa Moses. *Sacred Bonds of Solidarity: The Rise of Jewish Internationalism in Nineteenth-Century France.* Stanford: Stanford University Press, 2006.

Lehrmann, Charles. *The Jewish Element in French Literature.* Translated by George Klin. Cranbury, NJ: Associated University Presses, 1971.

Leuilliot, Paul. *L'Alsace au début du XIXe siècle.* 3 vols. Paris: S.E.V.P.E.N, 1959.

Lewis, Reina. *Gendering Orientalism: Race, Femininity and Representation.* London: Routledge, 1996.

Lichtheim, George. "Socialism and the Jews." *Dissent* 15 (1968): 314–42.

Lindemann, Albert. *Esau's Tears: Modern Anti-Semitism and the Rise of the Jews.* Cambridge: Cambridge University Press, 1997.

Lucas-Dubreton, J. *Aspects de Monsieur Thiers.* Paris: Fayard, 1948.

Lyons, Martin. "Fires of Expiation: Book-Burnings and Catholic Missions in Restoration France." *French History* 10, no. 2 (1996): 240–66.

MacKenzie, John. *Orientalism: History, Theory and the Arts.* Manchester: Manchester University Press, 1995.

McMahon, Darrin. *Enemies of the Enlightenment: The French Counter-Enlightenment and the Making of Modernity.* New York: Oxford University Press, 2001.

McPhee, Peter. *The French Revolution, 1789–1799.* Oxford: Oxford University Press, 2002.

———. "The Changing Contours of 1848." In *The Sphinx in the Tuileries, and Other Essays in Modern French History, Papers Presented at the Eleventh George Rudé*

Seminar Held at The University of Sydney, 4–6 July 1998. Edited by Robert Aldrich and Martyn Lyons. Sydney, 1999: 104–26.

———. *A Social History of France, 1780–1880*. London: Routledge, 1992.

Malino, Frances. *The Sephardic Jews of Bordeaux: Assimilation and Emancipation in Revolutionary and Napoleonic France*. Tuscaloosa: University of Alabama Press, 1978.

Malino, Frances, and Phyllis Cohen Albert, eds. *Essays in Modern Jewish History: A Tribute to Ben Halpern*. Rutherford: Fairleigh Dickinson University Press, 1982.

Malino, Frances, and Bernard Wasserstein, eds. *The Jews in Modern France*. Hanover, NH: University Press of New England, 1985.

Manuel, Frank. *The Broken Staff: Judaism through Christian Eyes*. Cambridge, MA: Harvard University Press, 1992.

Margadant, Jo Burr. "Gender, Vice and the Political Imaginary in Postrevolutionary France: Reinterpreting the Failure of the July Monarchy, 1830–1848." *The American Historical Review* 104, no. 5 (1999): 1461–96.

———. "The Duchesse de Berry and Royalist Political Culture in Postrevolutionary France." *History Workshop Journal* 43 (1997): 23–52.

Marrus, Michael. *The Politics of Assimilation: A Study of the French Jewish Community at The Time of the Dreyfus Affair*. Oxford: Clarendon Press, 1971.

Marx, Roland. "Les Juifs et l'usure en Alsace: réflexions sur un mythe." *Saisons d'Alsace* 55–56 (1975): 62–7.

Merriman, John, ed. *1830 in France*. New York: Franklin Watts, 1975.

Merriman, John, and Elise Kenney. *The Pear: French Graphic Arts in the Golden Age of Caricature*. New Haven, CT: Mount Holyoke College Art Musem, 1991.

Moss, Bernard. *The Origins of the French Labor Movement, 1830–1914; The Socialism of Skilled Workers*. Berkeley: University of California Press, 1976.

Muhlstein, Anka. *Baron James: The Rise of the French Rothschilds*. New York: Vendome Press, 1987.

Murphy, Kerry. "Berlioz, Meyerbeer, and the Place of Jewishness in Criticism." In *Berlioz: Past, Present, Future: Bicentenary Essays*. Edited by Peter Bloom. Rochester, NY: University of Rochester Press. 2003. 90–104.

Necheles, Ruth. "The Abbé Grégoire's Work in Behalf of Jews." *French Historical Studies* 6, no. 2 (Autumn 1969): 172–84.

Newman, Edgar, ed. *Historical Dictionary of France from the Restoration of 1815 to the Second Empire*. Westport, CT: Greenwood Press, 1987.

———. "The Blouse and Frock Coat: The Alliance of the Common People of Paris with the Liberal Leadership and the Middle Class during the Last Years of the Bourbon Restoration." *Journal of Modern History* 46, no. 1 (March 1974): 26–59.

Nirenberg, David. *Communities of Violence: Persecution of Minorities in the Middle Ages*. Princeton: Princeton University Press, 1996.

Nochlin, Linda, and Tamar Garb, ed. *The Jew in the Text: Modernity and the Construction of Identity*. London: Thames and Hudson, 1995.

Nye, Robert. *Masculinity and Male Codes of Honour in Modern France*. New York: Oxford University Press, 1993.

Ockman, Carol. "Two Large Eyebrows à l'orientale: Ethnic Stereotyping in Ingres's Baronne de Rothschild." *Art History* 14, no. 4 (1991): 521–39.

Pagels, Elaine. *The Origin of Satan*. New York: Random House, 1995.

Pasto, James. "Islam's 'Strange Secret Sharer': Orientalism, Judaism, and the Jewish Question." *Comparative Studies in Society and History* 40, no. 3 (July 1998): 437–74.

Perrot, Jean-Claude. *L'Age d'or de la statistique régionale française (An IV – 1804)*. Paris: Sopan, 1977.

Perrot, Jean-Claude, and Stuart Woolf. *State and Statistics in France 1789–1815*. New York: Harwood Academic Publishers, 1984.

Phayer, Michael. "Politics and Popular Religion: The Cult of the Cross in France, 1815–1840." *Journal of Social History* 11, no. 3 (1978): 346–65.

Philippe, Béatrice. *Etre juif dans la société française, Du Moyen Age à nos jours*. Paris: Éditions Montalba, 1979.

Pierrard, Pierre. *Louis Veuillot*. Paris: Beauchesne, 1998.

———."Deux Catholiques antisémites au 19e siècle. Louis Veuillot, H.R. Gougenot de Mousseaux." *Rencontres chrétiens et juifs* 6 (1972): 267–75.

———. *Juifs et catholiques français*. Paris, 1970.

Pierrot, Arlette, and Roger Pierrot. "Notes sur Balzac et les juifs." *Revue des études juives* 146, no. 1–2 (1987): 85–99.

Piette, Christine. *Les Juifs de Paris (1808–1840): la marche vers l'assimilation*. Québec: Presses de l'Université Laval, 1983.

Pilbeam, Pamela. *Republicanism in Nineteenth-Century France, 1814–1871*. London: Macmillan, 1995.

———. *The 1830 Revolution in France*. New York: St Martin's Press, 1991.

Pinkney, David H. *Decisive Years in France, 1840–1847*. Princeton, NJ: Princeton University Press, 1986.

Poliakov, Léon. *The History of Anti-Semitism. Vol. 3, From Voltaire to Wagner. Translated by Miriam Kochan*. London: Routledge & Kegan Paul, 1975.

Posener, Solomon. "The Immediate Economic and Social Effects of the Emancipation of the Jews in France." *Jewish Social Studies* 1 (1939): 271–326.

———."La Révolution de juillet et les israélites de France." *Univers israélite* 85, no. 42 (1930): 453–6.

Price, Roger. *A Social History of Nineteenth-Century France*. London: Hutchinson, 1987.

Raphaël, Freddy, and Robert Weyl. "Juifs d'Alsace: histoire, archéologie et art." *Encyclopédie de l'Alsace*. Strasbourg: Éditions Publitotal, 1984.

———."La presse juive en Alsace." *Encyclopédie de l'Alsace*. Strasbourg: Éditions Publitotal, 1984.

———."Rabbinat d'Alsace." *Encyclopédie de l'Alsace*. Strasbourg: Éditions Publitotal, 1984.

———. *Regards nouveaux sur les Juifs d'Alsace*. Strasbourg: Librairie Istria, 1980.

———. *L'Imagerie juive en Alsace*. Strasbourg, 1979.

———. *Juifs en Alsace*. Toulouse: Privat, 1977.

Rapport, Michael. *Nationality and Citizenship in Revolutionary France: The Treatment of Foreigners, 1789–1799*. Oxford: Oxford University Press, 2000.

———."Robespierre and the Universal Rights of Man, 1789–1794." *French History* 10, no. 3 (1996): 303–33.

Ratcliffe, Barrie. "Some Jewish Problems in the Early Careers of Emile and Isaac Pereire." *Jewish Social Studies* 34 (1972): 189–206.

Reddy, William. "Marriage, Honor, and the Public Sphere in Postrevolutionary France: *Séparations de Corps*, 1815–1848." *Journal of Modern History* 65 (1993): 437–72.

Rémond, René. *The Right Wing in France from 1815 to De Gaulle*. 2d ed. Translated by James Laux. Philadelphia: University of Philadelphia Press, 1969.

――――. *Lamennais et la démocratie*. Paris: Presses universitaires de France, 1948.

Rivers, Christopher. *Face Value: Physiognomical Thought and the Legible Body in Marivaux, Lavater, Balzac, Gautier, and Zola*. Madison: University of Wisconsin Press, 1994.

Roth, Cecil. "The Reconversion of Simon Deutz." *Journal of Jewish Studies* 17 (1966): 83–4.

Said, Edward. *Orientalism*. London: Penguin, 1978.

Sartre, Jean-Paul. *Réflexions sur la question juive*. Paris: Gallimard, 1954.

Schechter, Ronald. *Obstinate Hebrews: Representations of Jews in France, 1715–1815*. Berkeley: University of California Press, 2003.

Schwarzfuchs, Simon. *Du Juif à l'israélite: histoire d'une mutation (1770–1870)*. Paris: Fayard, 1989.

Sellards, John. *Dans le sillage du romantisme. Charles Didier (1805–1864)*. Paris: Champion, 1933.

Sepinwall, Alyssa. *The Abbé Grégoire and the French Revolution: The Making of Modern Universalism*. Berkeley: California University Press, 2005.

Sevrin, Ernest. *Les Missions religieuses sous la Restauration, 1815–1830. Vol. 1, Le missionnaire et la mission. St Maudé: Procure des Prêtres de la Miséricorde, 1948. Vol. 2, Les missions (1815–1820)*. Paris: Vrin, 1959.

Sewell, William. *Work and Revolution in France; the Language of Labor from the Old Regime to 1848*. Cambridge: Cambridge University Press, 1980.

Shaftesbury, Anthony Ashley Cooper, Third Earl. *Characterstics of Men, Manners, Opinions, Times*. Edited by Lawrence Klein. Cambridge: Cambridge University Press, 1999.

Silberner, Edmund. "The Attitude of the Fourierist School towards the Jews." *Jewish Social Studies* 9 (1947): 339–62.

――――."Charles Fourier on the Jewish Question." *Jewish Social Studies* 8 (1946): 245-66.

Spitzer, Alan. *The French Generation of 1820*. Princeton, NJ: Princeton University Press, 1987.

Stearns, Peter. *Priest and Revolutionary: Lamennais and the Dilemma of French Catholicism*. New York: Harper & Row, 1967.

Stow, Kenneth. *Jewish Dogs: An Image and its Interpreters. Continuity in the Catholic-Jewish Encounter*. Stanford, CA: Stanford University Press, 2006.

Sutcliffe, Adam. *Judaism and Enlightenment*. New York: Cambridge University Press, 2003.

Szajkowski, Zosa. *Jewish Education in France, 1789–1939*. New York: Ktav, 1980.

――――. *The Jews and the French Revolutions of 1789, 1830 and 1848*. New York: Ktav, 1970.

――――."French Jews during the Revolution of 1830 and the July Monarchy." *Historia Judaica* 21 (1960): 105–30.

————. "The Jewish Saint-Simonians and Socialist Anti-Semites in France." *Jewish Social Studies* 9 (1947): 33–60.

Szapiro, Elie. "Le prosélytisme chrétien et les juifs à Toulouse au XIXe siècle." *Archives juives* 15, no. 3 (1979): 52–7.

Tinterow, Gary, and Philip Consibee, eds. *Portraits by Ingres, Image of an Epoch.* New York: Metropolitan Museum of Art, 1999.

Trachtenberg, Joshua. *The Devil and the Jews: The Medieval Conception of the Jew and its Relation to Modern Antisemitism.* New Haven, CT: Yale University Press, 1943.

Trigano, Shmuel. "L'apostasie du messie: le paradoxe de l'Emancipation." *Esprit* 5 (1979): 6–18.

Tudesq, André-Jean. *Les grands notables en France (1840–1849): Étude historique d'une psychologie sociale.* 2 vols. Paris: Presses universitaires de France, 1964.

Tulard, Jean, ed. *Dictionnaire du second Empire.* Paris: Fayard, 1995.

Ullmo, Jean. "Considérations sur l'antisémitisme." *Revue de la pensée juive* 2 (1950): 117–33.

Viatte, Auguste. *Un ami de Ballanche: Claude-Julien Bredin (1776–1854) Correspondance philosophique et littéraire avec Ballanche, publiée et commentée par Auguste Viatte.* Paris: De Boccard, 1927.

Vidal-Naquet, Pierre. *The Jews: History, Memory, and the Present.* Translated by David Ames Curtis. New York: Columbia University Press, 1996.

Vincent, K. Steven. *Pierre-Joseph Proudhon and the Rise of French Republican Socialism.* New York: Oxford University Press, 1984.

Weber, Eugen. *Action française: Royalism and Reaction in Twentieth-Century France.* Stanford: Stanford University Press, 1962.

Wilson, Stephen. *Ideology and Experience: Antisemitism in France at the Time of the Dreyfus Affair.* East Brunswick, NJ: Fairleigh Dickinson University Press, 1982.

Wistrich, Robert "Radical Anti-Semitism in France and Germany 1840–1880." *Modern Judaism* 15, no. 2 (1995): 109–35.

Woolf, Stuart. *Napoleon's Integration of Europe.* London: Routledge, 1991.

Zinguer, Ilana, and Sam W. Bloom, eds. *L'Antisémitisme éclairé. Inclusion et exclusion depuis l'Epoque des Lumières jusqu'à l'affaire Dreyfus.* Leiden: Brill, 2003.

Index